My 6th grade class photo. I am second from the left on the front row.

I'll Be Good

TOMORROW

RALPH B. LAO

Dedicated

in memoriam
to my mother, Maria Ayxa Lao
(who encouraged me to write my stories,
so others could enjoy them)

and

to my wife, Lois Marie Lao
(who pushed me to finish writing them)

Table of Contents

I'll Be Good *Tomorrow*

FOREWORD

I first met Ralph four years ago in the YMCA pool, doing water aerobics. It is a great way to exercise, with a plus. You have a chance to talk to people and get to know them. I am a bit of a social butterfly and visit with everybody, and often help new people with the exercises, which opens the way to conversation.

Ralph and I found many common interests and I began a close friendship with him and his wife. He told me many stories about his life of 79 years. A few months into our relationship, he told me that he was writing a book about growing up in Spanish Harlem in the 50s. I expressed interest and offered to read it and help him with editing.

It wasn't long before the first installment of the book was handed to me. I totally enjoyed it and had only a few comments on editing. I encouraged him to continue and asked if I could have the next installment ASAP.

As the chapters unfolded, I grew to know and appreciate all of the characters, each with his or her own charm, be it positive or negative. Every remembrance was touching on many levels. There were many laughs, lessons, a few tears, but a wonderful set of memories I felt privileged to have shared.

One of the lessons I learned was what it was like to be REALLY POOR. I was raised in a middle class family and, thank God, never knew abject poverty. I remember driving through the Deep South with my folks as a kid and seeing the many hovels. I always wondered why—if they were so poor as to have to live like that—did every one of them have a Cadillac and a TV antenna, both of which cost a lot of money. Now I know why.

RALPH B. LAO

Other lessons were that no matter how poor you are, you can laugh, play, have loyal friends. No matter how young you are you can have a beautiful, loving, gentle romance.

While I was reading Ralph's book, a new couple came to the pool and I found out the wife was a professional editor. So I introduced them to Ralph. They have become great friends and have a special working relationship. About then, a few other denizens of the pool were allowed to read the book and were enjoying it, too.

From the very first day that I and the other Y members at the pool met Ralph (probably in the spring of that year), he told all of us every day that his birthday was coming soon; it is on February 24. By the time February came around we decided to have a birthday party for him.

One of our water aerobics instructors makes amazing cakes, and she decorated one with a broken Parcheesi board and a giant crab on it. The rest of us made up a basket with many of the items mentioned in his book: a miniature couch with a big stain on it, a mini pool table, a pearl doll, rats, cockroaches, and many other things you will understand the importance of as you read the book.

I do hope you enjoy the book as much as I did.

Karen Walther

My surprise birthday cake, a creation by Benita Miller

10

I'll Be Good *Tomorrow*

CHAPTER 1

THE FIRST GOODBYE

Shooting someone had never been at the top of my to-do list. And killing a cop was nowhere on that list. Especially, since at the time, "Old Sparky," the Hot Seat at NY's Sing Sing Prison, was the reward at the end of that black rainbow.

But here I am, trapped in a room with this idiot next to me starting to panic. It's all been too much for him—running from the store, people chasing us, cops banging on the door—and now, he's pulling the gun out. "They're not going to get us. We'll shoot our way out!"

I put my hand over his mouth. "Cool it, man!" I whisper. "Do you want them to hear us?"

But he pulls away. That familiar look of rage has now appeared. "The first fuckin' cop that comes through that door, I'm going to shoot him. We'll shoot our way out of here."

I can't believe my ears. Shit, he's going to get the three of us killed, for sure. I want to take the gun away from him—fight him for it, if I have to. But I can't. The cops are right outside and I don't want them to hear us.

And now the third member of our ill-conceived group starts laughing and can't stop. He tries to muffle his laughter but to no avail. As always, he's out of control. "Ha, ha, ha, he thinks he's Dillinger. He thinks he's Dillinger," he repeats to me over and over.

I pray silently to my dead grandmother. I always turn to her when I'm in trouble. "Abuelita, please, help me get out of here. I promise I'll be good. I'll be good tomorrow."

But it's not doing me any good. One dumb bastard wants to shoot it out with the cops, and the other one can't stop laughing. Suddenly the thought of dying is becoming real.

But, the Bronx? Why the Bronx? Why die here?

I'm a Manhattan boy, born and bred. I HATE the Bronx. *How the hell did I end up here?*

I've always heard that when you are faced with death, your life flashes before your eyes—back to the beginning. I'm starting to believe it. To experience it.

* * * * *

For me the beginning was 1936, when I was born at the Flower Fifth Avenue Hospital in Manhattan, New York City.

The first four years of my life were spent in Spanish Harlem, East 112th Street just off Park Avenue. But because my father was a musician and was often on the road, my mother and I went along with him whenever we could. So, I have vague memories of living in other cities, such as Baltimore, Miami, Chicago, and even Havana, Cuba, for one or two weeks at a time.

My memories of my father as a musician were of his playing the clarinet or saxophone in a band. But playing in someone else's band didn't appeal to him because he had to be the leader. It had to be HIS band.

To me, he was Superman. I was sure my father could beat up the then heavyweight champion, Joe Louis. Once, I almost got into a fight with a guy at school because I said that.

He laughed and said, "No, he can't."

I'll Be Good *Tomorrow*

But I was so sure he could, I was ready to fight with the guy for not believing me. That's how convinced I was that my father "could beat up Joe Louis."

My father often told stories of living in Puerto Rico as a youngster and about how tough he was. How he was once shot by some guy he was fighting with, but although blood was gushing out of the bullet wound, he still managed to beat him up—and he had a bullet wound to prove it.

They were wild, scary stories. But I listened, because my father was a great storyteller. Friends loved inviting him to their parties because he'd start telling stories and dirty jokes, and would have everyone laughing all night.

But he had to be thought of as "the best" at everything he did. To me, he WAS the best. He was the original "Macho." His measure of a man was based on how tough a man was, and how many women he could attract.

My Dad and Mom

Me with Dad and Mom in Central Park

My mother always had problems with him because of his chasing other women. Conquest of a woman seemed to be proof of manhood to him.

He also spent a lot of time teaching me to fight—and to win—at all cost.

He told me, "Never give up! If you can't beat a guy with your fists, then grab a bat, a brick, or anything else you can get your hands on." His idea wasn't to have a good clean fight. His philosophy was to make sure that every guy I met respected me—feared me, if necessary.

My mother didn't care for that. She wanted me to concentrate on my studies. But my father preferred that I focus on being tough and not letting anyone push me around.

I'll Be Good *Tomorrow*

One time when I was eight, there was a kid, Pete, who was in one of my classes. He was about a year older than me, but he was one of those dumb kids who'd been kept back a grade or two. Pete lifted weights, and because of it, was the strongest kid in our class, and one of the strongest in school.

One day I was playing with Pete on 135th Street when we got into an argument. I said something, and Pete just swung out and hit me hard on the side of my face. It shook me up and I ran into my house crying, "Mom, Mom!"

I was running to my mother so she could hold and comfort me. Instead, I ran right into my father. I didn't know he was home, and it was too late to change my act. He'd already seen me crying and holding my face.

"What happened?" he asked.

I said "This guy, Pete, hit me in the face when I wasn't looking. He's bigger and older than me," quickly adding "and he lifts weights."

But my father didn't care about that. "When I was your age, size never mattered. Making guys respect me, afraid to fight me, was what mattered. Stop crying and act like a man," he yelled.

He then grabbed me by the arm and took me outside. "Come on, we'll find this guy and you'll fight him. You'll show him that you're not afraid of him."

Not afraid of him? Is he kidding? I wasn't afraid—I was terrified! Fighting Pete with my father watching was crazy. I was a dead man. Pete would kill me in a fight. But, if I didn't fight him, my father was going to beat the crap out of me. I was in trouble either way.

But fortunately, Pete had run into the alley and disappeared.

So, I got the crap kicked out of me by my father instead. "Men don't run. And men don't cry—ever," he repeated over and over.

It wasn't fun being beaten by my father. It hurt. But getting beat by him was still better than having to fight Pete, who would have slaughtered me.

"Losing" never occurred to my father. If I couldn't beat Pete with my fists, I was supposed to grab a rock and split his head open. I always found that way of thinking difficult—but that was what my father tried to instill in me.

RALPH B. LAO

Although many of those early memories are painful, I actually had a pretty happy childhood. It wasn't always about fighting and being tough.

My father spent hours at a time teaching me to hit and catch a ball, or to throw and catch a football. We also went to a lot of professional baseball games. He often took me down to Central Park to watch him play baseball in a local Puerto Rican league.

Dad batting for his baseball team in Central Park

I'll Be Good *Tomorrow*

But, my memory of everything from that time is blurry. I was nine years old when he left for South America. The word was that in Caracas, Venezuela, Latin music was booming and he could do very well there. His plan was to go to Venezuela, check the music scene out, and if it looked good he would send for us later.

The day he left, I lay in bed crying most of the day. It was the first time we had been separated like that, and I felt I was never going to see him again. South America was not just another country to me, it was another world—another planet.

My mother tried to console me, saying, "Stop crying. It's only for a short time. Soon he'll find another job and send for us. We'll all be together again." Then she added, "Until then you're the man of the house now." But her words meant nothing to me.

Before my father went to South America, life seemed fun and carefree. The life I remember started the day he left.

RALPH B. LAO

CHAPTER 2

MORE DEPARTURES

My mother was a perfectionist, and always pushed me to get high grades. She felt that I should always do better than anyone else in school.

I was a smart kid and I got good report cards. I'd come home with A's and B's, and I'd be happy. "Mom," I'd yell, "look at the marks I got."

But she was never content. She'd look at the report card and say, "Yes, they're good. But how come you don't have an A here?"

I'd respond with something like, "But that's a tough class, Mom," and any other excuse I could think of.

But, she'd always say, "I want to see a couple of A's here and here." She was never happy. She wanted my report card to read A's all the way down. When she was in school she was one of the brightest kids in her class, and she told me that she always got straight A's.

My mother expected me to get straight A's, just as she had. She would spend hours helping me with my homework and showing me how to study and prepare for tests. Those moments she spent with me served me well in later years whenever I had to take a test, or fill out an employment application.

RALPH B. LAO

She was as pretty as she was smart, and caught the eye of my father when she was only seventeen. Although he was well into his thirties, he charmed her, and she fell for him. They married, and that ended her school career. She never finished high school.

When my father left, my mother had to go out and work. Because of that, the way she dealt with me changed. She no longer behaved as the warm, comforting person I could run to when I was in pain. She no longer pushed me for better grades in school. She wasn't content to just remain my mother. She decided she was going to be both my mother and my father.

There appeared a sternness in her I had never seen before. She got tough, very tough. I was afraid of her when she got mad, because she'd hit me with anything she could get her hands on—a belt, a strap, anything.

We moved in with my maternal grandmother, my great-grandmother, and my great-aunt on the top floor of a large apartment building on 140th Street. From our front windows, we could look sideways and see the Hudson River.

Pictured are: Great-aunt Angie, a family friend, great-aunt Maria.
I am in front and Abuelita is standing alone to the right side.

20

I'll Be Good *Tomorrow*

My mother and I shared a room, while my great-grandmother had her own room. My grandmother and great-aunt Maria shared the largest room.

Both my great-grandmother and Maria loved and treated me as if I was their own child.

But my grandmother was different. She always seemed stern and demanding of my good behavior. I didn't like being around her. Being my grandmother, I always tried to show her respect. But I could sense she didn't care for me. It was depressing.

I never even called her "Grandma." I always called her by her first name, Sasita, which she preferred. Instead, I called my great-grandmother, *Abuelita*, which is Spanish for grandmother.

The life I knew growing up changed overnight, and wasn't fun anymore. They all tried—Abuelita, Maria, and my mother— but it wasn't enough. They couldn't fill the void that was left after my father went away.

There had been another great aunt, long before my father left. Angie was Maria's sister. She loved me and spoiled the hell out of me. Anything I wanted—I mean anything—Angie would give it to me.

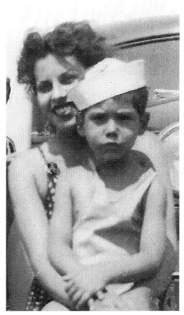

One time when I was three years old, I was on my little tricycle in the park with Angie. It was time to go home, but I didn't want to ride it back. I wanted Angie to pick up the tricycle and carry it. She said, "No, you ride it."

But I wouldn't move. I sat there crying, until I made good old Angie come over to pick up the tricycle. Suddenly, I saw my mother

Great-aunt Angie holding me

21

standing there, angrily looking at me. I hadn't expected her to show up at the park.

She surprised me by being there, so I quickly started peddling. My mother made me ride it home, and then punished me. Angie would've carried the tricycle back if my mother hadn't been there. I could do anything with her.

That same year as I was sleeping in my bedroom, I woke up when I heard a lot of people outside in the living room, sobbing and crying. I got up to see what was happening. Everyone was there. My mother, Abuelita, Maria, Sasita—my entire family were sitting around crying. It was as if I was floating in a sea of tears. I asked, "What's wrong?"

My mother held me and said, "Angie left us. She's in Heaven now."

Our family couldn't afford a funeral parlor, so we had to have Angie's coffin in the living room of our apartment. She lay there with flowers all around her for three or four days. I remember leaning in and kissing her for the last time. I will never forget the feeling of my lips pressing against her cold cheek. Nor can I forget the smell of roses flooding every room in the apartment. To this day, the smell of roses instantly reminds me of death.

When I was fourteen, I came home one day to find that Abuelita, my great-grandmother, had died. It was a little different then. We could afford to have her in a funeral parlor. Some men came into the bedroom where she was and carried her out in a large basket that looked like a hamper.

That day, *Abuelita* became my "Guardian Angel."

She had taught me that each of us has an angel looking over us, who protects us from harm. Each night she would sit next to me at bedtime and together we would recite, *Oracion al Angel Guardián*—a Prayer to My Guardian Angel—a short Spanish prayer that she'd taught me.

After my Aunt Angie died, Abuelita had told me that Angie was my guardian angel. Angie would look over me, and protect me. But

I'll Be Good *Tomorrow*

now, Abuelita became that angel. Abuelita became the one I prayed to whenever I was in trouble—whenever I needed help.

Her death left me with Maria and my mother—the only two people I felt close to and who I believed really loved me. Although Sasita was still alive, I never thought of her possibly caring about me.

Throughout my life I've seen far too many loved ones die. I've been at their bedside, or held them in my arms as that last breath took place, although, to me, it has always sounded like a low pop rather than a breath—a "pop" that often haunts me.

I've seen death up close too many times. So many that I've often felt everyone I got close to would suddenly leave—that everyone I loved died. Even my father, who'd left me to go to South America, seemed like another death. it's as if I've lived with death all my life.

Great-Aunt Maria holding me

RALPH B. LAO

CHAPTER 3

JOHNNY RIDES A PONY

People think of Harlem as being a scary, tough, dangerous place—a ghetto. But Harlem to us was just "the neighborhood." A fun neighborhood. We made it fun. We made it exciting. There was always something happening. We woke up every morning thinking, asking ourselves, "What are we going to do today?"

Our neighborhood wasn't like your average small town where a couple of guys get together, ride around in a car talking shit and smoking pot, and that's the big event of the day. In our neighborhood we had as many guys living in one block as other places have in an entire town. With that many guys to hang around with in our neighborhood, something was always going on.

Although I lived on 140th Street, I hung out on 135th Street. That was the fun block. On 140th Street I was known as a nice, obedient kid with good manners. On 135th Street I could relax, enjoy myself—just be one of the guys.

Suburban kids don't know what it is to create street games. To not have the money for baseball gloves or footballs, and have to invent ways to have fun. To create games like Stoopball, Ringolevio, Kick

25

the Can, Skullsy, Boxball, and a score of others—and all played on concrete, asphalt, or cobblestone.

One of the games we created was Chinese handball. It was like handball, but instead of hitting the wall directly, the players had to bounce the ball first and then hit the wall.

We each had a box marked up for ourselves, lined up side by side, facing the wall. Then we hit the ball to each other, trying to get someone to miss, or to hit it out of bounds, out of a box. If a guy missed or hit it out, he got a point against himself. Whoever reached a certain number of points first, was the loser.

We enjoyed playing that game with "Asses-Up." That meant that whoever was the loser had to face the wall, bend over, and put his ass up in the air. The other guys stood across the street with a rubber ball, and threw it as hard as they could. Each guy got two shots to try to hit the loser on the ass with the ball. "Pow!" Anyone who hit the loser's ass earned another shot. Meanwhile, the loser had to make sure he kept his legs closed, hiding his nuts, so as to not get hit there.

Then there was Johnny Rides A Pony. Two teams were picked, with one team chosen to be the "Pony." That team then picked a guy— usually the biggest, fattest guy—to be their "pillow," who had to stand with his back against the wall. Then, one after another, the guys would bend over at the waist, and hold onto each other tightly while facing the "pillow." They held on, heads down, end-to-end, while the first guy held on around the waist of the "pillow." This formed the "Pony," which extended out from the "pillow" to the end of the line.

The guys on the other team would come running one by one, as fast as possible. Each one would put his hands on the back of the end guy, leap up high in the air, and land as hard as he could farther down the line. The object was to break the chain by landing hard. The "pillow," seeing them coming, would then yell, "Here they come!"

If the chain hadn't broken after everybody landed, they would rock from side to side and yell, "Johnny rides a pony. One-two-three!" three times. After that, the teams switched sides and started all over again. Whichever team broke the chain first, won.

Of course, Stickball was always the most popular street game we played. It was just like baseball or softball, same rules, but we used a rubber ball that we had to bounce once before it reached the batter. The bat, or "stick" was usually a broomstick with the broom part cut off.

Those were some of our games, and when we got tired of playing them, we invented new ones. But, the neighborhood was constantly changing—we were all constantly changing. Just as we were outgrowing Johnny Rides A Pony, our group moved into its next stage—a gang.

RALPH B. LAO

CHAPTER 4

THE FIRST TIME

As far back as I can remember, almost to the age of six when I was in the first grade, I always had girlfriends. In those days, if a boy liked a girl and she told her friends she liked him, everyone would take it for granted that she was his girlfriend. It was that simple. No asking her to be your girl, or to go steady. That's the way it was in elementary school.

As I got a little older, nine, ten, and eleven, I had lots of girlfriends. I liked girls. Girls liked me. I was never without a girlfriend for long. I've been told that I looked like the actor, Robert Blake, when he was a youngster, so I was fairly good looking.

I was always courteous, and I treated girls right. My mother had instilled a certain code of honor in me. "Treat a girl with the same respect you'd want me, your mother, to be shown," she said.

But it wasn't until I was twelve, almost thirteen, that I had my first sexual encounter with a girl. It was a couple of years after my father left and I lived with my mother on 140th Street. On the first

29

floor of my building there lived a girl named Pearl. She was sixteen, very pretty, but four years older than I was.

The guys on my block all knew Pearl as the "neighborhood whore." The friends I had living on that block were all my age or a year younger or older. But they all knew anyone could screw Pearl. None of them had ever done it—not with Pearl or any other girl—but they knew about screwing.

They would say, "You go with a girl, kiss her, touch her, and if you're lucky and she lets you, you screw her." But none of us had ever screwed a girl. We'd all talked about it, but no one knew what that was like. Except Pearl.

Pearl and I got along great. She was a tomboy and a lot of fun. She'd play ball with us and do everything the guys could do— and better. I always enjoyed competition, and Pearl gave it to me. I enjoyed her.

I could tell that Pearl liked me, but there was that four-year gap. To me, Pearl appeared as a real "woman of the world," with lots of experience, while I was just a twelve-year-old kid.

Whenever the guys got together, we'd talk about how we'd like to kiss Pearl, feel her up, and screw her. Whenever we'd see her going somewhere, we'd kid around with her and make little remarks. But Pearl could always put us down.

We'd ask, "Pearl, where are you going?"

And she'd say, "Oh, I'm going to take a walk."

Then someone would ask, "Can I go with you?"

And she would turn around, look right at us, and answer, "Sure, come on."

The guys would laugh and shuffle around, but no one knew what else to say or do. She'd smile, and keep on going.

One day I went outside and Pearl was there alone, sitting on a stoop. One thing led to another, and we decided to go to her apartment to play Chinese checkers. Her mother had to go out to the store and left the two of us alone.

Pearl and I started kidding around on the sofa and wrestling. She was a strong girl—strong as a guy. You could wrestle with her and if you didn't watch yourself, she'd beat you. I didn't like getting beat. Not because she was a girl. I just didn't like getting beat by anyone, period.

While we were wrestling, Pearl grabbed me and started tickling me, slipping her hand under my belt, around my waist. I was laughing, and she stuck her hand down towards my crotch, reaching around and tickling me. I pulled away, but I was starting to get excited. And curious.

After all the talk with the guys about feeling up girls, and screwing Pearl, I realized this was it. This was my chance. But I had to act cool. I wanted Pearl to think I'd already screwed a girl, even though I'd never even come close to doing it.

So I asked her, "How would you like it if I did that to you? If I put my hand inside your pants, and tickled you?"

"Sure, go ahead," she answered. We were lying on the floor and she just grabbed my hand and put it inside her panties.

She said, "Here, see, I'm not ticklish. Go ahead." And she just lay there.

I don't remember the exact sensation I had then. I think it was more surprise and fear than anything else. I had my hand inside her panties and I started moving my fingers around, playing with her. But this was happening too fast. I was scared. I wasn't ready for it. I'd never done this before.

My hand was inside her panties, my fingers moving around, but I couldn't feel anything. I rubbed, but all I felt was hair. I knew that a man's joint is just above the crotch, higher up, so that's where I was touching her. That's where I expected to find her pussy—above her crotch.

I had seen women taking showers—my aunt, my mother—I'd grown up in a house full of women. But with all the hair a woman has there, I had never seen the actual pussy—the opening. So I didn't know where it actually was.

And there was no sex education in school back in the 1940's. Not in my school. Everything I learned about girls was from other guys on the street. I learned that girls had pussies and boys had dicks. But I

31

never had a girl show me or say, "My pussy's here, underneath, right between my legs."

So with my hand in her panties, I continued gently rubbing the area above her crotch—while searching. I'd always heard girls liked it when you rubbed their pussy. But instead, Pearl started laughing.

I asked, "Why are you laughing?"

She reached down, took my hand and said, "Silly, what are you doing there? You should be here." She pushed my hand down, right between her thighs, where I actually felt the warmth and softness of her lips, her pussy. Wow, it was amazing. I never expected it to be there.

But the awe and excitement of actually putting my hand on her pussy, any pussy, quickly turned to confusion. *What do I do now?* I thought.

I was so nervous she had to have felt my hand trembling a little. I was trying so hard to act cool, but I didn't know if I should continue rubbing her pussy or just keep my hand pressed against it.

Suddenly, her dog started barking at the door. Pearl's mother was coming back, and we had to stop. It was back to Chinese checkers. I made what I thought were a few cool remarks to Pearl. "Maybe some other time," and this and that. But I was so glad to breathe again that we finished our game and I left.

After that, I had mixed feelings. I had just become the first guy in my group to actually touch a pussy, to actually put my hand on one. If I could just get together with her again, maybe Pearl would let me go further and screw her.

Holy shit, at twelve years old I could be the first guy in my group of friends to actually screw a girl. But I also felt embarrassed because it all happened so fast I didn't know what to do once she placed my hand where it belonged.

Pearl had an intimidating way about her. She knew so much more than me, but I didn't want her to know that. All these things together made me realize I had messed up. And I felt stupid. I must have looked silly and immature to her. I had to try and fix that image.

A few weeks went by before I had the next opportunity. There was a couple in our building who had a young boy named Kenny, and they sometimes had Pearl babysit him whenever they had an evening out.

Since I lived on the same floor as them, I sometimes kept Pearl company while she took care of Kenny. We'd play cards or checkers.

One day Pearl asked, "Hey, Bobby, I'm sitting with Kenny for a couple of hours tonight. Want to come over and keep me company? We'll play some cards, or we can finish our Chinese checkers game." She smiled in a teasing way as she said it.

By now the guys had started getting on me for running around with Pearl a lot. They'd see me, and say, "Hey Bobby, did you get into Pearl, did you screw her yet?"

I would answer, "Well…" I didn't come right out and say yes, but I never said no. I'd just smile, leading them to think that I had. Or I'd say something like, "That's between me and Pearl."

But they didn't let up. They thought I did, but they weren't sure. So when Pearl asked me to come over to Kenny's apartment I quickly answered, "Sure. What time are you babysitting? When should I come over?"

Since I had looked so foolish the last time I'd been alone with her, I had to make amends. This felt like the perfect time and place for me to try and fix things. Especially since we both seemed to understand that the next time we were alone, we would pick up where we'd left off.

We started the night off by playing a few hands of Go Fish, and then we switched to poker. But I was nervous, and she could see I was trying to stall. So she made it hard for me.

She kept coming up with cute little remarks, or touching my hand and smiling. I knew I couldn't stall any longer, and I couldn't chicken out. I had to make some move.

When it was my turn to deal the cards again, I figured it was now or never, so I asked her, "Why don't we play strip poker?"

She said, "Okay, great! Let's do it. Let's play strip poker."

Holy shit! I never expected her to agree that quickly. I figured she'd hem and haw a few times, letting me act cool. But instead she said, "Okay" right away.

So we set the rules, and started playing. A belt counted as one item, a sock as only one, and so on. But I was not about to strip in front of this girl. No way. I never pictured ME losing. I only pictured HER losing and having to take HER clothes off. What I was going to do then, I didn't know.

Sure, I wanted to screw Pearl. But I'd never screwed a girl before. I didn't know where to start, or what to do next. I wasn't quite sure how the hell I was going to do that.

Not too far into the game, I realized that this goddamn girl was beating me. My belt was off, my shirt was off, a shoe, a sock, and I was getting nervous. I was laughing, but trembling at the same time. Pearl was laughing and making remarks, like, "Oh, your pants come next, and then we're going to see your boo-boo."

Oh, Jesus, I thought. *What am I going to do?* She really had me on the spot. She was making me take off my clothes—one item at a time.

So I figured I'd throw it all in one heap and gamble. I'd really put it to her and shake the girl up. I had to get out of this situation. I wasn't going to strip in front of her. I was too embarrassed.

I looked at her and said, "Instead of all this nonsense, why don't we play a hand of poker and whoever wins fucks the other one?" I said it just like that. "Whoever wins fucks the other one." And I sat back, smugly waiting.

I was sure she was going to turn around and say "Oh, no!" I figured when I confronted her with it, she wouldn't go for it, just like any other girl. Then I would call her bluff and say, "Why should we keep playing this stupid game if we're not going to do that?" That would get me out of it.

"Okay," Pearl said. "Let's play." No hesitation. No second thoughts. She just sat there smiling and said, "Go ahead and deal the cards."

Shit! My plan had backfired. But I had to keep acting cool. I had to act as if I'd expected her to go along with it. As if this was what I wanted her to say.

I dealt the cards; we played a hand of poker, and Crap! She beat me again.

"Okay, you won. Ha, ha. You have to fuck me," I said, still pretending I knew what I was doing, that all was going as I had planned. While in reality, shit! I was nervous. What the hell was I going to do now?

Pearl laughed and got up. "All right," she said. "But wait a minute. I have to go to the bathroom. I'll be right back."

She went into the bathroom while I sat there waiting. I figured it was something girls did. They probably always went to the bathroom just before screwing. That was part of the game. Part of the fun for them, getting a guy excited, and then making him wait.

So I sat there waiting for her to come back. I was nervous, praying my mother would come looking for me and knock on the door, or Kenny's parents would return, or anything that would get me out of this.

But nothing happened. Pearl came out of the bathroom, smiled at me, and I got up. "Come on," she said. "Let's go over to the bed."

She was leading. This girl knew I was nervous. But I kept trying to act as if I knew what I was doing. And all the time she had a smile on her face. She was playing with me.

Pearl put the chain on the door and we went into the bedroom. We walked up to the bed. She stood with her back to the bed and I was facing her, just standing there, trembling inside. I was waiting for her to do something. I figured she was the experienced one, so she would do something now.

But she just stood there smiling and waiting for me to make a move. But I was trying to get myself together, to figure out what the hell to do next, and I was taking too long.

Pearl asked, "Well, what are you waiting for?"

So I said, "Oh." And I pushed her on the bed, thinking to myself, *Well, I'm the man, she's the girl. A man's supposed to take the initiative and make the girl get on the bed.*

She fell back and said, "No, stupid. Are you going to use your finger? Your hands? Are you going to keep your pants on?" She really had me now. She was laughing, but not out loud. She just had a smile on her face.

I didn't take my pants off. I was not about to take my pants off. I opened my fly and fumbled around trying to get my dick out. I could always get a hard-on very easily, lying in my bed at night, thinking about girls. I only had to touch myself, and Bingo. But here I was, so nervous I couldn't get a hard-on. I was too scared. Too nervous. Nothing worked. I couldn't get hard.

When I finally pulled out my dick, I quickly got on top of her so she wouldn't see it. But she reached down and took me in her hand, playing around with me for a few seconds so that I was able to get a semblance of a hard-on. She didn't take her panties off, she just pushed them aside, and she put me inside of her.

As soon as I was there, I started moving. Moving up and down, up and down, because I thought this was what I was supposed to do. It wasn't what I felt like doing. But I didn't like her holding me in her hand, so I kept moving up and down, hoping that would work.

Unfortunately, I popped out right away. I fumbled around trying to find the opening to get back in, and I couldn't. I was just making a mess of it.

"Wait a minute, wait a minute," Pearl said. "This isn't going to work. Roll over on your back."

I rolled over and Pearl got up and took her panties off.

While I was lying there, I started playing with myself, rubbing myself, trying to get hard. I would start to, but I was so nervous I couldn't go all the way.

Then Pearl straddled me, putting one of her knees on each side of me. I looked up and felt I had to say something. I couldn't just lie there. I had to keep acting cool. So I said, "That's right, you're the one who won. You're supposed to fuck me. I've got to see how you're going to do this."

I thought that was a very clever thing to say. Acting as if this is why it didn't work before—because I didn't want it to. It wasn't

36

supposed to be me screwing her. She'd won the card game, so she was supposed to screw me.

She laughed and placed me inside her. And that lasted less than a minute.

All I felt was panic. I was disgusted with the whole thing. I didn't like it at all. For one thing, she was wet inside. Not just wet, but soggy. I figured she must have peed and hadn't cleaned herself, or something. This must be what a girl did to get wet so that the man could slide into her.

And I didn't like that. I couldn't get hard enough, so every time she moved up and down I'd pop out of her. Finally she just stopped, laughed, and said, "Come on Bobby, let's get up. This isn't going to work."

"What do you mean?" I asked. "Why won't it work?"

"Because you're too young Bobby. Come back when you're a year or two older. Maybe then it'll work," she said.

Me (when I first met Pearl)

So, we got up and finished a game of cards. I was so happy to get out of the bedroom, I didn't realize just how put down I'd been until much later.

When I finally learned what it was all about and got to make love with a girl, I kept hoping I'd get another chance with Pearl. I'd show her that "I'm older now and I know what to do. I'm a good lover now."

But Pearl got married, moved away, and I never saw her again. So I was cheated out of that one.

That day, when she let me off the hook, saying, "Come back when you're a year or two older," I was so happy to stop, that I told myself I would never try to screw a girl again. If this was what it was all about, NO THANKS!

Floating around inside a girl's pussy, all wet and soggy—I hated it. It was terrible. All that crap I'd heard about how great it was, and it was nothing.

I didn't want any part of it. EVER!

CHAPTER 5

BUT FOR A WATERMELON

It's strange to sit back and remember the mischief, the thefts, the burglaries, and realize that it all came about because of a watermelon. If it hadn't been for a watermelon, I might never have ventured into a life of crime.

It happened in my early teen years, after I'd just met Orlando, Manny, Tommy, and the other guys from 135th Street. We were going through our game-playing thing: Chinese Hand-ball and Johnny Rides A Pony.

Our neighborhood wasn't like some of those suburban towns where there might be sail boating and horseback riding, or indoor basketball courts, swimming pools, and all that crap. We didn't have any of that.

If we wanted to play ball, we had to play in the street, constantly dodging cars. If we wanted to go swimming, we'd go down to the Hudson River with all that crap floating in the water around us.

Sometimes we'd play stoopball, hitting the ball off the steps of a stoop while the other team tried to catch it. Each bounce, before it was caught, counted as another base—just like the bases in baseball. We sometimes called the game "Single, Double, Triple." We kept score, and whoever had the most runs after nine innings, won. But most of the time, the supers would come out and chase us off, so we rarely made it to nine innings.

We couldn't go down to Central Park, because that was too far from home. Riverside Drive had one softball area on 138th Street, a dirt field. But we could never use that because the "big guys" always had it.

We'd go down and grab the field, but before we knew it, the older guys would come and say, "All right, you guys, you've got five minutes to finish up your game. We got a game coming up and you have to leave."

After a while we got tired of that shit, so we didn't bother trying to get the field. We kept playing in the street, and we were getting too big for that, too. In those days there were no basketball courts available to us either—the schools just closed up. They didn't let anyone in. With little or no money, there was not much for us to do but hang out on the corner, looking for excitement.

One day we were playing stickball on 135th Street. We'd just chosen up four- or five-man sides when an old man came down the street with his horse-drawn wagon selling fruits and vegetables— just like he always did—yelling, "Fruits, vegetables," trying to sell his goods.

As the wagon passed us, I was leaning up against a car with Orlando and Manny. (Our team was up and we were waiting to hit the ball.) Orlando turned and looked at everyone as he pointed at the wagon. "Hey guys, how about a free watermelon," he asked.

A couple of us looked over at him, and I said, "Yeah, let's grab one and run."

Some of the guys started laughing, and said, "Yeah, let's do it." But I think most of us were scared. We'd never done anything like that before. We'd do it at the candy store—grab a candy bar and put it in our pocket, some dumb thing like that—but to steal something in broad daylight? A watermelon? The size of it—just the size of it—made it look like such a big thing.

Orlando quietly ran up behind the wagon, reached up, and grabbed a big watermelon from the back. He spun around and Boom! He put it right into my hands.

I caught it and ran with him. He held one end of the watermelon and I held the other. Manny and Tommy started running with us, and we all took off.

We heard the man behind us yelling, "Hey, hey!" He'd seen us, because he'd been sitting sideways in his wagon looking around. Obviously, other guys had pulled this shit on him before. I guess it was one of the hazards of his business.

We cut down to the alleys off 135th Street. Once there, no one could catch us. We knew those alleys. They were like home. We ran to the "Old Lots," an empty lot in the back of 135th Street.

About five or six of us got there, sat down, carved up the watermelon, and ate it. Deep down I think we all thought it was so stupid, especially since we could easily have just bought the watermelon. It wasn't that expensive.

But it was the excitement—the thrill of it. Here we'd done something different, different than anything we'd done before.

Looking back at it, I see the pattern, almost like climbing a ladder. We'd take a step, do something that was fun, then tire of it and take another step. It was never enough, so we kept climbing, step after step. Always moving up.

That's the way we went from stealing a car and going for a joyride, to later breaking into places. It never seemed to be enough.

We had so much energy we had to keep burning it up. We were impatient. We'd try one thing, and then we had to try something else, something more exciting. Something more dangerous.

Me, Rosie, and Manny at the beach. I am on the left

Orlando and Chino

I'll Be Good *Tomorrow*

CHAPTER 6

THE GLADIATORS AND
THE UNITED DUKES

It's interesting how a neighborhood evolves, goes through its cycles. I was about six years old when I had my first fight. At that age fighting wasn't fun. But when I got to be twelve or thirteen, it was different. I started to enjoy fighting. I wanted to assert myself. I wanted to take my place in the neighborhood. That was when I realized I had to belong to a gang.

Once every week or two the "West Siders," an Irish gang that hung out on the corner of 135th Street and Amsterdam Avenue, would come down the street and beat up any Puerto Rican kids they ran into. These guys were sixteen or seventeen years old, while we were only twelve to fourteen. But they hated Puerto Ricans moving into the neighborhood, especially on their block.

My friends and I would be playing Stoop Ball, Ringolevio, or something, and suddenly someone would yell, "The West Siders! The West Siders!" We knew what that meant, so we all ran like crazy. If those guys caught us, they'd kick us in the ass, and knock us around. Bam! Bam! All the while yelling, "You dirty spics, get the fuck off our block!"

Finally, we got tired of being pushed around. We realized that although they were older and bigger than us, we had more than enough guys to fight back. Three or four of us could grab one of them and beat the crap out of him.

We asked The Rainbows, a gang from 146th Street, to help us. They called themselves The Rainbows because they were all different nationalities, different colors—white, black, brown, yellow—you name it, they had it.

The Rainbows didn't like it that an Irish gang was beating up on us, so they agreed to help us. They came down to our street, hid in doorways with a bunch of our guys, and said, "Okay, get them down here. We'll just wait."

A few of us went up to the corner in the West Siders' territory, and made sure they saw us. They didn't like that. It pissed them off, so they chased us back down the block.

Our guys came out from hallways and from behind cars. We surprised them and beat the shit out of them. I remember the panic on their faces when we grabbed them. I had one guy down, and he looked scared. He was trying to get up and pull away, while Orlando and Tommy were punching him.

We were young then, just starting out, but it felt great to grab a big guy we'd always been afraid of, and find out we could beat the crap out of him. That we didn't have to be afraid of him anymore.

The West Siders took off, and they never pulled that shit again.

There were just too many of us now. The Irish guys were outnumbered. Too many Puerto Ricans and Cubans had moved into the neighborhood. We had the power now. We had the numbers, and it was a great feeling.

That's when we got together and formed the Gladiators. From then on, it was like every few blocks there was another gang springing up. We started with the Gladiators. Then the Buccaneers appeared.

I'll Be Good *Tomorrow*

There were already the West Siders, the Rainbows, and further uptown the Jacobins.

Almost overnight belonging to a gang became a necessity. Being in a gang meant you had help if you got jumped by guys from another gang. And then there were the parties and the girls. The Jacobins, the Gladiators, or any of the gangs might throw a party. Belonging to a gang meant you could throw your own party, or be invited to some other gang's party.

You had to form or join a gang in order to fit in. It's like guys that belong to school clubs or teams. They go to school and join the baseball team, the football team, or the basketball team. Well, these were our basketball teams, our social clubs. Except that our clubs also had war counselors.

Whenever two gangs met for a fight, the war counselors were the two guys who got the fight started. They'd walk up, face off, and start talking shit. Occasionally, they'd work things out without a fight. But when talking didn't work, the war counselors would start swinging away at each other.

One war counselor, Archie from the Rainbows, was famous for saying, "The shit is on." That was his signal to start the fight. So every time I saw Archie, I'd joke, and yell, "The shit is on." He'd laugh, and continue on his way.

I was voted captain of the Gladiators. We were a fun group. We'd known each other since our elementary school days. And although we were more interested in parties and girls than in gang fights, becoming a gang was necessary. But we also had some pretty bad guys. Guys who could fight.

As I got older, Chino, a guy who was about twenty-one years old, pointed out how the gangs were foolishly fighting each other most of the time. Why fight each other? Why not form one big gang, and call it the United Dukes? One gang with different divisions—the Manhattan Lords, the Rainbows, the Jacobins, the Gladiators, and so on—would all be part of the United Dukes.

We all respected Chino because he had a reputation as a bad guy. Everyone had heard the story of how he'd fought some guys from

110th Street, Spanish Harlem, when he was sixteen. How he stood in the middle of the street with two zip guns, one in each hand, yelling, "Come on you motherfuckers, I'm going to kill you!"

Wow, we thought that was so cool. We thought he was bad. But now he was twenty-one and he was still mixed up in this fighting shit. However, he got the neighborhood together, all the gangs, and we formed the United Dukes.

The Gladiators became the United Dukes second division under this new arrangement. The idea was that each group could maintain its own members. The group's captain could still be captain, and the group would still have its own co-captain and its own war counselor.

Now that we were the United Dukes, we were the biggest gang in the area. Other gangs, like the Dragons from 110th Street, now knew that, and had to respect us because of our size, our numbers. They knew they were no longer fucking around with only the Gladiators or the Buccaneers. They were fucking around with all of us. With the United Dukes. And that was cool.

But while the gang fights and partying were a lot of fun, other things started to get my attention. I started to get very close to two of the guys in our group—Orlando and Manny. While we enjoyed hanging out with the gang, the three of us found another common interests—money.

Fighting, gangs, and partying was one thing, but our need for money was another. Orlando, Manny, and I were quickly getting a thirst for it.

We went from stealing cars to breaking into grocery stores, clothing stores, jewelry stores, and stick-ups. It just evolved as we got older. Suddenly, the three of us had earned the reputation of always having money in our pockets. We were quickly graduating from one level to another. And along the way, we were getting a tough reputation as well.

I'll Be Good *Tomorrow*

CHAPTER 7

BERNADETTE

The first time I saw Bernadette, I was fourteen years old, and she had just turned thirteen. I was at a "jump" that a couple of our guys were having. A jump was a small party that was usually put together quickly, and held in someone's apartment, in a dimly lit room. They usually played slow music—rhythm and blues records—that a guy and his partner could dance and grind to.

While there, a couple of the girls from our group came in with a girl I'd never seen before. One of the guys in our gang, Richard, knew her and said, "Hi, Bernie," and he introduced her to me. "Bobby, this is Bernadette."

I wasn't going with anyone then, so I was glad to meet someone new, especially since she was really cute. She was an Irish girl with freckles on her face. She looked a lot like the actress Jodie Foster—the thirteen-year-old version of Jodie Foster. We started dancing together and were getting along really well. I found her very easy to talk to.

Suddenly, there were a couple of guys at the door wanting to "speak to Bernadette." She looked out, saw who they were, and said she didn't want to go out there. She got very upset.

"Don't worry. Wait here and I'll go see what they want," I told her.

When I got to the door, I recognized one of the guys. He was a member of the Manhattan Lords, the diddy-bops of the neighborhood. "Hi Jamie" I said. "I'm not sure what this is all about, but Bernadette doesn't want to come out here. She seems upset and a little scared."

"We're not going to do anything to her," he said. "We just want to talk to her. She's going out with one of the guys from our gang, and we don't like our girls hanging out at parties without telling us first."

It sounded like a lot of crap to me, so I repeated, "Look man, it's like I said, she isn't going to come out and talk to you guys right now. She's too upset."

They stood at the door, sizing us up, and apparently decided we didn't look like pushovers. There were a lot of us, and we looked determined, ready to fight if necessary. None of us was going to let Bernadette go with them. She was crying in a back room, scared.

After talking it over for a few minutes, everything cooled down. They finally understood that she really didn't want to leave with them or be part of their gang anymore, and they left.

The party ended fast. Everybody had gotten into a fighting mood and it was difficult to get back into a party mood. I told Bernadette I would take her home because I didn't want her to go out there alone. Richard came along with us. He knew her and I felt comfortable with him there because I'd just met her.

The three of us walked to her building in the middle of the block on 135th Street. She lived on the first floor in the back. But since the party ended earlier than expected, we sat on the stoop and talked for over an hour.

I asked her "What was all that about, Bernie? Why were they so upset because you were hanging out with us?"

She explained, "I went out with this guy, Tico, from the Manhattan Lords for a few months, but he was kind of a jerk, so I broke off with him last week. Unfortunately, while I was going out with him, he talked me into joining the Debs. But I don't want any part of them, either. I told him I didn't want anything to do with the gang anymore. That's what led to all this."

She went inside, and I walked along with Richard, feeling pleased. I could see she liked me. I could feel it. I had come off looking great in her eyes. She was scared and I told her not to worry. I'd gone out there to talk to them, and had come off like a hero to her. And I liked her, so that was great.

I pumped Richard on the way home for

Bernadette at age 15 years

everything he knew about Bernadette. But there wasn't much more to tell, other than that she had been going with that guy for a few months.

By the time I got home, I was thinking about her a lot. I came around the next day to see her. Before I knew it, I started seeing Bernadette regularly. We went to the movies together on weekends. Whenever we had parties, I would always go with her. I don't remember asking Bernadette to be my girl then. But because we were always together, everyone took it for granted.

I would come around and they'd say, "Your girl was looking for you." Or to her, "Your guy was looking for you, Bernie." Or someone would ask one of us, "Where's your other half?"

RALPH B. LAO

When I wasn't hanging around with the guys, I was with Bernadette. If we all went down to Riverside Drive to hang out, some of the guys would go with their girls, and I'd be with Bernadette. Everyone knew we were a couple.

I had long since forgotten the incident with Pearl. Since then I had gone out with Rosie and her sister Peggy, and made out with lots of girls. But I wanted a steady girl. A girl I could be with all of the time. And Bernadette was just at the right age where she could feel tender towards a guy.

Before long we'd been together for about six or seven months. When we went to a movie, we would kiss, and make out. She made me feel good. She made me like her, and want to be with her.

When we were together, we would do everything short of touching each other. But, it had gotten to the point where I could feel my hand wanting to touch her and her wanting to feel my touch.

Bernadette was just starting to develop and she had fairly nice breasts. Soft breasts. I could feel them pressed against me when we were kissing or making out. "Making out" then was nothing more then just kissing and holding each other, feeling each other's warmth through our clothing.

We'd do that a lot. We'd hold each other tightly, and slowly rub and press against each other. I was afraid to go beyond that. I wanted to touch her breast, her bare skin, but I felt shy about it, and I didn't want to mess up, and scare her off.

After school there was no one in Bernadette's apartment. Her father worked at a place that made prescription glasses. He was a lens grinder. He worked during the day and came home around 5:30 in the evening. Her mother was a waitress, and worked at Bickford's, a cafeteria chain, in downtown Manhattan.

So, we'd come from school, and if nothing were going on around the neighborhood, we'd go into her place and hang out. Sometimes we kissed; sometimes we played games like Parcheesi or cards.

One day, after we'd been going together for a while, we were in her parent's bedroom in the back of the apartment, on the bed. I don't remember exactly how we got there, but we were lying there kissing, while slowly rubbing our bodies together, and getting each other excited.

For the past few months, I'd been thinking, *One of these days I've got to touch her. I've got to feel her breasts.* By this time she had just about put her breast in my hand. I felt that she wanted me to touch her, but I was still too shy.

Every night when I lay back in bed, I thought about how I would do it. About how I was going to put my hand on her breast and gently touch them, but the opportunity was never there. That is until this day.

There we were on the bed. I had my hand on her side and I felt it was now or never. I kissed her and slowly got on top of her, just rubbing my body against hers, and I moved my hand up on the outside of her blouse. She didn't stop me. She liked it. She got excited and started making sounds.

Bernadette was great for making sounds. Whenever I was kissing her and did something she liked, she'd go "Ah." She'd always let me know if I did something good. She'd signal me this way—her way of letting me know she enjoyed what I was doing, that it felt good.

The first time I touched Bernadette's breast I felt different than I had with any other girl. It felt right. It wasn't like with Pearl, where I felt I had to. With Bernadette it was something I wanted to do, I needed to do. We'd been going out together and we really liked each other.

Suddenly there I was with my hand on her blouse, and through it I could feel her breast. It was the softest breast in the whole world.

That was the nicest feeling I could've possibly ever imagined. It was just what I expected and more. I didn't think I could ever feel that way again.

I kept kissing her, feeling great, because I had touched her and she had let me. I had accomplished something I had wanted to do so badly.

Now I was going to try to go a little farther. As long as I was touching her breast, maybe I could kiss them, just put my lips on them. Again, I was afraid she wasn't going to let me go any farther. But she didn't stop me.

RALPH B. LAO

So, I gently unbuttoned her blouse and started kissing her neck and moving down. She had her bra on and I just slid it down and kissed her. She let me do that, and she liked it. She made moaning sounds.

I wanted to take her bra off, but I had no experience with bra hooks and I just fumbled around. I couldn't get the goddamn thing off. Finally she reached back and unhooked it herself.

I was afraid to look at her. I had my eyes closed because I felt that was the right thing to do. I didn't want to make her feel self-conscious. After all, it was daytime, right after school.

Finally I put my mouth right on her breasts and played with her, slowly moving my tongue over them. It was just the greatest feeling—and what the guys always talked about.

When the guys got together and they talked about being with a girl, this was what I'd imagined it should be like. I had completely forgotten about Pearl. This was something else. It was Bernadette, and it was right.

We were there like that for a while. Then we got up because her mother and father were due to come home soon. But as I walked home that night, I felt like I was floating. I had my girl. I'd had her bra off. I'd kissed her breasts.

I went back to her apartment the next day. When the two of us saw each other, I could sense that we both felt the same way. I could see she wanted to repeat what we had done the day before.

We did, and she felt as good about it as I did—and she made sure I knew it.

We were like two kids with a new toy. We'd just discovered something new about each other. A new level in our romance. And something completely different than anything we had done before.

That evening we went down to Riverside Drive and started kissing again. I loosened her bra and started kissing her breasts. She liked it. She enjoyed having me kiss her breasts, gently sucking on them. It excited her.

To us, experiencing this, which was something new for both of us, was the ultimate in sex. This was further than we had ever gone before.

I'll Be Good *Tomorrow*

After that, it got to be a frequent thing. We couldn't wait to get away from everyone and go down to Riverside Drive, just the two of us. Or come home from school and go to her apartment during the day, before her mother or father came home, and start kissing. I'd start touching her and kissing her breasts, while she gently held my head close, both of us wishing it would never end.

Weeks went by before "the ultimate" got to be a common thing. Like everything else we did then, once we started doing something new, something that felt good to both of us, it became an everyday thing. It became normal.

But I wanted to go farther—and I could feel she wanted me to, also.

RALPH B. LAO

CHAPTER 8

BERNADETTE: THE NEXT STEP

Nick, one of the guys in our group, had a small clubhouse in the basement of his building on 136th Street. It was small and dark, but it was next to the boiler room, so it was always warm. It was a great place for him to hide whenever he played hooky or wanted to make out with girls. The super never used it for anything, so he let Nick use it whenever he wanted to. In return, Nick helped him clean out the boiler room.

Nick didn't mind some of us using it as a make-out place, as long as we were quiet and kept it clean. The super was a pretty cool guy, so he didn't mind, either, and never told Nick's parents about it.

After going together for six or seven months, Bernie and I could just look at each other and know what the other was thinking. We didn't have to say much of anything, yet we kind of understood what we each meant, or wanted.

One rainy day Bernie and I didn't feel like going to school. We just looked at each other and we both knew school was not where we wanted to be that day. So we decided to play hooky. Wanting to stay out of the rain and be together away from everyone, we went down to Nick's clubhouse.

Bernie and I were there alone, and we started making out, which meant we were standing against the wall, kissing, and slowly grinding against each other.

That was normally the way we'd start. Usually then I unbutton her blouse, or she would take her sweater off and loosen her bra so I could kiss her around her breasts. I would gently suck on her nipples, or nibble away. That was "making out" for us. It was what we had done a hundred times before. It was a great feeling. But again, like before in her father's bedroom, I wanted to go farther.

For weeks I'd been thinking about how I would go about it when the time came. I wanted to touch the most forbidden place she had. I wanted to put my hand right on her pussy. I wanted to do to her what I'd hoped to do with Pearl that time in her apartment. But, with Bernadette it was different.

It was something I was ready for, and something I really wanted to do. Everything was leading to it, and I could sense that she wanted me to touch her, also. But I was still too shy and I didn't know just how to go about it. I had a million ideas in my head on how I would get around to this, but I knew I had to wait for the right opportunity. The right moment.

Sometimes when we were kissing, I would start a conversation, say something a little suggestive, hoping to lead up to it, but it just never worked out.

That is until this day when we were kissing and grinding against the wall. I touched her breasts while she moved her hips around, in and out, both of us making sounds, getting ourselves hot and excited.

We'd never touched each other with our hands below the waist, but we would slowly grind our bodies together so I could feel the warmth between her legs, and she could feel me getting hard.

This particular day Bernadette had on a pair of dungarees with a thick buckle on her belt, and it was pressing against my stomach. It gave me an idea and I thought, *Maybe this is it. Maybe she'll take the belt off and loosen her pants, or even take them off.*

I'll Be Good *Tomorrow*

All kinds of crazy thoughts went through my mind. Finally, I said, "Bernie, the buckle on your belt is hurting my stomach."

"Then move it," she said. She didn't make any motion towards the buckle herself. It was like a signal.

I put my hand down and covered the buckle with the palm of my hand, just pressing it against her stomach. I kept kissing her and grinding with her, all the time keeping my hand there. I wasn't going to let this moment escape. I was afraid she would say something, but she didn't.

I could sense she was enjoying it, so I kept kissing her, little by little rotating my hand down the outside of the front of her dungarees, slowly moving my fingers around. I kept doing that until I finally got my hand down between her legs, right over her pussy.

I'd never felt anything as warm, as magical, as I did in that moment. I felt her warmth shoot up from my hand, through my arm and into my brain, until I could almost taste her.

We spent a long time in the basement that day. All I did was just gently rub Bernadette and play with her over her pants. I didn't dare put my hand inside them. I felt I'd gone far enough. I didn't want to push it. I didn't want to go any farther than that, because she might get scared and pull back.

It always had to be done step by step, just the right way. Whenever I reached one point, I stayed right there at that point. I just made sure that she enjoyed it, and I enjoyed myself. I wanted the magic of that moment to last as long as possible.

I remember the warmth of her pussy on my hand, even through the cloth of her pants. It was a moment burned into my brain. Into my soul. It was nothing like it'd been with Pearl, when she'd put my hand in her pants. There had been no magic with Pearl. The magic was now, here with Bernadette.

This was something Bernadette and I had both grown into. Our entire relationship was one discovery after another. Everything was a natural extension of what we'd experienced before. This was the next step.

When that day was over, we were like little kids again. We'd discovered something else.

That night when I went to bed it felt like it had all been a dream. I knew I'd wake up the next day and wonder, *Did that really happen or was I just dreaming? Did I really touch her?*

I couldn't wait to see her again. The day after one of these moments of new "discoveries," I'd always feel a little awkward, a little clumsy. Like maybe it didn't happen, or maybe the next time she'd stop me.

But the next day would come, we would see each other, and we'd do it again. Just like the day when I'd finally kissed her breasts. A little clumsy, a little scared, but I was able to do it again. And we both knew it wasn't a dream; it was real, it had happened. We had just gone another step farther in discovering each other.

For months after that day in Nick's clubhouse, in addition to kissing her, taking her bra off, and smothering myself in her breasts, I could touch her—I could play with her.

After a while I got my hand inside her pants. That was just as daring as the first time I'd rubbed my hand over the outside of them. I don't remember exactly how we led up to it, but before I knew it I had my hand inside her pants. This was not inside her panties, but just over the outside of them. However, I was now inside another layer of clothing. And I was better able to touch and play with her there.

By this time, about a year had gone by since Bernadette and I had first started going together. We'd reached that point where we'd touched each other just about everywhere. She enjoyed having my hand on her, playing with her.

We'd go down to Riverside Drive and sit there, and I'd play with her. Or we'd go to a movie where we'd sit in the back, up in the last row in the balcony. We'd start making out and I'd always end up with my hand inside Bernie's pants. If she was wearing a skirt, I could just put my hand under it.

By then, Bernie had started playing with me, too, but I felt a little shy about her putting her hand inside my pants. I guess she felt shy about it, also, so she'd just touch me with her hand over the outside of my pants. That was fine.

That went on for months. By then, naturally, I had to experience the next step. I'd gotten to the point where I had to have her. Then one day, rather by accident, we started talking about her first boyfriend, Tico, the guy from the Manhattan Lords.

I asked her if she'd ever done anything with him—had let him touch her. She jokingly said, "Oh, yeah, all the time."

I knew she hadn't, but we kept joking about it. I said, "You won't let me get into you, but Tico?…"

She kidded back a little, but I could tell she didn't like it. She seemed to feel a little hurt I'd think that way about her. But, I kept joking with her about Tico until she said, "You'll see, you'll see. One of these days I'll show you. You'll get a bloody dick."

I could see she was ready. It was just a matter of when and where. I knew she hadn't done anything with Tico. It wasn't about getting her to prove I was the first. It was about giving her something to hang her hat on. She wanted to, and I wanted to. But, she needed an excuse, a reason to say, "This is why I'm doing it."

One day after school we were in her house looking at a dirty comic book about Moon Mullins that I'd gotten from one of the guys. Mullins was delivering a package to a woman's house, and the woman was standing at the door, naked. She told him to come in and put the package down. One thing led to another, until finally Moon Mullins was on top of her.

It was really a dumb story. The only thing I remember about it was that Moon Mullins was on top of the woman, pushing in, when she said, "What are you trying to do, get your balls in there, too?"

Bernadette and I both started laughing.

I said, "Here's this guy trying to get his balls in. If I could just get the point of my dick in, I'd be happy."

Next thing I remember, Bernadette and I were making out, kissing on the sofa in her living room. We went through the usual—my kissing her breasts, and my playing with her beneath the free-flowing skirt she was wearing. Then I started taking her panties off.

She didn't stop me. She didn't say anything. I took them off and slowly put my hand back on her. I gently played with her, although I was afraid any minute she would say, "Stop! No more."

I kept playing with her for a little while, hoping to relax her and let her know everything was all right. Then, with her skirt up and her panties off, I slowly moved on top of her. I kept my hand right there between her legs, playing with her and rubbing her thighs. Reassuring her, while trying to excite her.

Little by little, I loosened the buckle of my pants, and pulled the zipper down. I went back to her, and gently touched her a little. With one hand I was touching her, and with the other trying to pull my pants off.

Finally, they were off. I grabbed my dick and I started playing around with her, while still lying on top of her. She didn't say anything. She kept kissing me, moaning softly. I held my dick in my hand and rubbed the head of it against her pussy, the same way I had been doing with my hand.

The next thing I knew, I was slowly—and gently—sliding into her. Everything with Bernadette was very gentle. I didn't want to scare her. I was at Heaven's door, and I wasn't going to push in and hurt her.

We must have been there like that for about half and hour. I would slowly push in a little, stop, and kiss her. Push in a little more, stop, and kiss her again, keeping my hand there all the time. Always gently, always passionately.

Finally, I was all the way inside Bernadette. It was as if my entire body was wrapped in her warmth—wrapped deep in the warmth of her body. When we finished (I don't remember what "finished" meant to us then) we got up.

Oh, Jesus! Bernadette had kept her skirt underneath her so that if she started to bleed, the skirt would soak it up. And from my place inside her, I could feel she was bleeding a little. But, we figured with her skirt there it was all right. However, the blood had gone through her skirt onto the sofa. There was a big red spot right on the brown sofa!

We panicked. Poor Bernie was so scared. She went and got a wet rag, and we tried to clean it up. She was scared, but we were laughing, too. What was her mother going to say?

Finally, she said, "Well, I'll just tell her. I'll say something like, 'Ma, Bobby and I love each other and we were making love on the sofa.'"

We laughed, but we had mixed feelings. We were happy and we felt good. This was something we'd both wanted. But, we hadn't meant to stain the sofa.

"Remember when I told you," she said, "one of these days I'll show you. You'll get a bloody dick?"

"Yeah, I remember. But you didn't say anything about a bloody sofa," I answered. And we both laughed.

She cleaned it up the best she could, and made up a story about spilling an ice cream soda she'd been drinking, which is what she told her mother.

Her mother was very nice about it. She used to spoil Bernadette.

For example, all the money she made in tips at Bickford's she would give to Bernadette. She was always buying her blouses, skirts, and things. So, anything Bernadette said to her was pretty much okay, although I suspect a lot of the things we told her she didn't really believe.

That stain was still there years later. Every time we looked at it, we'd remember. It was a mark we'd left there from the first time we'd made love. Bernadette and I were making love regularly. I just wanted to be with her. I had to spend every day with her.

Sure, I was still running around with Orlando, Manny, and the gang, but now every spare moment I had I'd run over to Bernadette's apartment. Every night — Bernadette. After school — Bernadette. Every free minute — Bernadette.

When school let out and our summer vacation started, I didn't work. It was the first time I didn't have a summer job.

I'd been working at Armando's Bodega for a few summers. Then for two years, I'd had a job as a bicycle messenger in the Times Square area — weaving in and out of downtown traffic, darting between cars, almost daring one to hit or stop me. I was a bicycle messenger long before it became trendy—long before movies began to glamorize it.

We had set up a little system for the summertime. Bernadette would let me know if there was anyone in her home. Her mother would leave first, because she had to be at Bickford's early to serve breakfast. Bernadette would get up and make breakfast for her father, who left about an hour later. Since it was summertime and school was out, Bernadette would get back in bed and go to sleep. But first she'd unlock the door for me.

We had it all timed. Every weekday I'd get up early. When it was time for Bernadette's father and mother to both have left for work, I'd head over to her apartment. I'd check the number on the door before I came in. If her father or mother were still in the house, Bernadette would put a piece of scotch tape over the apartment number. It was her signal to me that someone was home, and the door was locked. If there wasn't any scotch tape over the number, I knew it was safe. I could open the door and walk in.

Bernadette would be lying in her bed, sometimes almost sound asleep. I'd go in quietly, take off my clothes, and get into bed with her. She enjoyed being awakened by me kissing her and making love to her while she was still half asleep. She'd have nothing on, and I'd pull back the sheets and start kissing her thighs. I would then slowly kiss my way up to her breasts, and back down, making frequent stops along the way to taste and savor her.

Bernadette was very sensual and enjoyed being kissed in every bare part of her body. The warmth of my mouth and the feel of my lips excited her—and me. Every touch, every kiss, every sensation she felt, I felt. It's as if we were one.

Before Bernadette opened and invited me in, I'd spend an eternity just kissing her up and down, drawing each minute out as long as possible, as if I wanted to make time stand still, to stop. She would then gently hold my head between her thighs, while our lips met, and the taste of her would seem to melt my brain.

Until Bernadette, I didn't know a girl could taste so good—so sweet—so magical. And then finally, we'd embrace, and make love.

I'll Be Good *Tomorrow*

When I was inside Bernadette, she always felt like a flower opening her petals, allowing me in. I'd whisper to her that she felt so warm inside I could feel myself spinning away somewhere, unaware of time and space, that the taste of her had been locked in my brain. And she enjoyed hearing my words.

Everything we did was right. Everything was beautiful. Bernie and I started really falling in love with each other. She was my first love—and I was hers.

That first summer, we'd get up together after making love and we'd go into the shower. Taking a shower together was a big thrill for both of us. It was like playing house. We'd just slept together, and now we were taking a shower together. I'd scrub her back and she'd scrub mine. We'd wash every part of each other's bodies, up and down.

One day, we were both in the shower, giggling, holding each other close, when suddenly we heard the door slam. I thought, *Oh my God, her mom, or dad!*

But, poor Bernadette. All I could think of was her, really, because she was trembling so.

The two of us froze; we didn't say a word. The last thing we wanted to do was make a sound. If her mother or father didn't hear me, she could always tell them she was taking a shower.

But, damn it! My clothes were in her room. They could look in there and see my clothes.

We stood there for ten or fifteen minutes—an eternity. There was nothing I could do. I wasn't going to climb out the window with nothing on. But, since the door of the bathroom was locked, we at least knew that no one could get in. So we just stood there, waiting. Waiting. Waiting.

Finally, Bernadette called out, "Mom? Dad?" There was no answer.

We got out of the shower, dried off, and I hid behind the door. She opened it and stuck her head out. Then she went out and looked in her room. Then she came back, searching room by room. No one was there. Everything was all right.

What really happened that day, we never knew. I suspect her

mother may have come home early, and had heard us inside. Her mother, being the way she was, wouldn't want to rush in and yell, "What are you two doing?" She probably wouldn't have known how to handle it. Bernie meant so much to her. But, if it had been her, she wanted to give us a good scare, so she'd slammed the door.

After that, Bernadette felt a little shy around her mom, so we cooled it for a while. We were a little more careful about spending time together in the house during the day.

But we had to be together. Being alone during the day wasn't enough, anymore. We wanted to spend a whole night together. We wanted to have dinner together, go to a movie, then go home and sleep together for the entire night.

Bernadette came up with a plan. She had a girlfriend, Louise, who she'd known for years, and who had recently moved to Long Island. Her mom knew and liked Louise. So Bernie called Louise with a plan. She asked her to call her mother and ask her if it would be okay for Bernie to come out to Long Island for a night.

Bernie then explained to Louise that what she really needed was an alibi, since she was actually going to Kathie's house for the night. Kathie was another friend of hers, who'd moved to Greenwich Village a year before, but Bernie's mom didn't like Kathie.

Bernadette begged Louise, "Please, please, just do this for me this one time, and I promise I'll really come visit you later in the summer. Mom doesn't like Kathie very much, and would never let me go down to the Village alone."

Louise laughed, understood, and called Bernie's mom, who said it was okay, and gave Bernie permission to go.

Bernadette packed an overnight bag and took off to catch the subway to Grand Central for the train to Long Island. Louise didn't suspect anything. She really thought Bernie was going to spend the night with Kathie, and would come out to Long Island for an overnight visit some other time.

Bernadette's mother walked with her to the subway station on 137th Street, where Bernie kissed her goodbye and got on the express train downtown.

I'll Be Good *Tomorrow*

A few subway stops later, at 96th Street, she got off. As planned, I was waiting for her at the front of the station. Together, we took the subway back uptown to 137th Street where we'd started, and went to the Hamilton Place Hotel. We knew anyone could always get a room there—no questions asked.

This was the first time we had done this, and it was really exciting. We had our bags and walked in like a husband and wife from out of town. I told the clerk I wanted a room for the night, because we had just come from some place or other.

I was fifteen then, Bernadette was fourteen, going on fifteen. We were both trying to act very grown up. Bernadette was pretty well developed, so we looked about seventeen or eighteen.

But the clerk didn't care, or question us. We went up to the room and set our two bags down. It was exciting.

We went out and had a Chinese dinner—she loved Chinese food. Then we went to a movie. Heading "home" after the movie was an incredible feeling. It had been great to have dinner together, go to a movie, and then come home together.

But this time we didn't have to say, "Goodnight, I'll see you tomorrow." This time is was just like husband and wife. We had a little alarm clock to make sure we would wake up in the morning.

We didn't get much sleep that night. We made love for a couple of hours, dozed off in each other's arms, then woke up and made love again. We spent the whole night that way.

That was the first time of many. The Hamilton Place Hotel became our secret hideaway, our own love nest.

By then, for all practical purposes, Bernadette and I were just like a married couple. We weren't working and supporting a household, but we'd gone far enough with each other that we felt the only thing left to do was to sign the papers and get married. We started making plans. We were going to get married. We were sure of it.

I am 16 years old in this photo

I'll Be Good *Tomorrow*

CHAPTER 9

MY REPUTATION AND HOW IT GREW

I always found it interesting how reputations in my neighborhood grew out of nothing. Out of shit. Its as if they grew overnight. That was the way mine was growing, although I always felt and saw myself as just another scared kid.

One time Tommy, one of the guys on the block, got beat up by some of the Villains, a gang from 132nd Street. Poor Tommy, he never bothered anyone. He was too scared to fight. But, after an argument with him they grabbed Tommy and started hitting him. All he did was cover up and let them hit him.

I had just come on the block when one of my friends who was trying to break up the fight, said to them, "What kind of bullshit is this? What are you hitting Tommy for? You pick on him because he won't fight back. You don't pick on somebody like Bobby Lao over here, cause he'd fight you back."

He just casually threw this comment out. I thought to myself, *Holy shit, that's me—Bobby Lao*. It meant something. It made me feel good, although these guys could've beat me up almost as easily as they beat up Tommy. But I would've fought back. That was the difference. I would've fought back, and I was getting a reputation because of it.

I never really thought of myself as a tough guy, as a fighter. We all got into fights. We all had to. It was part of growing up in our neighborhood. A guy got into some fights and he won. Or he didn't really win, but the other guy didn't win, either.

The one thing that sticks in his mind each time is the fear he felt. There's always that fear. But each time he does better and better, and each time the fear is less and less, until he realizes it disappears once that first punch is thrown. And the other guys are noticing. All of a sudden he's got a reputation, and guys don't mess with him any more.

I got to be captain of the Gladiators because of that reputation, although underneath I was just another scared kid. Afraid, until that first punch was thrown. Just like any other guy.

Orlando, Manny, and I got that reputation, which seemed to soar overnight. Word spread around the neighborhood that nobody had better mess with us because we'd kill him. It was all because Manny had gotten into an argument with one of the Manhattan Lords.

Their gang was throwing a party at the apartment of one of their girls, and they invited all of the guys in our gang—all except Manny. They told us Manny couldn't come.

Orlando got mad and said to us, "What kind of bullshit is that? Half of our gang is at that party, putting money into the Manhattan Lord's pockets."

"How much are they charging to get in?" Manny asked.

"It's a quarter to get in, and a dime to check your coat or jacket. If you want a drink—a Coke or something—it's another ten cents. And it's all going into their pockets," Orlando repeated.

"It's okay," Manny said. "You guys go. I don't care about the party. Besides, I can use the money for something else."

"Bullshit," I said. "If you can't go, Orlando and I aren't going, either. We stick together. Besides, I know how we can scare the shit out of them, and maybe screw up their party."

I'll Be Good *Tomorrow*

At that time we had a '36 Ford and an old shotgun Manny had stolen from a neighbor. If my idea worked, we would get even with them for the bullshit they were pulling on Manny.

We got into the Ford with Orlando driving, Manny in the front next to him, and me in the back with the shotgun. We knew the layout of the girl's apartment. She lived on the ground floor, in front.

We drove by the building slowly. It was eleven o'clock at night, and the party was going on. We could see the lights in the living room and people dancing. Right next to the living room was the bedroom where they kept the coats. There was always a guy at the door to make sure everything was paid for and no one stole anything from the coats. They kept that door locked.

We figured we'd just pass by and fire a shot right through the window in the coatroom, and then take off. We didn't want to hurt anyone—just scare them, and maybe break up the party. So we pulled up and I fired. Boom! And we took off. But, on the stoop across the street there was a couple who saw us. They knew our car and they saw us shoot and drive off.

There was also a couple inside the room where the coats were, making out on the bed. I'd fired a shot right through the window, but never considered anyone being in there. That never occurred to me. I could've killed them.

That's what happens a lot of times. Someone picks up a newspaper and reads: "Gang War," and a story about how some kid shot another kid. But, in fact, I, as "some kid," didn't plan on actually shooting anyone.

A kid goes to a gang war with a zip gun, and "Bang, Bang," he thinks he's Roy Rogers firing his gun, and he runs off. But, suddenly the bullet hits someone and kills him. And some dumb kid, who was just another one of the bunch, is up for murder—twenty to life. I saw this happen so many times. Yet, here I was shooting a shotgun through a window.

I think my guardian angel saved me that day, because no one got shot. They didn't get shot, but they did get the shit scared out of them.

When we pulled away, the couple across the street went inside to the party and told them we had done the shooting.

Wow, what a reputation we were getting. It was almost as if we were killers.

The Manhattan Lords didn't mess with us after that. Nobody did. From then on, the word was, "Don't fuck with Orlando, Manny, or Bobby, 'cause they'll shoot you."

They never knew, never realized, that we didn't know there was a couple in the coatroom making out. They assumed we were trying to kill somebody. After that, we all got invited to every party, including Manny. I guess they figured it was better to have us there, than not.

This is the way it happens—this is the way a guy gets a reputation—pulling dumb shit like that.

Another time as I came around 135th Street, Tommy and Richard ran up to me, looking back behind them and shouting to someone, "Here's Bobby. Now we'll see."

Now we'll see what? I wondered. I looked up and there was Gus. Gus was a weightlifter who later became a professional boxer. He could easily beat the shit out of me. That guy was mean.

He and Angelo, a guy who worked in a gas station, were fooling around with Tommy. Between the two of them, they could almost lift up a car and change a tire. They were that strong.

They didn't belong to any gang. They were just big strong guys, messing around with Tommy, throwing his hat back and forth, playing catch with it. When Tommy saw me coming, he ran up and shouted, "Now we'll see."

There I was, suddenly in the middle of it, knowing these two guys could tear me apart. But my ego was on the line. Once a guy gets caught in this reputation thing, he has to keep moving, because he can't get out of it. He's trapped.

So I had to ask, "What's going on?" Fortunately, I wasn't stupid. I could quickly figure things out.

I sensed Gus and Angelo were a little surprised to see Tommy suddenly run up to me as if I were his savior. They didn't know what to make of it. I didn't know if they'd heard of the shotgun incident, and thought they would get shot or what, but whatever it was, it was enough to convince them to give Tommy his hat back.

"Here, take your stupid hat. It's too small. It doesn't fit on my head, anyway," Angelo said.

"Our brains can't fit into that small head of yours, Tommy. For our heads, you need a bigger hat," Gus added.

"Or a better looking one," I said. "A cool Pork Pie hat. Or a Stetson, like Roy Rogers wears."

We all laughed. "Yeah, a cowboy hat would look cool on Tommy."

However, to Tommy and Richard it looked like I had stepped in and put a stop to it, although I knew I could've gotten my ass kicked by either of those two guys.

But, God, that reputation crap can be great one day, and pressure the shit out of you the next.

Later, Orlando, Manny, and I learned to use it to our advantage. Like the time we put the shotgun in Vince's face and beat the shit out of him for breaking into Manny's apartment. We made sure everybody heard about that. It was our protection—our invisible shield.

Now, we didn't have to be fighting all the time—proving ourselves—or defending ourselves. Guys respected us, some were even afraid of us, and we were able to tend to business. To take care of other things we wanted to do.

RALPH B. LAO

CHAPTER 10

THE GUINEA AND HUNTLEY

Orlando and Manny were the best friends I ever had. From the ages of fourteen to seventeen we were as close as three people could be.

Manny was a happy-go-lucky guy. He was a dark-skinned Puerto Rican, taller than Orlando and me, about six feet and a few inches tall, not very bright, but a nice guy to have around, willing to go along with us on anything. We could always rely on Manny.

Orlando was totally different. Brought up in Cuba, he came to the United States when he was about eight or nine years old. His father had been involved in the shady side of Cuban politics, so Orlando had grown up with cunning, learning when to talk and when not to. He was sharp, and he was always scheming. Everything Orlando did had a purpose. He just didn't get involved unless there was money to be had or something to be gained.

Orlando was the main reason Manny and I got mixed up in stealing. He was always looking to get something for nothing.

73

RALPH B. LAO

Orlando's big goal in life was to be in the mob, just like his father in Cuba. His father had been some kind of political mobster over there, and had enjoyed certain comforts. Orlando wanted them, too. That was the way he'd been brought up, and that was what he wanted.

One night the three of us were down on Riverside Drive around midnight trying to score some money. One of our little gimmicks was to go along a row of parked cars and check the doors to see if any were open.

We'd always check the doors, then check the windows. If a window was partly open, we could get our hand in, open the door, get inside, search the glove compartment, and maybe find something.

We'd also look for new Buicks with the double lock ignition, where we could start the car without the key. A lot of their owners would shut the car off, take the key out, but not really shut the ignition switch off. If they didn't turn the key all the way to the end, they'd leave it in the second position, where the ignition switch was still active. We stole a few cars that way.

To go out at night and not break into something was considered a loss. Just breaking into one dumb car, or stealing the wheel from one bicycle, was exciting. There wasn't any money involved, but we had accomplished something, and we were staying sharp.

That was Orlando's philosophy: always stay sharp. Keep your hand in there. A bicycle today, a car tomorrow, a bank the next day, anything—just keep sharp, stay in shape. Keep your mind going.

So one night we were on 137th Street and Riverside Drive, and we noticed a big tree with branches hanging out over the sidewalk. We knew this neighborhood like the back of our hands, but we'd never noticed this tree before.

"You know, Orlando," I said. "One of us could climb that tree, crawl out on one of those branches, and be sitting right over the sidewalk. It's perfect. Just sit there and wait. The first guy who comes along, Bingo! Just jump down on him."

"Yeah, just like in the movies," Orlando said. "Two of us can wait in the bushes and come running out before the shock wears off. Grab his wallet and take off. Quick money. An easy hit. It's beautiful."

"What if he has a dog?" Manny asked.

Orlando and I looked at each other, and laughed. Good old Manny.

"If he has a dog, we don't do it," I said. "Unless it's a small dog. A Poodle or something. All they do is yap, yap, yap."

"That would even be better," Orlando said. "He'll be taking care of his dog and he won't follow us."

Although we'd never done something like this before— something this bold—we were always looking for a little adventure, something different.

Okay, great, I thought. "Manny, you get up there." I said.

"What do you mean, 'Manny, you get up there'?" he asked.

Manny wasn't too hot on getting up there, but Orlando and I always voted for him on these jobs. I knew Orlando wasn't going to buy it. I wasn't going to buy it. But Manny was dumb enough to get talked into it. Whenever one of us needed to be lifted up to a ledge or window, it was always Manny who got "boosted" up.

Every once in a while he would ask, "Why me? Why does it have to be me?"

Orlando and I would always answer, "Because you're the tallest, Manny."

He never quite figured out that whether being the booster or the boostee it still added up to the same total height. After a while, we just got used to saying, "Manny, we'll boost you up."

I think that, deep down Manny already knew he'd be the one to get up there.

So, we were fooling around trying to help Manny climb the tree, looking for the best position and how to get him up there, when out of nowhere we heard a voice. "Okay, you bastards, don't move!"

Holy shit. We didn't have to see him to know who it was. The Guinea. The meanest, most sadistic detective anyone could imagine. This guy delighted in smacking someone around for nothing. He'd catch someone on a corner, walk up and slap him for no reason—just slap him.

If the guy asked him why, he'd just say, "Shut up. Don't say a fucking word." And the guy wouldn't dare say anything.

Then The Guinea would walk away, and the guy would wonder, *What was that all about?* It was as if he just wanted to assert himself. Just wanted to let people know he was around.

Everyone called him "The Guinea," though never to his face. The name was meant as a derogatory term for people of Italian birth. Years before, someone called him The Guinea, and the name stuck. It then got handed down over the years from group to group.

So, we turned around. Sure enough, it was The Guinea, with his sidekick, Huntley, and another detective.

"All right, you spic bastards, what are you doing? We've been watching you up there. What are you guys up to?"

"Nothing, officer. Just playing around," Orlando answered.

"At midnight? Come on, you lying sons of bitches. Up against the wall over there."

They took us across the street to where their car was parked, and put us up against the wall of an apartment building. They made us face the wall and put our hands up, while they searched us. They weren't searching us for guns or knives, because they knew we never carried anything like that on us. They were looking to see if we had any stolen goods.

If they could find a ring, a watch, or a wallet, they had us. They probably wouldn't even bother taking us down to the stationhouse; they'd just delight in beating the crap out of us, knowing they had a reason this time.

They couldn't find anything. The Guinea didn't like that—searching us and not finding anything. He made us turn around to face him with our backs to the wall, while he just stood there looking at us. Studying us. Finally, he asked, "Okay, you pricks, what were you up to?"

Orlando said, "Nothing, officer. I told you. Nothing."

I'll Be Good *Tomorrow*

Bam! Out of nowhere The Guinea slapped him, right across the face. Orlando didn't like anyone touching his face. Orlando's face was immaculate. He went out of his way to take care of it. If he got one little pimple, he made sure he put medicine on it and walked around with a Band-Aid over it. So The Guinea came right up to Orlando, looked at him and, Bam! hit him.

Orlando reeled back and bounced off the wall. Then he charged forward, yelling, "You bastard!" and pushed The Guinea back.

The Guinea, taken by surprise, went flying on his ass. Huntley and the third detective (I don't remember who the hell he was) just stood there, surprised.

Orlando hauled ass across the street, heading for the park area on Riverside Drive. The Guinea got up and took off after him. He wanted to catch Orlando. He wanted to kill him.

Huntley and the other cop followed along behind, but both of them stopped at the corner and just watched as The Guinea ran after Orlando. They were only about forty feet away from us.

But instead of turning around and running away, Manny and I just stood there like assholes. We were so involved in what was going on we never thought of taking off in the other direction. All we did was stand there, looking at each other, and saying, "I hope he makes it." We were both thinking, "Run, Orlando, run!"

It was such a wild scene, and it happened so quickly, we were caught off guard. Imagine Orlando pushing The Guinea like that!

All of a sudden, Huntley and his buddy turned around and came running back toward us. They yelled, "Okay, you bastards, down. Sit your asses down."

Holy shit! Manny and I looked at each other. We didn't have to say anything, we both knew. What a pair of dummies. We were in trouble, too. We hadn't shoved The Guinea, but we were going to get it, just the same.

They made us sit against the wall of the building on the cold sidewalk at one o'clock in the morning. Waiting. They weren't taking any chances with us. Orlando may have taken off, but they weren't

77

going to have us get away from them. So we sat there waiting for The Guinea to come back.

Orlando filled us in on the details of the chase later. When he took off, he had run towards an area of Riverside Drive, along the Hudson River, that we knew well.

He'd crossed the street and headed towards the bushes along the park. A picket fence, about four feet high, separated the bushes from the sidewalk. On the other side of the fence was a hill, filled with shrubbery, which dropped about a hundred feet toward railroad tracks that ran alongside the river.

At the bottom of the hill, before it got to the tracks, was another fence. If a guy made it over that fence, which was about six feet high, and hit the tracks, he was gone. There were always a lot of freight cars and junk there where a guy could "get lost."

Orlando would never just run wild, not in our neighborhood. We knew this neighborhood in and out. When we had nothing to do— when we were just walking around—we searched, explored, practiced, always with the idea that someday we might need an escape route. Someday we might be in a gang fight; someday a bunch of guys might have us cornered. Someday the cops might be after us. Anything might happen. So we had to know every corner, every hiding place—where to run.

Sure enough, as Orlando told us later, he knew exactly where he was going. He'd headed down the hill, reached the picket fence, and cleared it—something we often did. We used to practice jumping this fence without touching it.

Orlando said he cleared it in one leap, landed in the dirt, and slid the hundred feet down the hill. But just as he'd hit bottom, he said he heard a commotion behind him. Bam! Then he heard a loud, "Ahhh," followed by a thud, and then a groan. A painful groan.

Holy shit! The Guinea had hurt himself! He must have tried to clear the fence the same way Orlando had, but he didn't make it. He probably got his pants or sleeve caught on the fence, flipped over, and landed hard in the shrubbery.

I'll Be Good *Tomorrow*

That's when Orlando, now at the bottom of the hill, said he realized he was in big trouble. Up until then, The Guinea just wanted to catch him, and beat the shit out of him. However, Orlando knew he could outrun him, and he wasn't about to let The Guinea catch him.

But now he was terrified. The Guinea sounded like he was really hurt. We'd never seen that happen before. None of us had. It was one thing for him to fall on his ass when Orlando pushed him, but this sounded like he was dying.

Orlando said that when he first heard The Guinea groaning, he thought, *Good, you bastard*, and had laughed. But then he realized, *This guy is going to want to kill me.*

We all felt that The Guinea would just as soon pull out his gun and shoot us as look at us. And now there was reason enough for him to kill Orlando. If he got anywhere near Orlando, he might blow his head off and then say he was running away from a crime, or he'd plant dope on him, or something.

At this point in his story, Orlando said he really took off. At the bottom of the hill was a drainpipe that ran alongside the other fence. He told us he'd followed this drainpipe about a block or so to a concrete abutment, where he'd climbed over the six-foot fence and onto the railroad tracks. Once he'd hit the tracks, he was gone. No way The Guinea was going to catch him then.

Meanwhile, Manny and I sat on the sidewalk with Huntley and his buddy, listening to a lot of crap. It was the same old story we'd heard over and over from these guys. It was as if they had a script memorized, and they took turns repeating it.

One or the other would say, "You spic bastards. We're going to clean up the street with you. One of these days we'll put a fucking hole in your head, dump you in the river, and no one will ever find you, or even give a shit."

Manny and I just sat there and said, "Yes sir, yes sir." We had to say that. It didn't matter what they were saying, we couldn't look blankly away or they would smack us one. So we just sat, repeating, "Yes, officer, yes officer," over and over. Agreeing to whatever shit they said.

About fifteen minutes later, The Guinea came limping back. His face was scratched, his clothes were dirty. And he was mad! The Guinea was Italian but very light skinned. Now his face was so red he looked like an Indian! He was mad, and he looked like he wanted to kill someone.

I looked over at Manny and thought to myself, *Holy shit! Who's it going to be, you or me?*

The Guinea grabbed me by the hair and said, "All right, you bastard, get up," which I did like a shot. Manny wasn't far behind. They hustled us into their car, The Guinea swearing and bitching all the way.

Huntley drove. The Guinea sat next to him in the front seat. The third cop was next to Manny and me in the back. As we took off, The Guinea turned around and looked at us.

"All right, you bastards, you're going to tell me where that guy lives. You're going to give me the address or I'm going to break both your asses. Come on. Let's hear it."

I sat there wondering, *What do I do?* I'd never give them Orlando's address. But if I didn't come up with something, this guy was going to kill us.

Suddenly Manny jumped in. He was thinking the same thing I was. "512 West 134th Street, officer," he said.

The Guinea said, "Okay! Let's go." Huntley made a U-turn and headed for 134th Street.

Meanwhile I was thinking, *Holy shit, what did Manny do? Orlando lives on 135th Street. He doesn't live on 134th Street. That's Manny's address. He lives at 512 West 134th, not Orlando.* Then I realized what he was doing. He'd given them his own address, and temporarily saved us from a beating.

Good old Manny! The guy who always said the wrong thing, had finally come up with a good idea, and said the right thing. He bought us some time. And with a little time, anything could happen—a flat tire, a busted radiator, another call, anything. Not likely, but who knows?

I'll Be Good *Tomorrow*

After driving a few blocks, we pulled up in front of Manny's house and parked, waiting for Orlando to show up. I sat there praying, because I knew we were in trouble. These were three mean guys. At one o'clock in the morning, there wasn't a soul around. They could kill us, dump us somewhere, and no one would ever know what happened.

Every few minutes Huntley, who had a flashlight in his hand, turned around and Bam! He'd hit us on the head or in the ribs. The Guinea wasn't doing anything. He just sat there, cursing. Huntley was taking it out on us, but The Guinea was saving it all for Orlando.

About half an hour went by, even though it seemed a lot longer. Suddenly, The Guinea turned around and yelled at Manny, "You son of a bitch. When's that guy coming home? Don't you spics ever sleep?"

Manny looked up innocently and asked, "What guy, officer?"

The Guinea looked at Huntley. Huntley looked at The Guinea. They both looked back at Manny.

The Guinea screamed, "What the fuck do you mean, 'What guy'? Who the hell do you think we're talking about? Your friend— the bastard who ran off."

Then Manny calmly said, "Oh, he doesn't live *here*, officer. This is my building. I thought you meant, where do I live?"

Holy shit, here it comes. Our time's run out. Although I felt like laughing, all I could think of was, *Oh, my God, poor Manny.*

Huntley turned around with the flashlight and rapped Manny on the side of his head. The Guinea grabbed him by the collar and started hitting him. Between the two of them they must have beaten on him for about five minutes. Huntley was swinging the flashlight over my head and bouncing it off Manny's ribs, and The Guinea kept rapping him on the head.

I was bent over, praying, and trying to stay as low as I could, and trying to come up with a plan to save myself, because I knew I was next.

I'd had an operation on my side years before and thought I'd use it to try and scare him. I figured if I yelled, "My operation," it might scare him. Maybe he'd think he'd opened up the scar and he'd be in trouble.

That was my plan. If any of them hit me, I would bend over like I was in pain. I'd yell, "Oh God, my operation, my operation," and they would stop. Brilliant—or so I thought.

All of a sudden Huntley reached down, grabbed me, and rapped me with the flashlight. As soon as he hit me, I fell over and started moaning. "Ohhhh, my operation, my operation," I said, thinking I was pretty smart.

He looked at me and said, "Your operation? What operation?"

It didn't work. Huntley grabbed me by the hair and lifted me off the seat. "You bastard, I'm going to operate on you. I'll give you an operation!" Bam! A couple more shots in the ribs.

I never said "operation" again. I didn't want to risk having these guys operate on my ribs—or my head.

They beat the crap out of us for another ten or fifteen minutes, trying to find out where Orlando lived—although I think they just enjoyed beating on us.

We told them we didn't know, that we'd just met him when we were running around on Riverside Drive. "We think he lives on 136th Street. Yeah, 136th Street, down by Riverside Drive." Back where they'd found us.

"Maybe if we saw the house we would remember it, but we aren't sure," we said. Any bullshit story we could think of.

Finally they drove us back to Riverside Drive. It was too late now, and they knew it. Orlando was home in bed, sleeping—snoring by then.

They knocked us around a few more times, and then let us out of the car.

"Don't let me catch your asses out after midnight again," The Guinea warned us. But it sounded weak. He had lost, and he knew it.

The next day, Orlando, Manny, and I exchanged stories, and although two of us were still sore from the beating we'd taken, we all had a good laugh.

I'll Be Good *Tomorrow*

CHAPTER 11

ORLANDO AND MANNY

In our little trio, Manny was the joker. Orlando was the serious one. He was always thinking of something. When it came to larceny, his mind was sharp as a blade. Quick.

But I was the in-between guy. I joked around like Manny, but I was smart, and I could be slick like Orlando, who was always planning something. I was a little more happy-go-lucky than Orlando. I wasn't constantly thinking larceny.

I had other things on my mind. I had a girlfriend, Bernadette. I had the guys—the gang. I had lots of other things going.

One time when we were walking on Riverside Drive, trying to figure out how to make some money, Orlando said, "I've got an idea. Why don't we just push some guy up against a wall, grab his wallet, and take off?"

"In broad daylight?" I asked. "You're kidding, right? What if someone sees us?"

"No one'll see us if we do it inside a building," he said. "Grab a guy when he's coming home—in the hallway. If we're quick, we can be out of there before he knows what happened."

We'd never done anything like this before but we figured, Okay, why not? We'll give it a try.

We were up around 160th Street, far enough from our own neighborhood we figured no one would recognize us. So we picked a street that was fairly quiet, and hung out on one of the stoops. Soon, along came a skinny little guy. Great. He looked like he could easily be intimidated. So we went inside the building with him.

As he pressed the elevator button, we were talking amongst ourselves. "Do you think she'll be there?"

"She said she'd be here about this time," like we were there to see someone. We'd always have some conversation to make everything seem natural.

As soon as the elevator got to his floor and the guy opened the door, Boom! We shoved him back into the elevator and stuck a comb in his side (we didn't have a gun, nor did we carry knives).

"Don't say a fuckin' thing," we told him.

Right away the guy got all shook up. "Don't kill me," he begged. "Please don't kill me."

"Shut the fuck up and nothing'll happen to you. Just shut the fuck up and stay still."

Meanwhile, Orlando got his hands in the guy's pockets and grabbed his wallet.

"You stick your head out that door," I said, "and we'll blow your head off."

We left him and headed out. We figured we'd hit the street, walk to the corner and take off. But when we got outside, the son of a bitch didn't stay put.

As we walked up the street, he came charging out the door, yelling, "Thieves, thieves, stop 'em, stop 'em. They took my wallet!"

Holy shit! We started running. Now, when someone's yelling and running after you, it feels like there are cops everywhere and everything's a big blur. Everyone's coming after you. Doors are opening and cars are coming—all after you.

I'll Be Good *Tomorrow*

We ran up to Broadway—a busy street—so there were people all around us. But this guy was still right behind us. He was running and yelling, "Stop them, stop them, they robbed me!"

But slick Orlando saved our asses. Right away he started yelling, "Stop em, stop em," pointing ahead of us. Manny and I started doing the same thing.

Now, there were four of us running up the street—the guy chasing us, and the three of us—all yelling, "Stop em, stop em!"

Everybody looked ahead in the direction we were running, wondering who we were all chasing.

The confusion Orlando created with his quick thinking, allowed us to get out of that one. Another narrow escape, another four or five dollars.

Vincent (the Junkie), Orlando, and Manny

RALPH B. LAO

Manny was the opposite of Orlando. Manny was always good for a laugh. We'd pick on him when we wanted to kid around, because he was so good-natured, and he could take it. Except for his quick thinking that time with The Guinea and Huntley, Manny had a knack for always saying the wrong thing whenever we got into trouble. Manny would put his foot in it if we were stopped by cops for doing something, like looking suspicious, or anything.

One night we were going up to 176th Street, to the Highbridge swimming pool area, to fight with the Jacobins. We had a little problem with them and we were going to go there and have it out.

Highbridge Park ran from about 160th Street to around 180th Street, on the east side of Washington Heights, the highest part of Manhattan overlooking the Harlem River. It had a swimming pool where people would put their clothes in a basket, and it cost a quarter to swim. If anyone actually swam in the water, he could probably catch the Syph, the Clap, or some other scary disease. But it had one charm; it was in the middle of the park, so it was quiet at night. A great place for a fight.

Orlando, Manny, and I, together with a bunch of other guys, took the subway up to Highbridge Park. Bingo! There were the Jacobins.

Our war counselor walked up and talked some shit with their war counselor. These were all the preliminaries before the fight. We were kind of squaring off and picking guys out, waiting for the action to start.

All of a sudden, out of nowhere, headlights shone on us. The fucking cops drove right up on the grass and put their headlights on us. Somehow they'd heard about the fight and were ready for us.

Everybody took off in different directions. But Orlando, Manny, and I had a knack for running as a unit. Without saying anything, the three of us would always be together. So we took off.

We really didn't know the Highbridge Park area that well. But we saw a huge darkness opening up in front of us and we thought, *Great! Trees.* I headed right for them, figuring we could get away in their shadows.

But we could feel the cops right behind us. Shit, they'd picked us out. I guess they figured we were trapped and we couldn't go anywhere, because, unknown to us, the darkness in front of us was actually the edge of the park. It was almost a sheer drop off, a steep hill going straight down to the Harlem River Drive.

Because we were in good shape, when we got to the edge we didn't stop. We were used to leaping over fences and sliding down hills just for fun.

But this was a little scary. I thought, *Oh, my God, this is it. This is the end.* But I wasn't stopping, Orlando wasn't stopping, Manny wasn't stopping. We took off down the hill. There were rocks and bottles all the way down, but somehow we managed to stay on our feet.

I heard a "pop" sound—a bullet in the night always sounds like a pop—followed by "bing, zing."

Those goddamned cops were shooting at us. I don't know what they thought we were doing. Normally, cops wouldn't shoot at a guy for a dumb fight. We hadn't even started the fight yet.

Having bullets flying over your head is a scary, unforgettable sound. I could swear they were passing right by my ears.

We made it to the bottom of the hill and kept running. We headed west, until we were on Amsterdam Avenue, heading home.

"Shit, I'm glad we got out of that one," Manny said.

"Yeah, that was a close call," I added.

Suddenly a police car pulled up right alongside us. And it was too late for us to run. Before we realized it, a cop was out of his car and right on top of us. The cop looked at us and said, "All right, what are you guys doing up here?"

Orlando and I immediately pointed to Manny. "We came up to his sister's house."

Always Manny, always Manny. We weren't trying to screw him or anything. Partly, we had to come up with an excuse, and partly, we did it for laughs. We'd always be able to get together later on and Manny would say, "Why me? Why are you bastards always pointing at me?"

We told the cop we'd gone to Manny's sister's house to get some money from her, but she wasn't there. So we figured, what the hell, we'd just walk back to 135th Street.

The cop said, "This is 170th Street, and you live on 135th Street? That's a pretty long way to walk."

"Oh, that's not far for us officer, we're used to it," I answered, adding, "We do it all the time."

"Uh huh," said the cop, knowing we were bullshitting him. He looked at us and said, "Tell you what, get in the car, and we'll give you a ride."

Poor dumb Manny. He really thought the cop was extending a courtesy. He thought the cop was really concerned over our having to walk that far. So he turned around and said, "Oh no, that's alright officer, don't bother. Thanks a lot, but we'll walk."

The cop reached out, grabbed Manny by the neck, and said, "You black son of a bitch, get your ass in that car!" He flung Manny in the car, then Orlando, and me, and they drove us around.

The cops proceeded to beat the crap out of Manny. Not knowing him the way we did, they thought he was being a wise guy. Orlando and I didn't say a word, so they spared us.

After beating on Manny, and threatening us a few times, they finally dropped us off about ten blocks from where they picked us up. Having been through this many times before, we knew the routine. However, it didn't stop each of us from thinking, *"Will these bastards shoot us, and then say we ran, or tried to attack them?"*

But once safe, we just laughed, and joked with poor Manny while he asked, "Why me? Why am I always the one they beat on?"

Our answer was always the same, "Cause you're the tallest, Manny." And more laughter.

I'll Be Good *Tomorrow*

CHAPTER 12

DEBS AND OTHER GIRLS

I talk about the guys I hung around with, the fights we had, and the things we did. But we also had some pretty bad girls. "Bad" in the sense that they could fight, and could take care of themselves. If they got into trouble, they didn't have to come running to us. They could handle themselves.

Every gang had its debs back then. Sort of a girls' auxiliary. The Rainbows had the Rainbow Debs; the Manhattan Lords had the Manhattan Lords Debs. We had our own debs in the Gladiators. We treated our girls well. Not like a couple of the other gangs—the Villains, or the Manhattan Lords.

The Manhattan Lords used to treat their girls like they were their property. "These girls are our debs, and they do what we want," they'd brag.

To us that was bullshit. We always thought of the Manhattan Lords as a bunch of young punks. They were a year or two younger than us and we considered them the diddy-bops of the neighborhood.

RALPH B. LAO

The kind of guys who walked down the street with a little bounce, "diddy-bopping" along.

The first time I met Bernadette, she'd just broken up with Tico who was a member of the Manhattan Lords. Unfortunately, before she broke off with him he had talked her into joining the Manhattan Lords Debs. But after she had an argument with another one of their Debs, she figured, *The hell with it, I don't want to be a part of this anymore*. So she also quit the Debs.

One time Bernadette went up to 145th Street with another girl from our group, Rosie. On the way back they ran into Marian, a black girl who was captain of the Rainbow Debs of 145th Street. One thing led to another and they started arguing.

Marian, trying to sound and look tough, started talking a lot of shit, saying, "I'm gonna go upside your head. I'm gonna kick your ass." She reared back to punch Bernadette, but Bernadette quickly reached out and poked her in the eyes with her fingers.

Marian let out a scream and covered her eyes. Bernadette then grabbed her by the hair, brought her head down, and Bam! She hit her right in the face with her knee, knocking her back.

Marian covered her face, and started yelling, "Shit, my eyes! I can't see! I can't fucking see!"

End of fight! Rosie and Bernadette left her there, yelling, crying, and cursing.

The next day, when I came around the block, Rosie ran up to me and said, "Bobby, you should've seen your girl yesterday. Man, she put Marian away."

I thought that was so cool. "Where did you learn to do that, Bernie?" I asked. "I didn't know you could fight like that. I've never even seen you in a fight."

She said she had seen this done in a movie and she'd always wanted to try it. She had fast reflexes and she wasn't going to let Marian hit her. So when Marian came at her, she got her chance to try it. After that, she had her own reputation, that of a badass girl.

Everyone liked Rosie, the girl who'd seen Bernadette beat

I'll Be Good *Tomorrow*

Marian. But she had a sister named Peggy who was a little on the pushy side, and had a knack for pissing people off. Like her sister Rosie, Peggy was fun to be with, but she often seemed to make snide remarks, whether she meant to or not.

At that time we had three girls from "*El Barrio*," Spanish Harlem, hanging around with us. They had come to one of our parties, had a good time, and kept coming around. One of them was nicknamed "Poison," because she had earned a reputation around her neighborhood as being tough, someone not to be messed with.

One night a group of us—guys and girls—were down on Riverside Drive, talking and listening to music on the radio. We were having a good time, when Poison and her two friends showed up. Since they were new to our group, some of the guys started crowding around, flirting with them.

Poison was enjoying the attention. Then she overheard Peggy make some kind of snide remark about her. "What did you say, bitch?" Poison snapped.

They started arguing, and Poison, in keeping with her reputation, said to Peggy, "Bitch, I'll slap you one."

Everyone was watching. Wow, a fight. Girls getting into fights were always fun to watch. Usually guys would quickly break it up, but sometimes they'd let them go at it.

This time, one of the guys said, "Peggy did come on a little strong. She does like to shoot her mouth off. Maybe it's time she learned a lesson." So the guys decided to let them fight, and they all stood around waiting to see what would happen.

But Peggy backed away, and gave some lame excuse about how she had to leave, and she took off. That was cool. It made Poison look good because she'd scared Peggy off.

The guys started crowding around her again, flirting, and flattering her, telling her what a tough little girl she was, and a lot of other crap.

However, about twenty minutes later Peggy came back, looking mad. With fists clenched, she walked up to Poison and said, "Okay, bitch, you want to fight? Come on."

Everybody stepped back. Holy shit, what had happened? Peggy was ready to fight now.

It surprised Poison. She backed up wondering what the hell was going on. Finally she got herself together and said, "Fine." She'd been in enough fights before, so she knew what to do. She came right at Peggy. She reached out, grabbed Peggy's blouse, and ripped it off.

In those days when girls got into a fight, one of them would always try to rip off some of the other girl's clothes. If she could pull something off, she had an advantage, because the other girl would be busy trying to cover up.

The first girl to have her blouse or skirt ripped off would probably lose. The other girl would then swing away at her, and it would be difficult to fight and cover up at the same time—knowing the guys were watching.

Peggy was tall and she was stacked—built like a brick shithouse. Now, with her blouse ripped off, wow! Everyone was going to see her topless.

But, Holy shit! Cool Peggy. She had on a one-piece bathing suit. That's why she had run off. She'd gone home to remove her bra, and put a bathing suit on under her blouse. It surprised everyone.

And it shook Poison up. Poison thought she'd be the first to rip off something, and she'd have Peggy at a disadvantage. But Peggy was ready and proceeded to beat the shit out of her.

Poison was getting beaten up so badly by Peggy that she quit, and went into her act, acting as if she was fainting. She fell back on a bench, threw a hand over her forehead, and then had guys fanning and consoling her.

But Poison getting beaten up was actually an anticlimax. The real show was Peggy and her bathing suit. After that, everyone thought Peggy was cool, and everyone showed her a little more respect.

Not surprisingly, we never saw Poison or her friends again.

I'll Be Good *Tomorrow*

CHAPTER 13

THE GAY BLADES

The Gay Blades was a roller skating rink downtown on 52nd Street just off Broadway. They had skating sessions named "singles only," "couples only," and stuff like that. Every once in awhile we'd go there with our girls, or we'd go alone and try to pick up girls. We were always looking for some fun, some way to enjoy ourselves.

At that time, a gang of Italian guys who lived nearby was frequenting the Gay Blades. Every time we'd go there on a Sunday, they'd be there. And all those guys looked alike. They had what we called the "Roman helmet" haircut—the long sideburns, the long back squared off, and the big pompadour. And they all wore pegged pants with pistol pockets and saddle stitching on the side.

They'd skate around, standing very straight, without moving their bodies or their hands, except for a dip here and there. There'd always be about eight or ten of them, all acting cool.

One Sunday I went to the Gay Blades with Bernadette. Tommy, Hector, and Richard came along. We were skating, kidding around, and having a good time. Hector was going around the rink at the same time one of these "cool" guys was trying to spin around and skate backwards.

He fell right in front of Hector, and Hector laughed—a natural thing to do. After Hector laughed, he reached down to help the guy up, but the guy pulled back. He didn't want any help. He got up on his own and kept skating. Hector figured, no big deal, and he didn't think anything more of it.

That was the way we were. We'd joke around, and laugh, but we weren't trying to be "cool," putting on airs like those guys with their stupid Roman helmet haircuts.

But those guys didn't seem interested in having fun, or laughing, like we did. Their big thing was just acting cool.

When it came time to leave, we were taking off our skates, when Tommy came over and said, "Those guys over there keep pointing this way. They look pretty mad. Something's up."

We looked over where they were, and sure enough, they were glaring at us. That's when Hector remembered what had happened earlier, and said, "One of those guys fell right in front of me when he tried a spin, so I couldn't help laughing a bit. I tried to help him up, but he pulled away, and looked a little mad when he got up."

Without pointing at him, Hector said, "That's the guy over there, the one in the middle. They're all huddled around him, so I think that's what they're all talking about."

Holy shit! That was just what we needed. Here we were at the rink, far from home, only four of us and a girl: Hector, Richard, Tommy, Bernadette, and me. And now we were going to get jumped by these guys.

Hector was one of the Jacobins from 176th Street, uptown. He'd come down to one of our parties one day. He enjoyed hanging out with us, even though he still belonged to the Jacobins. But Hector could fight. He could take care of himself; he was pretty cool. If someone got into trouble and Hector was there, that was all right. He could be counted on.

Richard was the smallest one of our group. He lifted weights and was strong, but I'd never seen Richard in a fight. He didn't seem the type. Richard was more of a bookworm. Because he didn't ever get into fights, I didn't know if I could count on Richard.

Hector could fight. I could fight, but Richard? Jesus, I didn't know much about him.

And Tommy, the fourth member in this group, was the one guy we could never depend on in a fight. If there were a lot of guys, Tommy would be in there swinging away with all of us, but if things didn't look good, he was gone. Tommy was not a fighter. He hated it. He could never get over his fear of fighting. And it showed.

Deep down inside, we were all scared. Every time a guy goes into a fight, the fear inside him keeps building. But when that first punch is thrown—everything goes boom, and the fear is gone. One punch is thrown and he's rolling around, everything happens so fast the fear disappears. But before that first punch, he's afraid. Hector, me, anybody. No matter how many fights we'd been in, it was always there. Most of us didn't show it. We kept it inside. But Tommy just couldn't hide it.

The Gay Blades had a wide entrance on 52nd Street, with four or five glass doors. We could see outside through the doors. Sure enough, the Italians were all out there. There were about ten of them, lined up against the parked cars, waiting for us.

We decided to walk out as if nothing had happened. Hector walked out first. He figured that if the guy walked up to him, and was angry, he would just apologize. The last thing we wanted was to get into a fight so far from home. Especially over something as stupid as "laughing" at someone. Besides, we were so outnumbered.

Sure enough, the guy who had fallen walked up to Hector and started talking shit. "Hey man, why'd you laugh at me?" and a lot of other crap.

Hector answered, "You fell right in front of me and I almost skated into you. That's why I laughed. It was more at myself than anything. If I made you mad because I laughed, I'm sorry. Really."

"Bullshit," the guy said. "I think you were laughing because I fell. You thought it was funny. That's why you were laughing, not because you almost ran into me."

Hector finally said, "Look, man, I'm sorry you feel that way. But I don't know what else to say. If that's not enough, that's up to you."

The guy stood there just looking at Hector. Then he looked back at his friend, who was against a car and said, "You hear that shit?"

Then he turned back towards Hector, and threw a punch. The old trick of turning to your side, saying something to someone, winding up and, as he comes back around, throwing a punch.

But, we'd pulled this shit ourselves, so it wasn't new to us. When the guy came lunging forward with the punch, Hector wasn't there. He'd moved over to the side and stuck out his foot, tripping the guy, who went flying on his ass.

Hector jumped back, and I thought, *Now, the first punch is thrown. Here we go!* The guy jumped up and charged Hector.

Hector was a good fighter. Bam! Hector clipped him. He then grabbed the guy, picked him up, and slammed him on the sidewalk. Then he fell on top of the guy, hitting away at him.

This was when the other guy's friends came off the cars. They'd been watching, making sure there were only four or five of us—not too many. As soon as they saw their guy was losing, Zoom! They all jumped in, grabbing and swinging at Hector.

Richard really surprised me. He spread his hands out like a skydiver and leaped on the pile. I didn't expect that from him. After he did that, I jumped in. Then Tommy.

I think Tommy was more afraid that if he didn't fight, Bernadette would see, and then tell all the girls in our group he was scared of getting beat up. So, he also jumped in and started swinging away.

Suddenly, someone grabbed me by the arm, lifted me up in the air, and threw me to the side. It felt as if my arm was being ripped off.

I realized it was one of the bouncers. The Gay Blades had a bunch of big strong guys whose job was to make sure there were no fights—that all was cool. They didn't want any trouble, inside or outside, of their place. So they grabbed us, and pushed us aside.

After the fight was stopped, we headed for the corner, looking for a cab. A couple of the Italian guys came charging towards us from across the street. Tommy and I grabbed a bus stop sign—one of these heavy things with a solid cast-iron base—and lifted it up, threatening to throw it, to hold those guys back while Bernadette and Hector stopped a cab. We flung the bus stop sign at them, squeezed into the cab, and took off.

We got out of there without getting beaten up, because the bouncers had come just in time. But we didn't like it. We were used to being kings in our neighborhood.

So, when we got back home we told everyone what had happened. All the guys in the neighborhood said, "Wow, we gotta get 'em."

We figured those guys were probably not going to show up for a few Sundays. Or, if they did, they'd make sure they had plenty of backups. So, we'd just wait. When enough time had gone by and we figured they wouldn't expect us to come back, then we'd go down there and surprise them. We'd get back at them for that shit they'd pulled on us.

One to two months went by, and finally we decided, "Now is the time. Let's do it."

One thing about our neighborhood, any time we had trouble with a gang from outside, we could always count on getting lots of guys. Hector got his Jacobins, I got the Gladiators, and we got the Manhattan Lords. So, we had three gangs, with about fifty guys, ready that Sunday.

We'd fight amongst ourselves, but if it were a group from outside, we'd fight together. That's why it was so easy for Chino to form the "United Dukes" later.

Everyone in the neighborhood was willing to fight. Guys who didn't even belong to gangs would join in. We'd go down the street saying, "We're going to have some shit with those guys," and more would follow.

This time we came up with a good plan that involved the girls. We had all chipped in with some cash, and we gave it to Bernadette, Rosie, and Peggy, and sent them down ahead of us.

"Here, take this money and the three of you go inside and make sure they're there. They won't know any of you, or even remember Bernadette. But Bernie, you'll know them," I told her. "If you see them there, call us. We don't want to go all the way down to 52nd Street, with forty or fifty guys, for nothing."

The girls took the subway downtown, arriving at the Gay Blades, and went inside. A few minutes later Bernie called me. "They're all here, about ten of them. And the guy who started the fight with Hector, is definitely here," she said.

"Do you think they recognized you?" I asked.

"I'm sure they don't remember me. I walked right by them with Rosie, and they didn't even look at us. They're too busy trying to look cool," she said as she laughed.

"Great! Okay, thanks. Just wait for us till we got there." We headed down. Cars, subways, buses, every which way.

Half an hour before closing time, we were there, waiting outside the Gay Blades. We were going to pull the same shit they'd pulled on us. We lined up against the cars—just the four of us: Hector, Richard, Tommy, and me. Tommy was feeling brave.

Backing us up were about fifty guys. Some sitting in cars, some leaning against buildings across the street, some at the frankfurter stand on the corner, and guys spread out along the street.

Bernadette, Rosie, and Peggy came out and said, "They're still in there, all of them. It was fun skating around, watching them, and knowing you were all coming down here."

Great! We were ready and waiting for them to come out.

Bernie then asked me, "Can we stay and watch? We'll stay out of the way, across the street."

"No, the three of you should head home," I said. "I don't know what's going to happen, and I'll feel much better knowing you're all safe back home."

"Okay," she said—and she, along with Rosie and Peggy, headed home.

Meanwhile, Hector, Richard, Tommy, and I stood there leaning against the cars, waiting for the guys to come out, just the way they had for us.

The Gay Blades had a large glassed-in area where skaters went before they actually bought their tickets to enter the skating rink. We saw them as they walked through that area on their way out, just as they saw us.

They could only see four of us, but they had to know we wouldn't show up with only us four. We could see them huddling inside. We figured if they didn't come out, we were going to have to go in there and get them before they called for help.

Suddenly, one guy came walking out, nonchalantly, like he wasn't part of anything, because he hadn't been there the day they jumped us. He thought we wouldn't know he was one of their group.

But these fucking guys all had the same haircut—the pistol pockets, the pegged pants—every one of them looked the same. And here was this guy, walking out, carrying his little bag with his roller skates inside.

Hector walked up to him and said, "Hold it, man."

We figured they couldn't get anyone on the phone, so they were going to send this guy out to try to get help, because they all lived around there. Living nearby, they could probably get twenty or thirty more guys within minutes.

But we weren't going to let them. We were going to get them here, just the way they were.

He asked Hector, "What's wrong?"

"Look man, don't bullshit me," Hector told him. "Don't tell us you're not with those guys. Turn your ass around, head back inside, and tell your boys to come on out. You do that now, or we'll kick the shit out of you right here."

He looked at us, turned around, and went right back inside. The guys inside knew they'd have to come out sometime, so they gave their girls their cases with their skates, and sent them off to the side. Then they spread out and came walking toward the door.

They were all bigger than us. And they were older, anywhere from seventeen to nineteen years old, while we were only fourteen to sixteen years old. We figured that was okay. They might have ten or fifteen big guys, but, although we were smaller and younger, we had about fifty or sixty.

One of them had been combing his hair as he started to come

out, looking kind of cool, getting ready for battle. They were walking very slowly, so we figured, "Let's go in and get it over with," because sooner or later the cops would come. We had too many guys for someone not to notice and call the cops.

We signaled the others and headed in through the glass doors. On my left was a little guy, Tony from the Jacobins.

Hector walked up to the guy he'd originally fought with and said, "Hi, punk. Remember me?"

Now Tony was the type who would pick out an opponent right away and start swinging. He just looked up at the guy who had been combing his hair, and threw a punch. As soon as that happened, everyone started swinging, and all hell broke loose.

When someone is in a gang fight, it's not like in the movies, where he grabs a guy, hits him, and the guy comes back and throws him over a table. Then he shakes it off, gets up, and hits the guy back. That's a lot of bullshit. None of the fights we were in were ever like that. Guys were just swinging away at anything that moved—anything that moved near or towards them.

If I had to explain to someone how to act in a gang fight, I would just say, "If you see a guy coming at you, swing away. Try to hit him first. Then quickly turn and get ready for another one. But you must keep moving, jumping, and swinging away, because you don't want to catch a knife, or a belt buckle."

Guys would sometimes take their belts and shave down the buckle like razor blades, and we'd have to constantly watch for this. Later on, we'd look back and tell ourselves, "I should've done this, or, I should've done that."

And someone would always ask, "Did you see me grab this guy, and hit that other guy?"

But it all happens so fast when the fight is going on, it's mostly just a blur.

From this particular fight, one thing stuck out. Two of the Jacobins grabbed one guy off to my right and threw him through one of the glass doors. Face first. I remember the shatter of the glass. Crash, boom! *Holy shit,* I thought. *That guy must be all cut up.*

I'll Be Good *Tomorrow*

I turned around to see some guy coming right for me. All I could think of was the glass doors behind me. I didn't want to go through them like the one I'd just seen. So I didn't back up. I stood my ground and watched him come at me, almost in slow motion.

Suddenly, an object from behind me came swinging around over my head. A chain lashed out right in front of me and caught him across the nose. I'll never forget the sound of chain hitting bone. I could just hear the bone cracking; it was as if his whole nose was opened up. Some of his blood spurted out on me.

One of the Manhattan Lords had a two- to three foot-long chain and had swung it at the guy coming at me. For months after that, the sound of the bone cracking rang in my head.

One thing led to another. By then the bouncers from Gay Blades were outside grabbing guys and pushing them aside. We figured the cops would soon show up, so we took off.

We'd already done what we'd come for. We ran down the street towards Broadway, and mixed in with the crowds.

I kept thinking to myself, *I don't want to get caught here. We just killed a guy, maybe two guys. One went through a glass door, face first, and another got hit with a chain; I know he's dead.*

We finally got back home, back to the neighborhood, with everyone accounted for.

Next morning I was up bright and early. I bought a *New York Times*, a copy of the *Daily Mirror*, one of the *Daily News*—every paper I could get my hands on. We combed the newspapers for stories about the fight. I was sure we'd killed at least one guy. If there'd been anything in the paper, then I'd know they were looking for us.

But there was nothing in any of the papers. No one had died. It turned out to be just another dumb fight.

RALPH B. LAO

I'll Be Good *Tomorrow*

CHAPTER 14

OTHER PEOPLE'S FIGHTS

In our neighborhood on 133rd Street and Amsterdam Avenue there lived a guy named Abrams. A big brawny guy, close to six feet tall, and built like one of the Green Bay Packers. But Abrams was a bit of a dummy. He could always be found playing with younger kids. And he let himself be pushed around by smaller guys.

Any time someone wanted to act tough and look good in front of their friends, they'd pick on Abrams. "Come on, Abrams, fight." They knew he wouldn't. They knew he'd back away because he didn't like fighting.

One day I was walking on Amsterdam Avenue with Orlando and Manny, and we saw Abrams arguing over a bicycle with a kid smaller than him. Abrams wanted to take the bicycle from the kid. The kid, almost half his size, looked scared, but kept holding onto his bike.

Abrams was pulling on one end of the bike and the kid was pulling on the other, practically crying, saying, "No! No!"

I started to walk over to help the kid when Orlando grabbed me and said, "What are you doing? Don't butt in."

Orlando could never understand jumping in and helping someone else out—like my always getting into fights for Tommy, because he was afraid to fight. Orlando didn't care for that. "Fuck 'em," he'd say. "If he can't fight, that's his problem. What're you doing, jumping into someone else's fight?"

But I couldn't help it. It was just something I did. When I'd jump in to help someone else, it was just instinct. Orlando, like a good friend, would help *me* if I needed him. But he didn't go for it. It was bad enough having to fight your own fights, but someone else's fights? That was too much for him to understand.

Anyway, I ran over and jumped in without thinking. I pushed Abrams back. "Get your hands off the bike," I said.

I was about five feet, eight inches at the time and must've weighed about 150. Abrams was six feet and weighed close to 200 pounds, and he was solid as a rock. He looked at me and backed up. He respected me, so he didn't try anything. He just backed away and let it go.

Suddenly, a figure came running out of an apartment building. It was Abrams father. Shit!

His father was a short, fat guy, but buck solid, like the ex-fighter, Tony Galento. He had a glass eye that made him look ugly and mean—a glass eye, a round face, and a short haircut. He ran up holding a knife—a carpet knife, which he used on his job installing rugs and carpets.

He stood there next to his son, looked at me, and said, "You want to fight him? Okay. You fight him, but the rest of you stay out of it." He looked at Orlando and Manny and said, "If one of you spics jumps in, I'll cut your ass off." And he told his son, "Go ahead, Junior. Beat his ass in."

There I was, facing this enormous guy while his father was holding Orlando and Manny off with that carpet knife. I knew Orlando would've just as soon taken off. With the father there, holding a knife, it wasn't worth it. All risk with no gain. But, I couldn't just back away. I felt compelled to fight—that stupid reputation crap.

By now, a crowd had started to gather. In that neighborhood kids could smell a fight; guys three blocks away could smell one. I looked first at Abrams, then his father. Out of the corner of my eye I could see the crowd forming. Guys were coming over to watch. They knew me. I couldn't back away now, even if I wanted to.

So, I looked at Abrams and thought to myself, *Maybe I can psych him out.* I knew he respected me. I knew that, normally, he wouldn't dare fuck with me. So I said, "You want to fight me, Abrams? You want to fight me?"

I was praying he'd say "No!"

But goddamn it, with his father there next to him, he felt brave. He looked at me and said, "Yeah, all right," and put his hands up. "Come on."

"*Shit,*" I thought, "*if I have to fight him I'd better not let him get hold of me. And I've got to hit him first. If I can land that first shot, I might just end this. Just one good shot.*"

With my hand still down, I asked Abrams again, "You sure you want to fight me?" I was buying time while I inched closer.

Suddenly, I lunged forward and hit Abrams right in the mouth. Bam! From the impact I was sure that was it; the fight was over. *This guy's going down,* I thought.

But all he did was take one step back and shake it off. It was as if I'd never hit him. He just shook it off. The fucking guy was like a rock.

Luckily for me, Abrams hadn't been in many fights. Although he was big and strong, he couldn't fight. If he had gotten his hands on me, he would've crushed me. So I kept circling around him, easily avoiding his punches, and looking for an opening.

Under normal conditions, without his father standing there with that carpet cutter in his hands, I would've swung my foot out and kicked him in the balls. If I got him in the nuts, Bingo! Fight's over.

I was a dirty fighter when I had to be. All that "clean fight" stuff was bullshit. When I got into a fight, it was a matter of Bam, Bam! Get it over with as quick as possible. Just like my father had taught me. If a guy went down, I'd stomp on him. I didn't let him get up. If I gave him a chance to get up again, he might knock me down and not let me up.

But, this time I couldn't do that because the bastard's father was right there—with his carpet knife. So I circled around some more. Every once in a while I'd charge in and throw a punch. But nothing seemed to hurt him. It was like hitting a wall.

Fortunately, he couldn't connect on me. He'd charge at me, swing a haymaker, but I was able to back away. A couple of times I blocked a punch. Holy shit, he was strong. I could feel my arm go numb. Man, I was glad he wasn't hitting me in the face.

Suddenly, I noticed that Abrams was right in front of stairs leading to a basement.

Most grocery stores along Amsterdam Avenue had basements where they stored their inventory. Leading down to the basement from outside were stairs with iron railings on each side. One railing had a chain that could be connected to the other and it closed off the top of the stairs. At the bottom was a door, which was locked until supplies were needed. They had solid doors down there, because guys were constantly breaking into those basements.

But, these stairs weren't chained, because the clerk must have been running up and down getting supplies.

Abrams was facing me with his back to the stairs. This was my chance. I wasn't getting anywhere with this fight. Eventually, he might get his hands on me or land a lucky punch. I had to act now!

I lunged forward into him. Abrams fell back, down the stairs, with me on top of him. It was almost like slow motion.

When we hit the bottom of the stairs, Abrams' back smashed against the door. And the door didn't give. Abrams was in front of me, so he hit the door. I bounced off him, and fell back against the stairs.

Abrams went "Ugh," and just slumped. As it turned out, (I heard later) he bruised a few ribs, but was all right otherwise. But, now I was worried because I still had to climb those stairs while his father was up there with that knife.

All of a sudden I heard a splat! Followed by everyone laughing. I ran up the stairs and found that his father wasn't there.

Later, Orlando, and Manny told me what had happened.

"It was funny as hell, Bobby," Manny said. "When you went flying down the stairs, Abrams' dad ran over to see what happened. At that moment, Orlando grabbed an apple out of a kid's hand, ran up to the old man, and threw it full force at his head."

"So that was the 'splat' I heard when I was running up the stairs," I laughed.

"Yeah, that apple hit him like a rock," Orlando said. "That fat fuck's head was so hard the apple splattered into about a hundred pieces. But it stunned him long enough for you to get up the stairs, Bobby."

"Damn, Orlando, that saved my ass. I was sure he was waiting up there for me to come back up," I said. "Thanks, man."

I don't know what would've happened to me if Orlando hadn't drawn the old man away from the top of the stairs. What I do know is that after getting hit on the head with the apple, the old man was pissed. He charged after Orlando, cursing and screaming "You bastard, motherless...."

Orlando ran back to Manny on the other side of the street. Both of them grabbed a garbage can full of coal ashes, picked it up, charged the old man and threw the ashes, followed by the can, at him. All the stuff hit Abrams' father, with everything pelting off him, sending him flying on his ass, into the ashes on the street.

That's when we took off. We left Abrams slumped in the basement and his father stretched out on the street.

After that, we never went back around 133rd Street. To this day I don't think I've been back. We knew he was looking for us. We spent months looking over our shoulders. Every time we saw a short, fat guy, we'd get ready to run.

I should have learned from that experience, not to jump into other people's fights. Or, I should have followed Orlando's advice not to do so. But I didn't. The next time I jumped in to help someone I didn't come out unharmed and looking good.

One day I was walking down the street with Richard and "Horny Felix," when we saw a guy pushing Richard's younger brother around. Both Richard and his brother, who was one or two years younger than most of us, didn't get into many fights. They were both pretty quiet, nice guys.

RALPH B. LAO

The guy doing the pushing was bigger and older than Richard's brother, and seemed to be bullying him. We ran over, and instead of Richard stepping in and saying something like, "Hey man, that's my brother," there I was—out of habit—the first one in.

I pushed the guy back, yelling "What the fuck you doing?"

He looked surprised.

I said, "You want to fight, fight me. What are you picking on him for?"

Suddenly, out of nowhere came two guys in army uniforms. This guy had a brother in the army who was home on leave with an army buddy. The brother came charging at me, grabbed me around the waist and I fell back.

I was only sixteen years old, and here I was fighting with an army guy who'd been trained to fight.

Shit! I was worried. But I wasn't doing badly. I kept circling and swinging away, while he kept charging. But, I wasn't getting beaten up.

Meanwhile, Richard and Felix couldn't do anything, because this guy's buddy was holding them off, making sure they didn't jump in. They were a little intimidated by the uniform, and they stayed back.

If I'd been with Orlando and Manny, they'd have probably jumped in and it would've been a free-for-all. But not Richard and Felix. Felix was a lover, and Richard...well, at the Gay Blades he had jumped in, but he wasn't going to do it this time.

Suddenly, the guy lunged and grabbed me, while I hung onto him. As we were wrestling around, we both fell back against a parked car.

Back then, most cars had hinges on the doors that protruded out. When this guy fell against me, the back of my head hit the hinge on the car door, and blood started flowing out. There was blood everywhere—on my clothes, on his suit, everywhere.

When they saw the blood, everybody jumped in and split us up. I was bleeding, holding my head, and cursing at the guy. The old angry bullshit: "I'm going to kill you, you son of a bitch!" Trying to look bad while everyone was watching. "I'm going to kill you!"

I'll Be Good *Tomorrow*

Me, a killer? Bullshit. Every time there's a fight where two guys are separated, they always threaten each other that way.

They rushed me into Richard's house to stop the bleeding with cold water and ice. But when they looked at the cut, Richard said, "Shit, Bobby, you got to go and get stitches. You got to get stitches."

I couldn't see a thing because it was on the back of my head, but I sure didn't want to hear that. All I had to hear was the word "stitches," and I'd freak out. No way. Forget it.

Our local place, Knickerbocker Hospital, was a joke—a bad joke. Word was that, if someone needed to get patched up, it was just "stitch, stitch," no anesthesia, and out the door. Knickerbocker's emergency room was always full. There were always guys with knife wounds, bullet wounds, broken jaws, and anything else one could think of. The doctors had to dispatch everyone as quickly as possible. It was a revolving door. In, stitch, and out.

So I told the guys, "Forget it. No way you're taking me to Knickerbocker."

Right away Felix said, "Don't worry, man, I'll take care of you. I'll patch you up. Let me do it." Felix came from a little town in Cuba where they didn't even have a hospital. Whenever they got into trouble, Felix and his friends used to patch each other up. No problem. They never thought, "Gee, I'm going to have a scar." Besides, scars made you look tough. Everyone wanted scars.

So I said, "Okay, Felix. Do it," and I bent over the sink, while Felix carefully snipped off the hair around the cut. I wouldn't let him shave my head; I didn't want him coming near me with a razor. Then he took a piece of gauze and stuck it on my head with surgical tape.

Next day, Felix was so proud of the operation, he showed me off to everyone. "Hey man, look at the job I did on Bobby."

They just looked and then laughed, because the bandage was just floating on these little hairs. It wasn't tightly secured, or even attached snuggly, because Felix didn't shave my head. I could feel the bandage bouncing up and down while I walked.

But it served its purpose. No Knickerbocker Hospital. No Stitches. No questions. To this day, I can still feel the scar.

RALPH B. LAO

CHAPTER 15

PERV ON THE ROOF

It's scary how many times we came close to killing someone, especially when the last thing on our minds was that someone could actually die.

Back in the forties and fifties, the "Sullivan Act" made buying and carrying a gun in New York almost impossible. But, although buying a gun was difficult, everyone in our neighborhood knew how to make one. To make a zip gun.

Zip guns were made by taping a piece of car antenna tightly to the top of a block of wood shaped like a gun. Then a shorter piece was taped to the wood with about an inch of space between the two. Both sections were carefully lined up with each other so that a long nail could be placed through them. Then a piece of thick rubber, from a car tire's inner tube, was wrapped from the front of the wood to the nail.

A guy tied the rubber piece tightly around the head of the nail and placed a 22-caliber bullet in the space between the two antenna sections. When he pulled the nail back and let it go, it hit the bullet with enough force to fire it.

RALPH B. LAO

When we walked through another neighborhood we could usually tell how many zip guns they had by the number of broken-off car antennas we saw.

I remember the feeling of going to a gang fight, all hyped-up, with twenty or thirty guys on our side. And there were usually some guys with a zip gun or a switchblade. They weren't planning on killing anyone. They just wanted to look BAD. Like in the gangster movies.

Although it wasn't a gang fight, I do remember one time when I believe a guardian angel stepped in and stopped us from killing someone.

Nick, one of the guys in our group, lived on 136th Street. He was about sixteen years old and was one of the best looking guys in the neighborhood. Because of that, old perverts (queers) were always trying to pick Nick up with offers of money or jewelry.

If a guy needed money he could always get a quick five or ten bucks by letting one of these perverts play with his dick, or give him a blowjob. "Horny" Felix made lots of money this way, but most of us didn't go for this shit. Especially Nick.

One day, Nick told us about a queer who was always trying to pick him up. Every time he saw Nick, he'd say, "Hi Nicky. If you go with me, you can make some money." Or, "How about a movie, dinner, and then we go to my place? I've got money if you want it."

So, Orlando said, "Look man, next time he tries to hit on you, say 'okay,' I'll go with you for a few bucks.' Set up a time and let us know. We'll make sure he never hits on you again, and make some money while doing it."

Nick said, "All right, cool."

One night, while hanging out on the corner with Orlando and Manny, Lefty showed up, showing us a zip gun he'd just made. Lefty was another guy from the Jacobins on 176th Street, and was one of Hector's friends. Like Hector, he started hanging out with us on a regular basis.

Suddenly Nick came running up and said, "I got him. I got that queer. He's waiting for me on my stoop. I told him I'd be right back. He wants me to go out with him."

I'll Be Good *Tomorrow*

I said, "Great, here's what you do. Tell the guy you can't go out with him, but you can go up to the roof with him. No movie, no dinner, none of that bullshit, but you can go up to the roof where he can give you a blowjob for ten bucks."

Orlando added, "You know the building next to mine, '612'? Take him up there. It's a good spot. If this guy has any knowledge of our block, he'll know this roof is pretty cool, pretty quiet, and it's nearby."

"Yeah," I said. "Tell him he can give you a blowjob up there and no one will see him doing it. Once up there, we'll jump him, take his money, and make sure he never hits on you again."

"When he sees my gun, he'll be too scared to move. It'll be quick." Lefty said. "We'll smack him around a few times, grab his wallet, and take off."

"But don't shoot him. Just scare him," Nick said.

"Don't worry," Lefty answered. "I'll be careful. I'll just point the gun at him to keep him quiet."

"Okay," Nick said, and he took off to get the guy.

The rest of us headed up to the roof to wait for Nick and the pervert to show up. There was a little section up there with a door that opened onto the roof. We hid behind that section and waited.

The door opened and we heard Nick say, "Yeah, come on over here, Pablo," or whatever the queer's name was. This was the signal to let us know they were there.

When the two of them stepped out, we ran around from behind the door, and leaned against it. Lefty put the zip gun up against the guy's head and said, "Okay, you son of a bitch, put your hands up and stay still!"

The queer looked around, scared and surprised. We were holding the door back, but this bastard didn't even notice there was a gun at his head.

He panicked, and all he could think of was getting out. He grabbed Orlando, who was against the door, and flung him aside. I jumped on his neck, trying to hang onto him, but he swung me off.

He was only about five foot nine inches, but he was strong. With

113

one hand he just swung Orlando out of the way and then threw Manny the other way. We kept grabbing at him, hitting him, trying to make him stop. But he kept trying to open the door.

Lefty had put the gun to his head and told him to stop. But he wasn't stopping.

Lefty fired. He pulled back on the nail and let it go, over and over. Click, click, click, firing right at his head, but it kept misfiring.

For some reason the zip gun didn't work. Maybe Lefty was too nervous. Maybe he wasn't pulling the nail back far enough—but he kept trying to shoot the guy.

Later he told us, "I wasn't trying to kill him. I wasn't thinking of that. I just wanted to stop him." But it was right at the guy's head, and if the zip gun had fired, Lefty could've killed him.

The queer flung the door open, threw us aside like rags, and headed down the stairs.

There was an old battered chair sitting up on the roof landing. I grabbed the chair and threw it with all my might right on him. The chair hit him, but the son of a bitch just kept on going, like nothing hit him.

I don't know where he got that strength. He had to be one of the strongest guys we'd ever come across.

We all kept running down the stairs after him. It was no longer a matter of grabbing him and taking his money. Now we just wanted to beat the shit out of him. This guy didn't listen, didn't stop, he just didn't pay any attention to us.

I was fast and got to the street first. But I didn't know what the hell I was going to do if I caught up with him. The guy was so strong he could've killed me. However, I couldn't stop, couldn't let up. Something just kept driving me.

But when he reached the street, the perv stopped and turned around to face me. He just stood there, waiting to see what I was going to do. Now, I was scared. The guy wasn't running anymore. I thought, *"Oh shit! Now he's going to take it out on me. He's going to kill me."*

Then I spotted an old floor lamp, with a long pole, in a garbage can just outside the building. I reached over, picked up the lamp, and swung it at him. But he just grabbed it when it hit him, and held onto it. There we were, him holding onto one end, and me holding onto the other.

Just then Lefty, Nick, Orlando, and Manny came down the stairs. When he heard them, he took off down the street. We let him go. We had to. We were not about to go running down Broadway chasing this guy in front of everyone. After all, we had been trying to mug him, which was a crime in itself. Although we didn't get any money from him, he never bothered Nick again.

However, Lefty could have easily killed him with that zip gun, and we'd have all been doing time—twenty years to life. And for what? For some excitement and a few bucks.

RALPH B. LAO

CHAPTER 16

HORNY FELIX

There were perverts all over our neighborhood. A guy could go along with one and make five or ten bucks, while getting a hand job or a blowjob. But, I didn't really go for this. Although I always could have used the money, I couldn't even stand the thought of a guy having his hands on me.

While in the eighth grade, my math teacher recommended me to Brooklyn Technical High School, one of the finest schools in New York City. After taking and passing their entrance exam, I became the only kid from the Upper Westside to pass the test that year. But, it also meant I had to ride the subway every day for forty-five minutes each way.

At that hour of the morning, it was almost impossible to get a seat on the subway. And when I did, I usually gave it up to a woman or older person. But every few days, standing in a crowded subway, Bingo, there'd be a hand crawling around my leg, touching me.

And what really pissed me off was that it was never a woman—

it was always a perv, a queer. I'd grab his hand and pull it up for everyone to see and really embarrass the bastard—making him stop, and usually exit at the next station.

None of our gang really cared for this crap, going with a perv for a few bucks. Except for one guy, Horny Felix. If he couldn't get a girl, he'd pick up a queer.

He'd find one, get a blowjob, come back, and say, "Look man, I made some money." And we'd know right away, Felix had been out with a queer.

Felix told us he came from a little town in Cuba where there weren't many girls. With more guys than girls, he didn't get laid as often as he wanted to. But there were always queers, perverts. So if he couldn't get a girl, he'd get a queer. When he got horny, and no girl or queer was available, he had other ways to satisfy himself.

Once he asked us, "Any of you guys ever do the 'Flies-in-the-bag' thing?"

"The what?" we asked.

"Flies-in-the-bag," he said. "You get a paper bag, catch some flies, put them in the bag and tie it around your dick. Then lie back in your bed with all the flies buzzing around your dick. If you close your eyes and think about a girl you like, you'll come."

"That's sick, man! Besides, how are we going to catch that many flies? We don't live on a farm, with shit all over the place," we told him.

"Damn, Felix, you're one horny bastard," we added, and we all laughed.

Queers, or flies—nothing was sacred to Horny Felix. But if a guy wanted to get laid, he could always count on Felix to find some pussy.

One night I was standing in front of the candy store where we all hung out, on the corner of 135th Street. But, because I'd stayed out late a few nights earlier, my mother had put a strict curfew on me. She wanted me home by nine o'clock, no later.

It was about 7:30 when Felix came running up to me saying,

I'll Be Good *Tomorrow*

"Hey, Bobby, I got these two girls I just picked up and I need another guy. Come on. We can get laid. I know it."

If Felix said he had two girls and he could get laid, I knew I was going to get laid, too. He had a knack, a nose for it. So I said, "Fine, let's go."

He introduced me to the two girls. Both were Irish, and pretty nice-looking. We headed down to Riverside Drive. I figured I could make it. Get laid and still be home by nine. I had plenty of time—an hour and a half.

But, goddam those girls. They didn't want to get right down to business. They wanted to fool around, giggling and teasing us, first. They enjoyed horsing around together, while we were trying to get our hands on them—trying to feel them up a bit, and pull off their drawers.

By then we'd walked all the way down to Grant's Tomb at 125th Street and Riverside Drive, to screw the girls.

Finally, I got my girl over to one side and Felix got his away. Bingo, we got laid, and everyone was happy. Everything was cool. When we finished, the girls headed home. I looked at my watch. Ten o'clock!

I broke into a cold sweat. Holy shit! My mother was going to kill me. She'd put this curfew on me because I was already coming home late. And she'd told me, "You come home late again and I'll kill you."

I mean, I could get into a gang fight with a bunch of guys and get beat up, and that was better than having my mother hit me. I preferred fighting with the guys, because I could always fight back or run. Anything could happen when it was a gang.

But with my mother? I couldn't run, I couldn't fight back, I couldn't do anything. All I could do was just cover up while she beat on me.

Now, I was scared. I knew I was in a shit-load of trouble.

Finally I said to Felix, "Man, do me a favor. You take off before me and head on home. As soon as you get home, call up my mom and say, 'Hi, Mrs. Lao, is Bobby there?' and act like you're out of breath."

"Why? Felix asked.

"Because then she'll ask you 'What's going on?' And you tell her we got jumped down by Riverside Drive around eight o'clock by a bunch of black guys," I answered.

Everyone in the neighborhood knew we were having trouble with the blacks on 125th Street. At that time, things weren't going well between some of the black gangs and us.

"You tell her you got away and you weren't sure what happened to me," I added. I had it all figured out.

I explained to him, "She'll be worried for a little while, and then when I walk in the door, she'll be so happy to see that I'm okay, she'll forget to be mad. Instead of hitting me, she'll hug me!"

"Okay," Felix said and he took off.

I started trotting slowly from 125th Street and Riverside Drive, heading for home on 140th Street. While I jogged, I started hitting myself. I ran down Riverside Drive, punching myself in the mouth, hitting myself in the cheek, biting my lips with my teeth, trying to draw blood and swell up my lips.

If my mother didn't see blood, she wasn't going to believe this shit. She wouldn't go for this story, and she was going to beat the crap out of me.

By the time I got home, I was exhausted and feeling a little groggy. My lips were swollen and my cheek was a bit puffed-up from me hitting myself. *Great. This'll work.*

I got to my place, opened the door, walked in, and there she was. I ran up to her with a sad face, all puffy-lipped, and said, "Oh, Ma, guess what happened!"

Before all the words were out of my mouth, Bam! She hit me. With a belt. She must have beat on me for ten minutes solid. She finally stopped.

I lay there in my bed and I couldn't believe it. I'd beat myself up for nothing. I'd punched myself for what?

She beat the shit out of me, anyway. She didn't give me a chance to get the story out. And what the hell had happened to Felix?

I'll Be Good *Tomorrow*

I found out the next day that Felix was just as scared of my mother as I was. He had called up, just as we'd planned. He said, "Mrs. Lao, this is Felix, is Bobby there?"

Before he could explain, she'd said, "Felix, I'm going to get the cops after you." And Felix just hung the phone up.

He was scared. He didn't want to mess with my mother. He didn't want the cops in his house and his mother finding out. So he never got to tell her the story I had cooked up to open the way for me.

After beating myself up while running home, I walked right into a second beating—two beatings in one night—one by me, and one by my mother.

RALPH B. LAO

I'll Be Good *Tomorrow*

CHAPTER 17

BROOKLYN TECH

My junior high school, P.S. 43, had a reputation for having lots of gangs, and lots of fights. It was known citywide as a very tough school.

It was on the edge of Harlem, at 126th Street and Amsterdam Avenue, and it was the only junior high in the area, an area referred to as "the valley." All the guys from my neighborhood—Puerto Rican, Cuban, Irish—we all had to go there, as well as all the black kids from Harlem. It was quite a mix.

School was fairly easy for me then, and I was always able to keep my marks up while I was there. My best subjects were math, English, and mechanical drawing. I loved drawing.

Just as I was starting my third year in junior high school, my math teacher, Mrs. Casner, told me she had recommended me to Brooklyn Technical High School. She discussed it with me, telling me that it was an excellent school and I should seriously consider going there. At that time, Brooklyn Tech and Bronx Science were the two top high schools in New York City.

RALPH B. LAO

It meant taking an entrance exam, which she was sure I could pass. If I passed it, instead of spending my third year at P.S. 43 Junior High, I would go right over to Brooklyn Tech.

I didn't know anything about the school, but it sounded like fun, and a challenge. I told my mother and she got excited as well.

She worked at the offices of the International Ladies Garment Workers Union (ILGWU), and the people who worked with her were all familiar with Brooklyn Tech. Some had kids going there, and they knew it was one of the best schools in the city.

My math teacher's recommendation paid off. A date was set for just four of us from upper Manhattan to take the exam. Only two passed, a Jewish kid and myself.

Paul, the other guy, lived a few subway stops below me, so we often met at his station and continued to Brooklyn together. But since we were not in the same classes together, we couldn't really help each other much with our studies. That, plus the fact that our neighborhood experiences were so different, made it a short friendship.

The first day of school they had all of the new students—the entire freshman class—meet in the auditorium. It was immense, with entrances on the second, third, and fourth floors.

The principal gave a speech about how tough it had been to pass the test, and only the "cream" of the city got accepted. However, if we thought it was tough getting in, we'd find out it was a lot tougher staying in. I came home very impressed and determined to do well.

My first year at Tech was exciting. It was like a new world to me. I managed to get excellent grades, with "High Achievement" awards in both English and Drafting—awards I've proudly kept to this day.

In gym class I was so good at rope climbing the gym teacher made me a rope-climbing monitor. My job consisted of teaching students how to climb a rope that extended from the floor to the ceiling of the gym. This particular talent proved quite useful a couple of years later. All in all, I had a very good first year.

But during my second year I started growing tired of Brooklyn Tech. By then I realized the other students at Tech were not the type of guys I was used to being around.

I'll Be Good *Tomorrow*

Besides, being only one of a handful of Puerto Ricans there, I also became self-conscious about my clothes. They weren't as nice, or as new, as what the other students wore.

I often wore shirts that were frayed around the collar, and worn out shoes, sometimes with holes in them. Most of the other students came from wealthy families and seemed to have plenty of money. This bugged me. I felt like one of the poorest guys in the school.

And, there were no girls at Tech. It was a goddamn all-boys school back then. No girls!

But I was the only one in my neighborhood going to Brooklyn Tech, a school that seemed like a million miles away. Everyone else was going to George Washington (G.W.), the neighborhood high school.

It was during my second year at Tech that I really started getting involved with Bernadette—and with Orlando and Manny. It was one thing to hang around with Orlando, Manny, Bernadette, and the guys at home. But it was quite another thing having to travel to Brooklyn Tech every day. It was tough as hell. Tough to get up in the morning, tough to go all the way to another world—Brooklyn—and tough to leave all my friends behind.

It took me forty-five minutes to get there. Every morning I'd have to get up at the crack of dawn, get on the subway and head to Tech—an all-boys school. It really was another world. A world without girls.

Not only had it been a long trip to Brooklyn, but by the time I got home after school, it was 4:00, 4:30, and the homework they'd piled on me would take one or two hours to complete. I always had other things I wanted to do, anything other than sitting down and doing homework.

Something was going on in my neighborhood all the time. So I'd get home and say to myself, "To hell with the homework. I'm going to 135th Street and hang out with some of the guys, and spend some time with Bernadette."

Every once in awhile, one of the guys would say, "Instead of going to school tomorrow, why don't we do…" this and that?

125

The first year I didn't go along with that, but the second year I'd say, "Great. Let's do it."

Besides hanging out with them, Bernadette and I also started playing hooky a lot, and spending more time together.

CHAPTER 18

TAKING THE CURE

Like the stain on the sofa, a Parcheesi board also had a special meaning for Bernadette and me.

When we were younger, someone would show up with a wrench, open the water hydrant, or "Johnny-pump," as we called it, and the kids would run in and out of the water, cooling off and having a ball.

Whenever a car or a bus went by, someone would grab a board and hold it tightly under the water as it came out of the pump. They could then maneuver the board at different angles so the water would spray onto the vehicle. That was half the fun of opening a Johnny-pump, especially if the car or bus windows were open. The spray would drench the people inside.

But, now at our age, a swim in the Hudson River was the perfect way to cool off. The Hudson River wasn't the cleanest place to swim, especially where we went, which was about a hundred feet from an open sewer line.

The condoms, sludge, and crap that flowed out of the sewer line made the "push-away stroke" very popular, since it allowed us to clear a path while continuously kicking to keep the water rats from following us around.

But when we dove in off the dock, we had to remember to keep our eyes and mouth closed. You never opened your eyes—or your mouth—until you surfaced. Other than that, it was great, and it was close to home.

One time I came around the neighborhood and the guys were all getting ready to head down to the river. Being in our mid-teens, most of us were too old now to be running in and out of a water hydrant on the street, which was what the younger guys did.

It was a really hot, humid day, and everyone decided to go for a swim. But because it was a spur-of-the-moment thing, totally unplanned, I didn't have my bathing suit. So, rather than me running home to 140th Street to get it, Orlando offered to loan me an extra one that he had, plus one of his towels.

Problem solved. I borrowed his bathing suit and towel. We went swimming, cooled off, and had a great time.

A couple of days later I started itching around my groin area. On and off, on and off. I'd scratch one spot, get relief, and then it would start in another spot. *Damn it, what the hell is going on?*

I immediately thought of the river. But I'd swum there about a hundred times over the years, and never felt anything like this. Then I felt something soft and wiggly on the tip of my finger when I scratched. I pinched it, held onto it, and pulled it off.

Holy crap! It was a small, round, bug-like thing with little legs that kept moving around, like a tiny spider, or cockroach.

What the hell is this? I felt itchy all over. Disgustingly itchy. Then I pulled off another one. Same thing. Goddamn little bastards, crawling around the hairs of my dick. *What the fuck?* I asked myself. It scared me, because I didn't know what it was. I'd never seen or had anything like this before.

I told Bernadette about it, and showed her one of the little bastards I'd pulled off, to see if she knew what they were. "I don't know what it is either, Bobby," she said. "I've never seen anything like that before. It almost looks like a tiny spider."

I'll Be Good *Tomorrow*

"Damn it," I said. "I can't go around with these things crawling on me. Let's go to the library and look it up. Let's find out what the hell I've got."

We raced up to the nearest library. After searching through a couple of books, Bernie suddenly turned to me and said, "Here it is, Bobby! Here's a picture of one of the little bastards. It looks exactly like the one you showed me, legs and all."

I looked, and sure enough, she was right. The picture in the book and the description of itching all matched. It all pointed directly to something called Pubic Lice—Crabs!

"Shit, Bernie," I said. "I've never heard of these before, or even knew they existed."

"Neither have I," she said.

The library book clearly stated that they're passed from person to person, either by sexual contact or by using an infected persons clothing, linens, or towels. You don't get them while swimming.

But the only person I was having "sexual contact" with at that time, was Bernadette. And we both knew I hadn't gotten them from her, so I had to have gotten them from someone else. It had to be the bathing suit or the towel I'd borrowed from Orlando.

Since he had a reputation for always being immaculate, I guessed he'd caught the crabs but didn't want anyone to know, so he kept it to himself. Orlando was always well groomed, trimmed, and spotless. He took great care to keep himself clean. Unfortunately, his bathing suit, or towel, weren't as well cared-for, or as discrete, as he was.

Because Bernadette and I were so close, so heavily involved sexually, it was only a day or two before she got them, also. Fortunately, she only found one or two of them.

But now that we knew what they were, we went to a drugstore and bought some over-the-counter medicine the book recommended. It was a liquid that was then poured on the infected area.

Both of Bernadette's parents were at work, so we went straight to her place and into the bathroom. After reading the instructions, we realized we had to shave all of our pubic hair off first. A person couldn't really get rid of the little bastards if he or she didn't shave, because they would hide and hold on tightly with their little legs.

We had to pour this crap—a black liquid—right on our shaved groin areas. And we had to repeat the process again after a week, because they might have laid eggs that would hatch a few days later.

The shaving actually turned into a fun experience for both of us. I helped Bernadette shave, and she helped me. We did it together, and it was nice. I shaved first, with her adding a few final touches in spots I couldn't see or reach. Then I helped her shave, and added a few kisses along the way.

She didn't care much for the shaving part, but as always, she enjoyed having me add the well-placed kisses. She would say over and over, "A little more there, Bobby. A little to the left. That's it. Now a little lower."

She laughed as I obeyed, kissing every spot she directed me to. Finally I felt her hands gently holding my head between her thighs, while she pressed her lips against mine, as she'd done so many times before, filling my brain with the taste of her.

After clearing my head, and steadying myself, I remembered why we were there. We had finished shaving each other and it was time to pour the liquid on. Not knowing what to expect, I chose to go first.

Bernie said, "Okay Bobby, here goes," and she poured the medicine on me.

"Holy shit!" I yelled. "It burns, Bernie. It burns like hell." I saw stars. "Damn, that shit burns!" I jumped up and down trying to stop the pain.

Poor Bernadette didn't know what to do. Suddenly she said, "Here, let me fan you, let me fan you, Bobby. Cooling should help. Hold on, let me get something. I'll be right back."

She ran to her room, grabbed the board from a Parcheesi game we enjoyed playing, ran back to the bathroom, and started vigorously fanning me with it.

All the time she was fanning me I continued jumping up and down in pain.

I'll Be Good *Tomorrow*

"Stay still! Stay still," she yelled.

Suddenly I spun away from her, yelling, "Oh shit! Oh shit, that hurt. You clipped me. Damn it, that hurts."

She was fanning frantically, while I kept bouncing around, unable to stay still. But my jumping around caused her to hit my dick by mistake with the board. She hit me so hard the Parcheesi board split in two. Boom. Oh, Jesus! Now I was in double pain—first from the burning, and now from being hit with the board right on the head of my dick.

Finally, the burning stopped, and the pain eased off. Then the two of us laughed while she still tried to fan me, cool the burning, with two halves of a Parcheesi board.

When it was time to pour the medicine on her, we were well aware of the dangers. I said, "Here goes, Bernie. Get ready."

She braced herself, and I poured the medicine on her slowly— very slowly. Then I carefully and deliberately used one half of the board to fan her, thus easing the burning sensation for her.

After that experience, a week later, when it was time to repeat the process, she was a lot more careful with the fanning, while I made sure to limit my jumping up and down, and keeping my dick from bouncing around.

After that, every time we sat down to play Parcheesi on the now taped-up board, we'd look at it, remember the day we "took the cure," and start laughing.

"Bobby, are you feeling warm? Burning up a little?" she'd whisper. "Do you want me to fan you?" And we'd continue laughing, at our own private joke.

RALPH B. LAO

I'll Be Good *Tomorrow*

CHAPTER 19

PARTNERS IN CRIME

Whenever we stole a car or broke into some place, it was always with guys—never girls. We never got the girls involved. Girls were for parties, making out, having a good time, and turning to when you needed nurturing.

But Bernadette didn't follow those rules. She was always looking for the next thrill, anything that was exciting, as long as it was with me.

One night we were walking on Riverside Drive towards Grant's Tomb, to make out. That area was always dark and had very few people around at night. We would find a bench and I would sit with my legs sticking through the slats that formed the backboards, while Bernie sat against them, and leaned into my arms, as we faced each other. We could kiss and make out without having to twist our bodies.

This particular time on the way up there, I happened to notice a Buick with the double ignition switch—two positions, one labeled "Off" and the other, "Locked."

Out of habit, I checked the door. It was unlocked. Next I looked at the ignition switch, and it was in the "Off" position. That meant I could just turn the key switch back up to "On," and the car would start. No key needed, no hot-wiring necessary.

I said, "Bernie, we could go for a ride." I said it as more of a boast, kind of like, "I'm so cool, I could start this car if I wanted to." It was a half-hearted boast, never really expecting Bernadette to go for it—nor really wanting her to.

In the blink of an eye, before I could stop her, Bernie opened the door, jumped in, and said, "Let's go, let's go for a ride."

I was startled. "Are you sure, Bernie?"

"Yeah, let's go. Come on Bobby, let's go," she insisted.

I started the car and pulled out, heading downtown on Riverside Drive. At 72nd Street we turned onto the West Side Highway and headed back to Grant's Tomb, where we left the car.

It was just a short drive, but I'll never forget the feeling of having Bernadette sitting there with me, all excited. It was a new thing to her, a new thrill, and a new form of excitement.

As we ran home, she kept laughing and saying, "Wow, that was fun. What a thrill!" Even though I didn't expect to, or want to, I couldn't help but feel some of her excitement. It was as if I was experiencing everything through her.

The next day she told all the girls what we'd done, and they couldn't believe it. "Damn Bernie, you stole a car and drove downtown in it. How'd it feel?" They almost seemed jealous of her.

She felt great and acted like, "I'm a badass girl. I stole a car."

However, I had mixed feelings. I felt good for her excitement, but I kept thinking, *What if we'd been caught?* I would have felt terrible—not for me, but for her. It would have been my fault for starting it all.

Fortunately, we didn't get caught. But the excitement stayed in her blood. She'd had a little taste of it, and she liked it.

About three months later, we were down on 124th Street where Bernie had a friend, Consuelo who lived in a small tenement house with five floors, and only two apartments on each floor.

On the left side of the stairs was a tiny apartment with one door. On the right side there was a "railroad" apartment. That was the name given to a long narrow apartment, with the rooms lined up one after the other, end-to-end, like railroad cars. Consuelo lived in the railroad apartment on the fourth floor, with one floor above hers.

We were at Consuelo's talking, when Bernie told her all about the car ride. One thing led to another and I jokingly said, "The next thing you're going to want to do, is break into a place."

Consuelo quickly jumped in and said, "I know this couple that has a large piggy bank. They live on the fifth floor, in the tiny apartment across the hall. It's an actual piggy bank, and they keep throwing in quarters and half dollars. And the bank is packed."

She'd been in their apartment and knew where they kept it. Besides, she thought the husband was a creep, often hitting on her, so this was a good way to get back at him. Since both of them worked, she was sure they weren't home. The people living above Consuelo, in the railroad apartment, weren't home, either. She was sure the entire fifth floor was empty.

Without any hesitation, Bernie said, "Let's go up there, break in and grab the piggy bank. We can break it open, and split the money."

Consuelo quickly agreed. The two girls were so excited, I was easily drawn into it, "Okay, let's do it," I said.

But it was a strange feeling for me. This wasn't like breaking into a store with Orlando and Manny. Plus, I'd never broken into someone's apartment. And this job was with two girls.

We climbed up the stairs and sat on the top step, waiting while Consuelo knocked on the door of the railroad apartment.

"Mary, Mary!" she called to the people living there, and kept knocking to make sure no one was there. If someone had opened the door, she had an excuse. She was coming to borrow something. But, no one answered.

Then she knocked on the door of the apartment where the couple lived. Nothing. So, now it was cool. We knew both apartments were empty—there was no one on the entire fifth floor.

Bernadette and Consuelo stood at the top of the stairs looking down. Both were lookouts for me, looking and listening to make sure they didn't hear approaching footsteps or see anyone coming up.

RALPH B. LAO

Those apartments had very thin doors. They had a thick fancy frame around the door, but the center was paper-thin. The hallways in the building were very narrow, only about four feet wide, so that the wall of the apartment across the hall was right there. I could press against the door with one arm and brace the other arm against the wall facing the door.

By using the wall as leverage, I could press my arm against the door and push it in, which is what I did. I put my arm against the door and just stood there like Samson between two pillars. I kept pressing until the wood cracked.

Once it cracked, we all stood still, and just listened. I could almost hear the girls' hearts beating, going "boom, boom, boom." When we were sure no one had heard the noise of the door cracking, I finished pushing in the wood. I reached in and opened the latch inside.

Now it was Consuelo's turn, since she knew exactly where the piggy bank was kept. She whispered to Bernadette, "Come on, you go with me."

"Okay," Bernie said. The two of them went inside. I stayed outside making sure no one was coming, while the two girls were in the apartment.

Consuelo grabbed the bank and they both came running back out. She handed me the bank, and Bernie and I took off. Consuelo trusted us. She knew we would be fair with her. We were always fairly honest with each other.

Bernadette and I took the bank and went to our favorite spot around Grant's Tomb. We cracked open the bank and took out a little under $60. We split it evenly three ways. Consuelo got $19 and some change. Bernadette and I—being a team—got about $38 or $39.

In the early fifties, that was a lot of money, especially for young teenagers.

Later the girls described the feeling they both had of being in the apartment, to me.

"Bobby, you should've seen the look on Bernie's face when we ran into the apartment," Consuelo said. "She looked so excited, I was afraid she wanted to clean the place out."

I'll Be Good *Tomorrow*

"No I didn't," Bernie answered. "I just wanted to grab the bank and get out of there. Also, I didn't expect that piggy bank to be so large, or so heavy. But it sure was fun — and exciting," she added.

Bernadette's description sounded like the same feeling I'd had when I first stole the watermelon with Orlando. But this was much more exciting because I had done it with Bernie, together — as a team.

First the joyride in the stolen car, now this.

To this day, every time I see the movie *Bonnie & Clyde,* and see their first robbery together, I think of Bernadette and our "Partners in crime" spree.

RALPH B. LAO

CHAPTER 20

THE KNIFER

One block from my building was a grocery store, a bodega. Armando, the owner, was a good guy. It wasn't a big bodega, but it was clean and he made a decent living from it.

I worked there delivering groceries on Saturdays until I was sixteen. When I worked at Armando's, I'd brag to the guys about how easily I could break into the place if I wanted to.

"I know Armando keeps a few hundred bucks in the store every night," I said. "I can get in through the basement window, go up the stairs, grab the money, and be out of there in ten minutes, tops. Easy as hell." We used to talk like this a lot back then, about how we could break into one place or another.

But I would always say, "I can't do it at this bodega, because Armando is a nice guy, and I know him too well."

Late one night, about a year after I quit working there, I was walking home and saw fire engines all around the store. The place burned to the ground while Armando stood watching. I felt bad for him, because the store was gutted.

A few days after the fire I learned that one of my friends, Rico, deciding to try what I had told them, had broken into the store. He and his friends went in through the basement, went up the trap door into the store, and started looking for the money.

But I hadn't told Rico or any of the guys about Armando's hiding place. Armando never kept the money overnight in the cash register. He hid it in a secret drawer behind some shelves. It was a perfect hiding place.

When he couldn't find the money, Rico got mad and started throwing things around and knocking stuff off the shelves. Then, he and his friends decided to start a fire. They lit a match, set fire to the place, and took off.

Luckily, one of them noticed there were tenements above the store, and had the presence of mind to turn in a fire alarm when they got outside. Then they'd crossed the street to watch the store burn.

It pissed me off when I heard this story. I couldn't believe Rico would do something like that. Armando had given me a job, sure. He didn't pay that much, and I worked hard for what he gave me. And I wasn't married to him. But, what got me mad was that, although I'd told these guys about the store, I'd also said I would never break into it because he was a friend.

It wasn't only that he broke into Armando's Bodega. Knowing I wouldn't do it or want it done, Rico had done it, anyway. I felt that now my reputation was at stake. I felt challenged.

But Rico had a bad reputation with a knife. A while back, he had pulled a knife on someone and gotten away with it. After that, the word got around that he was a knifer, and he liked that. He started carrying a knife all the time then, and flashed it for any reason. Rico's protection now was his knife. That's how he got what we were all looking for—a reputation.

If a guy could build a reputation and have people think he was bad, he wouldn't have to fight as much. People would quit testing him.

I started asking around for Rico. I didn't know what I was going to do when I found him. I knew Rico could take care of himself. He knew how to fight.

"That's stupid, Bobby," Orlando told me. "What are you going to get out of it? So he burned the bodega down, so what? The joke's on Rico, not on you. He didn't get a goddamn cent, he got shit."

I'll Be Good *Tomorrow*

Orlando took a different view. Reputation didn't mean shit to Orlando. Only money did. He could never see the advantage in fighting for nothing. Every move, every breath, had to be for gain.

But Orlando's words fell on deaf ears. I still felt like my reputation was at stake, and my reputation meant something to me. So, a few days later, when I learned that Rico and some guys were up at Rosie's, I told Orlando, "I'm sorry, but I'm going up there. I have to get that bastard." (Rosie was one of the girls who hung out with us, and was always nice to me.)

Orland and Manny joined me as I ran up to Rosie's apartment and knocked on her door. When she opened it, I just walked past her like I was Al Capone and owned the place. Stupid shit. Rico was sitting in the living room.

"You son of a bitch," I said. "You and your buddies broke into Armando's bodega, even though you knew the owner was a friend of mine. Then, when you couldn't find the money, you weren't man enough to just walk out again. If you'd just done that—walked out—I wouldn't care. But, you had to burn the place down." On and on I ranted.

Rico stared at me with a mixture of anger and shock. Then I remembered his reputation with a knife. *What if Rico pulls his knife on me? What do I do?* Using my fists was one thing, but I'd never been in a knife fight with anyone. Carrying or using a knife just wasn't my thing.

I kept on ranting, but I was thinking fast. I realized I couldn't wait. The slightest hesitation on my part, even just continuing as I was, he might pull his knife. Once he made that move, he would have to follow through; it was expected of him. That was his reputation, and he wasn't going to blow it.

I thought maybe he'd try to scare me with his knife first, because that was our game—always trying to psych each other out. But I knew if I waited until he pulled his knife, it was the first step down an irreversible path that would get one of us killed. I had to beat him to the punch. I had to act first.

"You lousy son of a bitch," I yelled. "I'm going to kill you!" I used the word "kill" deliberately, to hold him. If he was ready to go for his knife, that word might shake him up a little. I knew his game; it was just like mine. Bluffing. Bull shitting. Psyching each other out. But, I needed to be sure I had the upper hand.

Before he could recover from being yelled at and threatened, I ran into the kitchen and grabbed two steak knives from a drawer.

Rosie tried to stop me. "Bobby, what are you doing?"

"It's okay," I said, and pushed her aside. I ran back to the living room, threw one of the knives in Rico's lap, and stepped back with the other knife in my hand.

"Come on, you bastard," I said. "You've got your knife. Now I'm going to show you what a real knife fight is like. Come on!"

I stood back, looking mean and bad, as if I knew what I was doing. As if I'd done this many times before. But I was praying inside.

Rico just looked at me. He finally pushed the knife off his lap, and said, "I don't want to fight you, Bobby."

That was all I needed. I threw my knife on the floor, dramatically, and walked over to Rico. "You lousy bastard," I said, and started hitting him.

Orlando and Manny grabbed me and pulled me back. "Okay, okay," they said, "he's had enough. You can stop now."

I turned around and walked out, with Orlando and Manny behind me. That was the end of it.

I'll never know how close I came to losing that one. If Rico had pulled out his knife, his adrenaline might have given him the courage he needed to follow through. Falsely or not, he did have a reputation with that knife—and he would have fought to keep it.

However, the joke on all of us was that no one had actually ever seen Rico use a knife. No one had ever seen him cut or stab anyone. He was great at flashing and threatening with one. But no one had actually seen him use it.

So, when I threw the kitchen knife on his lap, I apparently got him worried that maybe I was the thing he was pretending to be— maybe I was a real knifer.

CHAPTER 21

JOHNNY LOCO

We had a friend who was known by everyone as "Johnny Loco." Crazy Johnny. He was twenty-four years old, about five foot, seven inches tall, and weighed two hundred pounds. We'd first heard of Johnny Loco when we were going to hook up with a new gang named the Buccaneers.

A couple of guys came over and said, "Hey, man, we're going to form a new gang, and Johnny Loco's going to run it."

We looked at each other. "Who's this guy, Johnny Loco?" Manny asked. "Sounds like a bad guy."

A couple of days passed and finally we got to meet Johnny Loco, a rather short, fat guy with a very short haircut, like a skinhead Marine cut. We could see scars on his head through his hair. He told people he had mental problems, and they had to operate on his head every once in a while.

Johnny Loco liked to act like he really was crazy. He'd go into a rage and grab a stick or a baseball bat, and he'd intimidate people this way. They figured he really was loco.

That bullshit didn't work for long with us. We noticed his scars when we first met him, but four or five months later he was still

143

wearing the same short haircut. Those scars were about two years old already. He wanted people to see them, and think he was really crazy. That he was a head case.

After a while, we got to know him better, and he was okay. He was a lot dumber than Manny, but he was cool. He didn't pull that "crazy" act on us anymore, and we enjoyed joking with him and listening to his tough-guy stories, which by now we all knew were bullshit.

One time we'd gotten into a fight with a gang, the Villains, from 130th Street. We were supposed to meet and have it out with them by Grant's Tomb. We got there with some of the Buccaneers and a couple of other guys from the neighborhood, all waiting by the tomb.

Grant's Tomb had a big circular street around it. On the Hudson River side there were benches overlooking the river. The sidewalk was about twenty or thirty feet wide, and a couple of us were leaning up against the fence. We had guys hidden all over the place—in the bushes, by Grant's Tomb, everywhere.

But we had to have some guys visible so when the Villains came they would spot us. Orlando, Manny, Tommy, a couple other guys, and I were the decoys. Plus, Johnny Loco—Johnny, with his zip gun, talking a lot of shit, acting bad—but always good for a laugh.

While we were joking with him, we spotted a car slowly coming around Grant's Tomb, making the circle. It swung up right in front of us, and a guy jumped out of the back. He had a rifle and he aimed it straight at us. Holy shit!

When we saw that rifle, everyone cleared the fence. It was just as high as the one Orlando had cleared when he was running away from The Guinea. This fence also had a steep hill on the other side, going down about two hundred feet, towards the West Side Highway.

Orlando and I were in great shape, and cleared the fence, the first ones over. I slid down the hill, grabbing bushes on the way down, to break my fall. Behind us we could hear "Pow, pow, pow!" The guy was shooting at us, or over our heads.

We were halfway down the hill before Johnny, fat and slow as he was, cleared the fence. But that son of a bitch came barrel-assing down the hill, flying right past us. He left us in the dust and beat us down to the highway.

We couldn't believe it! We kept asking each other, "How the hell did he do that?"

Another time Manny, Orlando, and I were sitting in a Chinese restaurant, right by the door, getting ready to order, when Johnny saw us. He walked in and asked, "Hey, man, how you guys doing?"

We looked up and said, "Oh, hi, Ace. Sit down."

Johnny sat down. "Hey, what you guys going to do—eat?"

"Yeah," we said, "we're going to order something and eat."

"Oh, wow, what did you do?" Johnny asked. "You pull a score? You pull a score?"

We poked him in the side. "Cool it, man. Don't say that shit so loud."

"Okay, okay, man," Johnny said. "You know me. I don't say nothing. These Chinese make good food. They sure know how to cook." He looked around and then after a pause, he said, "I'm a little hungry too, you know."

He was looking for a handout. He didn't weigh two hundred pounds for nothing. Then he said, "Like, man, when you guys pull a score, I wish you'd call me. I could always use a little money, for food and stuff."

"Okay, Johnny, cool. You want to eat something, then go ahead, man. You're our ace." Orlando grabbed a menu and said, "Go ahead, don't worry about a thing, just order what you want."

So, Johnny looked at the menu. He figured we'd made a score, and we had some money. We had a reputation. Every once in a while we'd go around the neighborhood and we'd have money. Other times we'd have nothing. Feast or famine. Johnny figured we were on one of our feasts. When we had money, we'd turn people on.

Johnny sat there, looking at the menu and said, "Great. I'll have one from column A, two from column B, and maybe a little from columns C and D." And when the food came, he stuffed himself.

Holy shit, I thought. *Johnny can really put it away.* We ate, but the rest of us didn't eat too much. We ate just enough to satisfy ourselves. But he was packing it in.

After we finished, Johnny noticed that we were laughing and smiling. He seemed to know something was going on with us. He said, "Hey, man, why you laugh? I mean, you laugh cause I eat a lot?"

We laughed and I said, "No, Johnny, no. We didn't laugh cause you ate a lot. I mean, you do put it away for a little guy. But, no, we're not laughing at you."

"I was hungry, man."

"Okay, Johnny," we said, "now what do you want for dessert?"

"Oh, no. No dessert. I pass on dessert, I've had a lot to eat."

"No, Johnny, you've got to order dessert. You don't have to eat it, but you've got to order it."

"Why?" he asked.

"Because," we told him, "we're going to order dessert and when the man goes back for it we're going to take off."

We'd been going through one of our phases. We'd go into a restaurant and order a meal. After we'd eaten we'd order dessert, and when the waiter went back to get it, we'd take off. We'd been doing this all over the city — uptown, downtown. We liked it; it was fun. And we were eating like kings.

Johnny looked at us. He asked, "Take off? What you mean, take off?"

"Johnny, man," we said, "we don't have any money, we didn't pull a score, we're broke. We're as broke as you. We're just going to eat and then we're going to take off. So, you order dessert and then we all run out of here."

"Oh no, man," said Johnny. "You don't do this to me. Oh shit, not after I ate so much. Now you tell me! I'm too full. I can't run."

"Bullshit, man, like we invited you? You invited yourself. We didn't tell you we pulled a score. You're the one who walked in and wanted to eat. Okay, fine. So you ate. Now we run."

I remember the look on Johnny's face when he glanced up and saw the Chinese waiter coming towards us. He whispered, "Oh man, you can't fool with these Chinese guys. They grab one of those cleavers, those big machetes in the back, and they chop your ass off."

I'll Be Good *Tomorrow*

"Bullshit, Johnny. Just watch us, and get ready to run."

We ordered dessert, and took off. Of course Johnny ran out with us, and for a short, fat guy, he didn't lose a step. Orlando, Manny, and I were in good shape, moving fast. But Johnny was right there with us, matching us step for step. Fat and stuffed, but man could he move.

We got far enough away that we were finally able to stop and catch our breaths. "See Johnny, that wasn't so bad. You had a good meal, and it didn't cost you a cent," we said. We all laughed about it, and headed home.

We liked putting Johnny Loco on. He was such a fathead, always shooting his mouth off about how bad he was. He thought we really believed his bullshit stories. But every once in a while, even Johnny would pull off a good one. He'd get lucky and put one over on someone.

Nick told everyone about one time when Johnny Loco was going with him and Richard to smoke pot at Richard's apartment. (We could get marijuana anywhere in my neighborhood then. I saw my first joint when I was about six years old. Some kids about nine or ten years old had one and they were going to smoke it.)

So Johnny Loco and the guys were going up to Richard's house to smoke pot when they ran into Tommy. Johnny got the idea that they should take Tommy with them and play a joke on him. He said, "Hey man, come up with us, we going to smoke some marijuana."

Tommy was the guy who was always too scared to fight. He didn't really go for that kind of thing, but he always wanted to be one of the guys. So he went along. At Richard's place they rolled their joints, but one joint they rolled with oregano in it. No pot, just oregano. That one they gave to Tommy.

When they lit up their joints, Johnny showed Tommy how to smoke. "See, you do this, you light it, you go..." He sucked in his breath. "Just hold it in, hold the smoke in."

Tommy said, "Okay man, okay." And he lit his joint, the one with oregano, and started puffing and walking around holding it in.

"Hey, Tommy, man" the guys said, "That's some bad shit, ain't it?" They were nodding and getting high.

147

But, although Tommy was on oregano, he agreed, saying, "Yeah man, this is some good shit."

Then they started laughing. Poor Tommy didn't know what was going on, so they explained to him that his joint was just oregano. Then they all took a drag from Tommy's joint, and the damn thing tasted terrible.

Tommy had smoked almost the whole joint. He wasn't getting anything out of it, but he wanted to be high. He didn't want to be left out, so he figured he had to be cool, like one of the guys.

To this day I think he really did get high. He wanted to so badly, that he convinced himself he was really getting high on pot.

Every time we saw him after that, we'd say, "Hey, Tommy, want to go with us and smoke a joint, some oregano?"

Tommy would laugh along with us, "Ha, ha," and turn red.

That was one of the only times I can remember Johnny Loco wasn't just bullshitting about something he did. That time he actually pulled off a good one on someone.

CHAPTER 22

THE HENRY HUDSON BRIDGE

A car is a big deal where people don't have anything. In a poor neighborhood a car is a way of escaping the place, even if it's only for a little while. It's not uncommon to see people who are living in a basement, with little food, owning a Cadillac.

But people who are well off don't understand. They ask themselves, "How can these people, who don't have anything else, own a big car?" They don't understand it's because a car is their escape, their way out of a filthy roach-infested neighborhood—that even just knowing they can drive off for awhile makes life more bearable for them.

I knew about this first hand. Every night when I went home and wanted to take a bath, I'd have to go into the bathroom with a pan filled with hot water (if I had any), which I then poured on the roaches crawling inside the tub. I'd have to flush them down the drain, before I could take a bath.

Then I'd have to keep looking up at the steam pipe that ran from the floor to the ceiling. At the ceiling in the corner was a hole where

149

the steam pipe went through. I'd have to watch out for roaches coming out of that hole, from the small space around the pipe.

If I wasn't careful, all of a sudden, Bingo! I'd have a roach floating in the water with me. They'd just drop down into the water. Needless to say, showers became very popular at home.

That was what people in my neighborhood had to come home to. But if we could get into a car and get out of the neighborhood, even for a short time, it was great. If we had a Buick or a Cadillac, it was even better. We could drive into a better neighborhood and nobody would know the difference. We could blend in.

Nick, the guy who had the run-in with the perv on the roof, and who also told everyone about Tommy smoking oregano, lived on 136th Street. His father owned a used car lot right there on the corner. It wasn't a big place, just a small lot that held five or six cars.

Nick's father would buy old jalopies for a few hundred dollars, work on them, and then sell them for twice as much. In that neighborhood you could always find someone who was looking for a car. And you could push off anything, especially if it had a new paint job.

One day, we were hanging around on the corner, when Tommy came up with a bright idea. "Why don't we get ourselves a car and go for a ride?" he said. "We can get out of the neighborhood for awhile, and have some fun."

So we pulled Nick over and said, "Look man, suppose we take one of your father's cars tonight and go for a ride. After the ride we'll fill the tank up with gas, put it back in the morning, and everything will be cool."

Nick thought about it for a few minutes, and then said, "Okay, let's do it."

His father kept the keys to the cars hanging on nails, on a wooden rack he kept in a booth on the lot. Nick went in during the day, when the place was still open, grabbed one of the keys, and put it in his pocket. Later that night, his father locked up the place, and went home.

We'd been watching, and when we saw him close up and leave, we were ready to take the car and go for a ride.

I'll Be Good *Tomorrow*

We chose Vincent the junkie, a pothead, to go get the car.

We gave him the key and said, "We'll be waiting for you on Riverside Drive."

None of our guys could get the car because everyone knew us too well. But Vincent was new in our neighborhood, and he knew how to drive. He could walk in, and if anyone saw him they wouldn't know he was one of us.

We waited down on Riverside Drive and finally Vincent came driving up in an old jalopy.

"What the fuck, Nick? Couldn't you have grabbed the keys to a better car?" Lefty asked. "This looks like a piece of shit."

"Sorry, guys," Nick said. "My dad just got this car and hasn't had a chance to fix it up yet. I didn't know I was getting this one. I just grabbed the first key I saw, and got out of there before he saw me."

"Fuck it," someone said. "Let's get in it and get out of here before some cops come along."

So we all piled into the old wreck. There were about ten of us, including Orlando, Manny, Nick, Tommy, Hector, Victor, Lefty, and me. Guys were everywhere. Sitting on each other's laps, kneeling on the floor—any spot they could grab. Only Vincent, the driver, was spared from having to double up.

Vincent asked, "Which way we headed, up or down?"

"Let's head up to Henry Hudson Parkway," Orlando said. "We'll go up a ways, then cut back down on the Harlem River Drive, and back home. Okay?"

"Yeah, sounds good," we all agreed, "But let's get going before someone sees us."

We headed uptown on Riverside Drive, hit 145th Street, and, click—a red traffic light got us. When we stopped for the light, the car died.

"The fuckin' car won't start," Vincent said. "It won't start. Damn, did you have to pick the worst car on the lot, Nick?"

"We have to get out and push," Orlando said. "Vincent, put it in second, keep the clutch in, and when I yell 'NOW,' let it out. It's a stick shift, so it should turn over then. Just keep giving it gas. Then we'll all jump back in and take off."

We all got out, pushed the car, and when it started, we all jumped back into it. But, we realized we'd have to go through the same routine every time the car stopped.

So Lefty said to Vincent, "Look man, keep this thing going. If you hit a light, throw the thing into neutral, stop it, but keep your other foot on the gas. Just keep it going. Keep giving it gas."

Okay, cool, no problem. Next time we came to a red light, Vincent shifted into neutral, braked for the light, and kept giving it gas. That time the car didn't stall. He'd kept it running. Great!

Vincent kept doing this until we made it onto the Henry Hudson Parkway, heading upstate, driving in the left lane.

We were all having a ball. Guys were getting elbows in their sides and joking around, like "Who's sitting on my lap, come on, get off, my legs are numb."

All of a sudden someone noticed a sign ahead that read, "Last Exit Before Tollbooth."

And, holy shit! We couldn't get over to the exit. We were in the left lane and there were cars all around us. There we were, heading towards the tollbooth, and all we could think of was the cops that were always there.

We were going to hit a tollbooth with all these guys in the car, and Vincent driving. I mean, Vincent looked like he was fifteen years old. The cops were going to look in the car and they were going to stop us. We knew we were going to get caught.

If the car stopped—if it stalled—we were in trouble. But now there was nothing we could do but keep going.

One of the guys had a hat and he gave it to Vincent, and said, "Here, put this on, so you'll look older." Vincent put the hat on, but it was too big for him, and it was floating on his ears.

We all started laughing. "Holy shit, look at Vincent with that hat," Lefty said. "He looks like Al Capone."

"Yeah, like Capone when he was fifteen years old," Manny added. And we all kept laughing.

I'll Be Good *Tomorrow*

Right before the tollbooth, Tommy, Manny, and Hector hit the floor. The other guys put their feet over them so the man in the tollbooth wouldn't see there were so many guys. We had to look cool, look natural.

There was Vincent with this big hat and we kept telling him, "Look man, don't take your foot off the gas, don't take your foot off the gas. You get to the tollbooth, give him a dime, and keep going. If you have to stop, just throw it in neutral, but keep your foot on the gas!"

"Don't worry, don't worry," Vincent said. "I've got it. I know what to do. I'm not stupid. I can handle it—relax."

But fuck! There was a car in front of us at the tollbooth, and the goddamn guy didn't have any change. He was waiting for change and bullshitting with the toll keeper. And while he talked, we waited, and waited—and waited.

And the car stalled.

The toll keeper looked out and saw Vincent trying to start the car. He waved toward a cop car parked over on the side, and the cop came over.

Holy shit, I thought, *we're in trouble now. We're in a stolen car, we don't have registration, and we don't even have driver's licenses. Even though it's Nick's father's car, we stole this thing. Now we're going to get busted. I do not want my mother to know that I am doing this shit.*

Orlando looked over and saw the bridge. "Bobby, the bridge," he whispered. "We'll jump off the bridge."

Right away I agreed, "Sure, that's it. Of course. This is the Henry Hudson Bridge. The cop comes over, and when he's getting everybody out we'll take off and jump off the bridge into the water, into the Hudson River."

We knew the river. We'd swum off the docks, jumped right into all the dirty water—rats, scum, everything. We were used to it. We knew how to swim in that crap.

Fine, I thought. *We'll jump off the bridge and into the water.* We got ready.

The cop came running up and said, "All right, you guys, hurry up. Out, all of you. Out."

Guys started piling out. About nine of us crawled out of the car. But when Vincent opened the door and also started to get out, ready to put his hands up, the cop looked at him and asked, "Where are you going?"

Vincent looked at him with a blank expression.

The cop said, "What the hell are you getting out for? Get you ass back in there. Who's going to drive?"

So Vincent jumped back in.

"All right," the cop said, "the rest of you, push this shit out of here. You don't think I'm going to drive it for you, do you?"

We all breathed a collective sigh of relief. "Yes, officer. Yes, sir." We were so happy. We pushed the car, got it started, and quickly drove out of there.

The cop hadn't come over to arrest us; he just wanted us to move out of the way because we were holding up traffic.

A couple of weeks later, Orlando and I were in Inwood Hill Park, looking up at the bridge that connects Manhattan to the Bronx along the Hudson River. We both realized it was the same bridge that our car had stalled on, the night of our joy ride.

"Holy shit!" Orlando said. "That fuckin' bridge is about two hundred feet from the water."

"That's what we were going to jump off?" I added.

That surely would've been our last adventure. Had we jumped off that bridge, we would've landed, Splat! Just like hitting concrete.

"Thank you, cop," for not asking Vincent for his registration and/or driver's license.

I'll Be Good *Tomorrow*

CHAPTER 23

CUBAN NIGHTMARE

During the time that Bernadette and I were together, we'd sometimes get into arguments and we'd break off. But we'd always get back together again. No matter how bitter the argument, we always came back to each other.

One day Bernadette and I got into one of our arguments and I walked off in a huff. I was sitting in the candy store on the corner of 135th Street having a soda, when Orlando came running in.

"Oh man, Bobby, I'm glad you're here," he said. "Carlos and I met some girls and they're hot. But we need a third guy. Come join us and you'll have a good time, a couple of drinks, and maybe we'll all get laid."

He and Carlos (one of the guys in our group) had just met three girls—two Irish girls, and a Cuban girl. Carlos invited them up to his place for a few drinks, and the girls quickly agreed.

This particular night I didn't really feel like hanging out, or meeting anyone. I was thinking of Bernadette and our argument, and I just wanted to head home and go to bed. But, it was Orlando. He would always help me out, and I'd help him out whenever we needed it. So I figured, *Oh, all right. What the hell.*

Orlando and I bought some beer and went to Carlos's place. On the way up to the apartment, he told me that Carlos had picked out one of the Irish girls for himself, and Orlando had chosen the other one. He said the Cuban girl, Carmen, was really good-looking, and was for me.

When we came in, Carlos was sitting with the girls in the living room. They all got up as Carlos said, "Bobby, come over here, meet the girls," and he started introducing me to them.

"Bobby, this is Rita, Janet, and Carmen. Girls, this is Bobby. He's not as good-looking as Orlando and me, but we couldn't find Cary Grant, so he'll have to do for now."

Everyone laughed, with Carmen adding, "He looks pretty good to me."

I could see as soon as I walked in the door, that sure enough, these bastards had picked out the best-looking girls for themselves. Carlos's girl, Rita, was a very pretty blonde, and Orlando's girl, Janet, was a redhead, and built like a brick shithouse.

Mine however, was a brunette who looked like she was about fourteen years old and was very plain looking. (I found out later that she was actually seventeen.)

She was small, thin, and had on a cheap-looking cloth coat buttoned up to her collar. Maybe it was because I wasn't feeling good that night, and I wasn't really up for it, but she really looked terrible.

We went into the kitchen to pour some drinks. "Come on, man," Orlando whispered, "grab the girl and help us out."

He and Carlos were trying to make it with their girls, but they couldn't while Carmen was sitting there.

He continued, saying, "Take the girl and do something with her—you know—so we can get on with the other ones. Even if you don't want to screw her, at least talk to her. Keep her out of the way."

So I figured, *Okay, I'll help them out and keep her busy.* I went back to the living room and sat in an armchair next to Carmen, talking to her.

Meanwhile, Carlos and Orlando were trying to get their girls into separate bedrooms. But their girls didn't want to go, because they didn't want to leave Carmen sitting there. Carlos and Orlando were giving me the eye, like, "Come on, man."

So, I said to myself, *All right, if that's what they want, I'll take this girl and try to make out with her right away. I'll get right down to business and scare the shit out of her.*

I figured I could scare her and make her want to take off—leave in a huff or something. That was fine with me, because all I wanted to do was go home.

The guys couldn't get mad at me if Carmen got upset and left, because that was exactly what they wanted me to do—be aggressive and keep her busy.

So I leaned over from my armchair and asked Carmen, "Why don't you come over here and sit next to me?"

She smiled and said "Okay." She got up from her chair and removed her coat. That's when I saw that she was really built. She was wearing a low-cut blouse, and she was stacked. She sat next to me, half on my lap actually, and half on the arm of my chair.

I realized the next move was up to me, so I put my hand on her lap and started kissing her. I slowly moved my hand between her legs. I figured she was going to let out a yell and jump up. Instead, she grabbed my head, cradled my face against her breasts, and started grinding on my hand.

I couldn't believe it. Holy shit, this girl was going crazy. She started saying things in Spanish, moaning, and rubbing the back of my head. I was kissing her breasts and all of a sudden I got really excited. I forgot all about trying to chase her away. She had managed to really get me going.

I got up and led her into Carlos's room. I locked the door and we got on the bed together. I couldn't believe how quickly she'd turned from the quiet plain-looking girl, to a spitfire. She was all over me. It's as if she'd been on a desert island all her life.

She didn't even give me a chance to unbutton my pants. She did that, and pulled them down for me. Everything I'd do or try to do, she was already there, one step ahead of me. She had me on my

157

back before I could move. She then straddled me and completely took over — smothering me in kisses, while pulling me into her.

Meanwhile, Orlando and Carlos were out in the living room arguing with their girls, who were giving them a hard time. The girls started knocking on the bedroom door saying, "Carmen, come on, we want to go home!" But I was still inside the locked bedroom with her.

"Just a minute, just a minute!" she yelled back at them. "Give me a couple more minutes, then I'll be out!"

Finally, after she was finished, completely satisfied, we got up. When we went out into the living room, Orlando and Carlos were really pissed off with their girls. The bitches wouldn't put out for them.

Orlando looked like he wanted to boot Janet in the ass, while Carlos just wanted them all out of his apartment.

Carmen kissed me goodbye, and the girls left. Carlos and Orlando kept looking at me, acting as if I was the one responsible for them not getting laid. But, after a few beers, we started laughing about the way the evening had turned out. Between bouts of laughter, Carlos kept bitching, and Orlando kept repeating, "You bastard, Bobby. You lucked out again."

The next day when I came around the block, some of the guys ran up to me and said, "Oh man, Bobby, there's a girl waiting for you. She's been asking all of us when you'd show up."

"Has Bernie been around?" I asked.

"No, not yet. But if she shows up while that girl's here, you're in a whole lot of trouble," one of them answered.

Holy shit, there she was! Carmen. Sitting in the candy store, waiting for me. She came out and said, "Hi, *Papito*." She'd called me "Daddy" in Spanish.

She put her arms around me and cuddled up. I was scared to death because I was afraid Bernadette might come around the corner. If Bernadette saw this shit going on, mad at me or not, she would've beat the crap out of both Carmen and me. So I grabbed Carmen and got her out of there fast.

It turned out that Carmen lived in a girls' detention home where the girls were locked-up all week and then allowed to go to their own homes on weekends. Being a Friday night, she was out for two days, and decided to spend it with Janet, one of the two Irish girls who lived in our neighborhood.

For the next two days, Carmen wore me out. We'd go down to Riverside Drive, and while lying on the grass, she'd say, "Come here, *Papito*." She'd grab me, and almost order me inside of her, until she was satisfied.

An hour or two later, she'd be horny again. Without hesitation, she would reach over and grab onto me, telling me where to touch her and where to kiss her, until she would bury me inside of her all over again.

Until that weekend, I'd never met a girl as sexually aggressive, or as sexually demanding, as she was. She didn't leave me alone until Sunday night when it was time for her to head back to the detention home.

Even then, with her two friends waiting for her, she scared me, saying, "I'll be back *Papito*. Don't forget me."

I don't know what happened to Carmen; I never saw her again. But when she left, although I'd enjoyed every minute of it, I was glad to go home and get some rest.

After that, I spent some anxious weekends for two or three months, worried she might show up again while I was with Bernadette.

I went back to Bernadette, and we continued breaking up for a day or two and then getting back together again, seemingly more in love each time.

But, that weekend and the Cuban nightmare is one I'll never forget.

RALPH B. LAO

I'll Be Good *Tomorrow*

CHAPTER 24

MRS. GONZALEZ' CANDY STORE

From the age of thirteen, until I was eighteen, my main hangout was on 135th Street, between Broadway and Riverside Drive. Everyone would usually meet on the stoop of Bernadette's building in the middle of the block. Or else we'd meet on the corner of 135th Street and Broadway in front of Mrs. Gonzalez' candy store.

It was more a luncheonette than an actual candy store. Mrs. Gonzalez' main business was making sandwiches, malteds, egg creams, and other fountain drinks.

The store wasn't very wide, but it had a long counter with about ten stools that stretched from the front of the store to the back. In the back of the store were three phone booths and a little space where people could stand around.

Mrs. Gonzalez would let us stay back there, because a lot of people from the neighborhood would come and hang out with us. We made it a popular place to meet and buy stuff. Without us, her business wouldn't have been doing as well as it was.

One winter day, we walked in and there was a jukebox in the

back. Mrs. Gonzalez figured that as long as we were all hanging out there, why not try and make some extra money from a jukebox. It was great.

Now we were able to hang out back there and hear the latest rhythm and blues records. We'd tell Mrs. Gonzalez which records were popular and she'd order them.

The candy store was really jumping then, and she was making more money off the music. And we grew to like the jukebox. It had spoiled us.

But, eventually Orlando, Manny, and I got tired of the shit of having to feed our hard-earned coins to the goddamn jukebox. It cost five cents a shot to play a record, and our money was quickly disappearing into the thing. We could go through twenty-five or fifty cents in no time. When we'd scored and had money it wasn't a problem. But during the tough times, when we didn't have any cash, it was a bitch to have to feed that machine.

The jukebox had a clear plastic front so we could see the records spinning on the turntable, and how they were selected. There was a series of little metal plates in a row with numbers on them. When someone dropped a nickel in and made a selection, a little arm would move down the row of plates and stop in front of the number that had been chosen. Then the little arm would swivel and hit the plate, and the selected record played.

One night as we were standing there looking at it, I watched the jukebox turntable for a few minutes. I realized that the object was to trigger the little metal plates. Once one of them was triggered, a record would play. Great.

As I watched it work, I got a bright idea. Being the mechanical one in the group, the details of breaking into anything, or any place, were usually left up to me. We'd all contribute ideas, but I'd always come up with the best way to get in. This looked like a pretty simple operation.

We talked it over, and I came up with an idea and a plan. "Orlando, do you have any wire hangers at home?" I asked.

"Yeah, I do," he answered. "Why?"

I'll Be Good *Tomorrow*

"You live the closest, just down the street," I said. "Run home and grab a hanger you're not using, bring it here, and I'll show you how we can play all the records we want, without having to pay for them."

Orlando loved the idea of not having to pay for something, so he quickly ran home and came back with a wire hanger. We straightened it out, and using one end of the hanger, we started digging a little hole in the clear plastic on the front of the jukebox.

We dug in the lower corner, about waist high, just before the plastic attached to the metal part of the jukebox. As we did so, we crowded around in front of the jukebox, and kept playing music so no one would notice what we were doing.

When the hole was just big enough, we inserted the straightened wire hanger, with a little hook bent over at the end. "Click." We tapped one of the metal plates, and sure enough, the record played. We waited until the record had finished, and then did it again. Beautiful!

We were able to go directly to any metal plate, tap it with the wire hanger, and play a record — any record we wanted.

We did that for about a month, and didn't let anyone else know how we were doing it. There were just four or five of us who knew the secret. But we'd always try to get other people to play records first, get them to use up their money, because we knew that at the end of the night there had to be some money in the box.

In between, when things were slow and there wasn't any music playing, we'd go over and hit a few plates. We'd let some of the other guys think it was our turn and we were paying now. So we had music whenever we wanted it.

But after a while, just playing records wasn't enough for us. We saw a lot of money going into that jukebox from other people.

One day Orlando pulled me over and said, "You know, Bobby, even with our little wire trick, there's still a lot of money going into that box."

"So?" I asked.

"Well, it's all because of us. All these guys come around and want to hang out with us," he said. "There ought to be a way to get some of the money they bring here into our pockets, instead of into the jukebox and into Mrs. Gonzalez' purse."

"You're right, Orlando," I said. "We do bring in a lot of business to this place. Mrs. Gonzalez is doing great in this store. Not only from the jukebox, but also from the sodas, and coffee, and other crap she's selling."

"Shit, if we're bringing in the business, we ought to get a cut," he said. "Besides, I hate that bitch and her stuck-up daughter."

There really was no love lost between Mrs. Gonzalez and us. It was all business. She lived in a big house up in Westchester, and she had a snotty-assed daughter—a conceited snob who always acted like she was better than any of us.

Besides the candy store, Mrs. Gonzalez' husband owned a bar a couple of blocks away. They were making money off of everyone in our neighborhood, then running home to Westchester and spending it there. So, it didn't bother us a bit to beat Mrs. Gonzalez out of some money.

We checked out the jukebox for a couple of nights and noticed that the moneybox was in front of it, on the bottom. Someone would put in a nickel and it would drop straight down, right into the box. I knew I could just pop the thing open, but I didn't want to damage it. We had to be able to open the box, help ourselves to a little of the proceeds, and then put it back, because we didn't just want to take money out of it only one time. We wanted to take money out of it frequently.

One night we came in with a screwdriver and huddled around the jukebox. We played some records, and acted like we were making selections. Meanwhile, I bent down, took the screwdriver, and inserted it into the metal box right along the edge.

It took us about half an hour. I'd go down and try to pry it open, and then Orlando would drop down and work on it. Whenever someone came into the candy store, we'd sit back, innocent like, and take a break.

Finally, we got the box open. Took out the money, and checked the box. Not a mark on it! After that, we went in every night—late—after we thought the jukebox had been played a lot. We'd take out some money, but we made sure we always left some change. Also, we put a napkin in the box to cushion the noise of a coin dropping in, so it wouldn't sound as empty.

We just kept taking money out of our private till over the next couple weeks. We could go in, play free records, and always have some quick spending money for hot chocolate, soda, or malteds.

Then one day we walked into the candy store and the jukebox was gone. The back of the store was empty, and our steady flow of cash was over.

She'd found out someone had been pilfering her proceeds. When the man had come in to get the money, he found it almost empty, and Bingo, Mrs. Gonzalez had the jukebox taken out. And she was mad.

We ordered a sundae and casually asked, "Where's the jukebox?"

She said, "The jukebox is gone. I had it removed."

She didn't go into details. I was sure she kind of suspected us, but she couldn't come right out and pin it on us. After all, a lot of people hung out there. But she knew everything usually centered around the three of us.

She gave us what we ordered, and then said, "I don't want anyone hanging out here anymore. From now on, you order something, you have it, and then leave."

Not only had we lost our jukebox, we'd also lost our winter hangout, and our steady cash—a couple quarters, nickels, dimes.

We didn't like Mrs. Gonzalez anyway, but now that she wouldn't let us hang out in there, we felt we had to get back at her. We had to spite her, but make some cash at the same time. Always, we had to make some money. Orlando didn't like doing anything just for spite. There had to be some cash in it.

So, one day, while Manny and I were sitting in the store having a malted, I eyed three small postage stamp machines in front of the store on the counter next to the cash register. Since she had removed the jukebox, Mrs. Gonzalez had figured out this was another way to make some extra cash.

"You know, Manny, those new stamp machines Mrs. Gonzalez has, aren't chained down. They're just sitting there loose," I whispered.

"So? What've you got in mind?" he asked.

"Let's wait for Orlando to show up, and I'll tell you. Okay?" I said.

"Yeah, sure," he answered. We finished our malteds, went outside, and waited about fifteen minutes until Orlando finally showed up.

I told him about the stamp machines and added, "We can go in there, sit right next to the machines and order some sodas. We wait until she goes to the back of the store for something, then we grab one, put it in a bag, and walk out."

"Hmm, sounds like a great idea," Orlando said. "We can take it up to my roof, break it open, take out the money, and get even with that bitch for taking away the jukebox."

"When she realizes it's gone, what if she knows it was us?" Manny asked.

"How's she going to know it was us?" I said. "If we plan it and do it right, she might suspect us, but she can't prove anything. She can't prove it was us."

"Let's do it!" Orlando said.

We went inside and bought some stamps, just to check them out, and we discovered one of the machines was already packed with money. We put our dime in, and Boom! It sounded like it hit lots of coins. So we figured, "That's the one."

We went out and got a shopping bag. Then the three of us went into the candy store, sat down right next to the stamp machines, and ordered something. While Mrs. Gonzalez went to the back to take care of some customers, we grabbed the stamp machine, and lowered it into the shopping bag. Then we stood around and waited a few minutes to make sure no one had seen us.

We had to stay cool, but we could hardly wait to head out, go up to Orlando's roof, and open up the stamp machine. Open it, take out the money, and be in stamps for months. Any stamps we didn't use, we planned to sell to the rest of the guys whenever they needed some.

I'll Be Good *Tomorrow*

But just as we were ready to leave, in walked detective Huntley — Huntley, The Guinea's partner. We froze.

Goddamn it! We couldn't leave now. And we couldn't just walk out and leave the shopping bag there, because he'd get suspicious. He'd see us leave, see the shopping bag on the floor, and know that we had left it there.

Messing around with the U. S. postal system was a federal crime. We couldn't take the machine with us — we couldn't risk it.

And, there was Huntley, a sadistic prick. He would've loved catching us on this rap. We were sure he'd relish beating us up every day for a week, before he would turn us over to the feds.

Manny and I stayed put, but Orlando slipped out. He was afraid Huntley would recognize him as the guy who'd pushed The Guinea on his ass that night on Riverside Drive. If Huntley recognized him, the three of us would be in trouble, even if he didn't see the stamp machine in the bag.

I ordered a pack of gum, just so we had a good excuse to stick around. Huntley ordered cigarettes. We hated that prick and he hated us. But we had to talk to him. We knew we had to say something and act friendly. So Manny said, "Hi, Mr. Huntley."

"Hi, what are you guys up to? Ha, ha, ha."

We kept talking a lot of bullshit. Dumb shit. Anything, to keep his attention away from the shopping bag. We were sweating.

Mrs. Gonzalez was right there with us, giving Huntley his cigarettes. If she noticed the stamp machine was gone, we were in trouble. The only thing we could have done then would be to look down and say, "Gee, I don't know, is this it?" We'd point to the shopping bag on the floor, and act as if we didn't know anything about it.

But that would've meant a busted head for one of us, for sure. So we stood there around that stamp machine in the shopping bag, for what seemed like an eternity, but was actually about two or three minutes.

Manny stood right in front of the shopping bag, with his knee slightly bent over it, to make sure he kept the bag closed so no one could see what was in it.

Finally, Huntley walked out with his cigarettes, and we walked out with him. We weren't taking the shopping bag or the stamp machine. We just wanted out.

"Well, keep your noses clean." All that bullshit cop talk he felt obliged to tell us. "Make sure you don't get into any trouble."

"Oh, don't worry, not us." A lot of crap. "Goodbye, Mr. Huntley."

We headed the other way, turned the corner, and took off running. We knew that encountering detective Huntley was a bad omen. To hell with that stamp machine. We just left it there. We didn't care what Mrs. Gonzalez would think or say when someone noticed it in the shopping bag. We wanted no part of it now. Not after running into Huntley.

A couple of days later I went back to the candy store acting as if nothing had happened. "Hi, Mrs. Gonzalez. Let me have a chocolate egg cream, please."

She mixed it, quietly, and then said, "Here, drink your egg cream, and get out."

I looked. The stamp machines were chained to each other. And Mrs. Gonzalez was mad. Again.

CHAPTER 25

OUR CLUBHOUSE

After Mrs. Gonzalez limited our stays at the candy store, we got a little pissed off. "Fuck her!" Orlando said. "We don't need to go in there anymore. We'll find a new place to hang out."

"Yeah, let's look into the basements around here and see if we can find a room like the one Nick's got on 136th Street, only larger," Manny said.

"If we find one, we can make some kind of deal with the super, like cleaning up, taking out the garbage cans, or something. Okay?"

"Fine," we answered.

We started looking, asking around, and a few days later we lucked out. The building next to where Orlando lived on 135th Street had an empty room in the basement. It was in one of the three buildings that Orlando's super took care of, so Orlando knew him, and they were on good terms with each other.

Orlando told us, "I talked to the super and he said he's not using the room for anything right now, so I made a deal with him. If we pay him a few dollars a month, we can use it as a clubhouse."

169

"That's great," I said. "How much does he want?"

"He said three or four dollars a month would be fine. But part of the deal is that we can't make any noise. We can't disturb the people in the apartments above us," Orlando said. "I told him that wasn't a problem, since all we wanted to do was hang out there to keep out of the cold."

We checked the room out, and it was great. The door was facing the back alley, and had a lock on it, which the super gave us keys for. Now we had a clubhouse where we could safely keep a radio and stuff. A private place where we could take girls, hang out, and stay out of the cold and rain. We didn't have to go to Mrs. Gonzalez' candy store anymore.

However, the room didn't have any furniture. It was a fairly large room, but except for a few chairs the super gave us, it was bare. So we started looking around.

We remembered some of the buildings along Riverside Drive had large lobbies with fancy-looking furniture in them. Sofas, little tables with lamps on them, and even plastic floor plants. Some of them had better furniture than we had in our apartments.

One of the buildings on 137th Street, facing Riverside Drive, had some beautiful furniture in the lobby. When we first went in there, Orlando said, "Damn, that sofa would look great in our clubhouse. I know it's only vinyl, but it looks just like leather. And it's in great shape, almost new."

"Let's take it!" I said. "We can carry it out of here tomorrow morning, right after everyone leaves for work, when it's quiet. All we have to do is go a few blocks, and Bingo, into our clubhouse."

"What if someone from the building sees us carrying it and recognizes it from their lobby?" Manny asked.

"We'll cover it," I said. "That way even if someone sees us, they won't know what it looks like."

"Yeah, that's cool, we can throw some old sheets around it and take it to the clubhouse," Manny said. "I can borrow a dolly from my super. He let my dad borrow it a few weeks ago. I'm sure I can get it.

I'll Be Good *Tomorrow*

That way we don't have to carry it, and we'll look like we're moving furniture for someone."

The next morning a few of us got up early and met at the clubhouse. Four of us—Orlando, Manny, Tommy, and I—showed up. We brought a couple of old sheets from home, and some rope. Manny was able to borrow the dolly from his super the night before, so we wouldn't have to carry the sofa. We could just roll it away. Cool.

But we still had to get the sofa out of the building without anyone seeing us.

We looked around and noticed that the next building, which was on the corner of the block, had a side door leading out to 137th Street, thus avoiding the front entrance facing Riverside Drive. Great, that's our exit.

The next thing we did was check out the doors on the roofs of both buildings to be sure they were both open.

Next we went into the lobby, grabbed the cushions, and put them on the elevator with Tommy and Orlando, who then rode it up to the top floor. When Tommy and Orlando got to the top floor, they removed the cushions from the elevator. Tommy stayed with them, and Orlando rode back down in the empty elevator.

The other three of us then grabbed the sofa, put it into the elevator, and sent it back up to Tommy. We were not about to get caught on the elevator with the sofa, especially since none of us lived in the building.

We climbed the stairs to the top floor where Tommy was waiting. He was holding the elevator door open with the sofa inside.

The four of us then carried it out of the elevator to the roof, then over to the adjoining roof, and repeated the entire process in reverse, going down the next elevator, to the side exit of that building.

When we got to the exit, there was nobody in sight. We'd made it! Two buildings, two elevators, no problems.

We carried the sofa to the side, wrapped the sheets around it, tied them on, and placed it on the dolly. We then rolled our treasure along Riverside Drive from 137th Street to our clubhouse on 135th Street.

Now we had a fine-looking sofa to sit on—and make out with girls. After that, we went to some other apartment house lobbies, and got a couple nice side tables and lamps to set it off.

We invited the super over to see what we'd done with the room he rented us, and he couldn't believe his eyes.

"Damn, Orlando," he said. "This room has better furniture than some of the apartments in the building. How much are you guys going to rent it out for?"

We laughed, as Orlando looked around the room, and said, "Hmm, not a bad idea."

CHAPTER 26

LASTING IMPRESSIONS

When we first got the clubhouse, even before we'd furnished it with the sofa, end tables, and lamps, we put a pool table down there. It wasn't fancy. It was just a fold-up table we bought from a friend of Tommy's who was looking for some quick cash. He sold us the table, including the balls and the sticks, for ten dollars. A steal, literally, since we figured he'd stolen the thing himself.

Now, along with our new clubhouse and a small radio Orlando had contributed, we had a pool table for recreation. Although a guy couldn't make some shots because he was up too close to the wall, it was kind of fun. And for ten bucks we couldn't beat it.

The place was starting to shape up. A pool table, some chairs, and a radio.

Then there was Mona. I think of her every time I see a pool table.

About a month before we got the clubhouse, I went to a party with some of the guys, and met Mona, a girl who lived on 133rd Street. She was very pretty, with dark brown hair, and extremely well built for a fourteen or fifteen year old girl. We danced together for most of the night before it was time for everyone to leave.

I walked Mona home and ended up making out with her between floors of her apartment building. No screwing, just a lot of kissing, grinding, and touching, until she had to head into her apartment.

I didn't see Mona again until after we'd gotten our clubhouse. One day I came around the block and ran into her. I hadn't seen her since the night of the party, and she looked good. Very good. Better than I remembered.

I thought to myself, *I've got a key to the clubhouse and I can take her down there. Check it out, and if nobody's there—Bingo. We can make out.*

So I asked her, "Would you like to see our new clubhouse? We have a radio, so we can play some music, and even play some pool if you want to. It's cool."

Right away she was willing. She knew what I had on my mind. She could see it from the moment we'd run into each other. And I sensed she had the same thing on her mind. She'd been asking about me, and now here we were, together. I had the feeling she was ready to go anywhere with me.

We went to the clubhouse, and luckily, no one was there. I showed her the room and told her, "It may not look like much now, but we're going to get better chairs, a rug, and fix it up."

She said, "It's nice!"

I wanted to try to get a little mood going, so I turned on the radio to a station playing slow music. "Come on, let's dance," I said. I folded up the legs on the pool table, placed it against the wall, and started dancing with her.

We held each other close, and started grinding slowly to the music. After a while, the music seemed to disappear into the background. All I could think of was her soft warm body in my arms. So I star ted kissing her on the neck, touching, and gently rubbing against her. She hung on to me, pressed tightly, kissing me back, getting me hotter and hotter.

I'll Be Good *Tomorrow*

I slowly leaned down and started kissing her on her breasts. Now she was leaning up against the wall, and I knew I had to get her on the floor.

I reached over and grabbed for the folded-up pool table, which was next to her. With one hand I tried to get the pool table off the wall and flat on the floor, and with the other hand I was holding Mona and kissing her.

Finally, I got the pool table on the floor and gently laid her down on it. I kept holding her close, kissing her. I could feel her getting as excited as I was.

I put my hand on her leg and started slowly moving it up under her skirt. I rubbed her thighs, slowly and gently, while continuing to kiss her.

Each time a guy does this, he wonders, *Will she stop me? How far is she going to let me go? Is this where she says no, or can I go further?* As excited as I was now, I wanted to go all the way. I wanted to have her, to bury myself in her. I definitely didn't want her to stop me. Not now.

I put my hand under her skirt, grabbed her panties, and slipped them off. She didn't stop me. Instead, she opened her legs, and seemed to be inviting me in. I undid my pants, took them off and threw them aside, and found myself caught in the warmth and softness of her thighs, as she wrapped her legs around me, and slowly pulled me inside her. We made love right there on the pool table.

We were on the pool table for over half an hour. We just laid there, nothing mad or crazy. Just holding each other very quietly, softly, gently.

Then, suddenly we heard someone turning the handle of the door trying to get in, and we heard someone calling "Hello? Anyone in there?" Fortunately, I'd locked the door behind us when we first got there.

But the knocking on the door shook Mona up a little. She was scared. She thought someone was going to come in, and she didn't want anyone to see her there. So I just held her close until whoever it was finally went away, assuring her that the door was locked.

We got up and I took Mona home. We started kissing again on the staircase for a little while until it was time for her to head inside.

The next day, I went down to the clubhouse to see what was going on. A few of the guys were there, including Orlando. He looked at me and said, "Ah ha, you bastard. You screwed somebody on the pool table, didn't you?"

"What do you mean?" I asked, wondering how the hell he'd found out.

Then I looked down at the pool table. Everyone knows a pool table needs to be flat all the way across. But, now this one started out flat on both ends and suddenly—right in the middle—there was a big dip.

Holy shit! I could see the imprint of Mona's behind right there in the pool table. I just hadn't thought of that. Our nice new ten-dollar pool table had Mona's shape on it. Forever.

Orlando was a little pissed. So were Manny and Tommy. Finally it blew over. They forgot about it once we brought in the sofa and the rest of the furniture.

But even then, every once in a while we'd go up to the pool table, and stand there looking at it, and Orlando would say, "Look at that. That was you. You did that—you bastard."

After that, I saw Mona for about four or five months, on and off. Every time Bernadette and I had a little argument and went through one of our short breakups, I could always get together with Mona.

If we couldn't get the clubhouse, we'd go to Riverside Drive and make out in one of our secret spots. I had a wonderful time with Mona that year, and she with me.

I'll Be Good *Tomorrow*

CHAPTER 27

MONA MEETS THE GUINEA

After the pool table incident, and our five-month on and off romance, one of the last times I saw Mona was at Carlos's apartment.

I was with Orlando and two or three of the guys, and we were all playing hooky from school that day. I was going to Brooklyn Tech at the time, but the others were from George Washington High School, or GW as they called it.

Carlos had put together a jump, a little party, and had invited some of the girls from 133rd Street. Since Bernadette was in school that day, he'd invited Mona. Bernie didn't know about the jump, or about Mona. If she did, she never confronted me about her, or let on that she knew anything was going on. At least I don't think she knew about Mona, although most of the guys did.

We were all dancing and having a good time, when suddenly there was a knock at the door. Carlos called out and asked, "Who is it?"

"You know who it is," someone replied. "Just open up."

Son of a bitch! It was The Guinea, detective Huntley's partner.

At first I'd been worried that it was Bernadette, but this was worse. Although, in reality, if Bernie had found me with Mona, it might have topped this.

All the guys took off in different directions as soon as they heard who was at the door. Nobody wanted The Guinea and Huntley to catch them playing hooky.

Orlando and I ran into Carlos's bedroom, and headed for the back window. But Carlos lived on the third floor, and after looking down we realized it was just too high to jump. Instead, we hid in the closet and held our breaths, trying not to make a sound, although, we both knew that if The Guinea or Huntley came into the room, the closet would be the first place they'd look. But with the window not being an option, this was it.

We knew if they found us, it was a busted head for Orlando, for sure—and probably for both of us.

We were there for about ten minutes when Carlos came into the room. He said, "It's all right, you guys can come out now!"

We came out slowly, and I asked Carlos, "What happened?"

"I'm not sure," he said. "The Guinea was alone. He wasn't with Huntley."

All of us guys were hiding because we were the ones who were going to get our butts kicked. But, Mona and a couple of the girls hadn't hidden. When The Guinea saw Mona he called her over to the kitchen and started talking to her. The next thing Carlos knew, Mona was leaving with The Guinea.

We didn't know it then, but Mona had bought our freedom.

When I saw her later I found out what happened. The Guinea had picked her up once before. He'd taken her out in his car and had made out with her. So, this time when he came up to Carlos's house and saw Mona, he took her with him. That bastard had hit on a sixteen-year-old girl, and screwed her.

I didn't go out with Mona much after that. The thought of her with The Guinea was difficult for me to forget. I know it was kind

I'll Be Good *Tomorrow*

of silly of me. She was fun to be with, and had been good to me throughout our short and steamy romance. But her being with The Guinea was too much for me.

About a year and a half later, I saw Mona again. I could sense that she still liked me, although she knew that I was really involved with Bernadette. She'd always known that, although she let me know she resented Bernie for being involved with me.

She looked great. She was with another girl, a black-haired beauty, and they were sharing an apartment somewhere downtown, while working as prostitutes. Mona had come around the neighborhood to see her mom.

That night I took a walk with her to Riverside Drive. We sat on one of our favorite benches down by the Drive and I could sense she was trying to impress me. She kept telling me about all the things she was doing, the places she'd been, and how much she'd learned and matured.

I asked, "How much could you have learned in that short time?" I was fishing, looking for proof. "It's only been about a year and a half."

She looked at me as she smiled. She knew what I was trying to do, and she was ready. "I'll show you," she said. She leaned over and started blowing in my ear, while gently nibbling. I could feel her breath going through my brain. I couldn't move.

Then she started to slowly unbuckle my belt and open my trousers. She put her hand down there and I could feel her warm hand starting to play with me. She'd done this to me before, but this was different. The nibbling, rubbing, blowing in my ear all seemed to happen at exactly the same time. Her timing and technique had improved so much I was barely able to catch my breath.

The next thing I knew she turned around and straddled me. "What are you doing?" I asked. "Someone's going to see us."

"So what? Don't worry about it," she said. "Just relax and enjoy it."

179

She sat on my lap facing me with her legs around me, through the back of the bench. And instantly I felt this flood of warmth spread through my body. She didn't have any panties on.

That was something she'd never done before. She then grabbed my dick and slowly, very slowly, rubbed it between her legs, until I could barely breathe. She then slipped me inside of her, while she continued blowing and nibbling on my ear.

Her slow movements were so deliberate and sensual, she had me completely unable to move, almost frozen to the bench. I never expected to be inside of her, and to feel her warmth, that quickly. I felt completely overpowered by her.

She just sat facing me, and, Bingo! We were making love, although I could barely move.

Once I heard footsteps on the walk. "Someone's coming," I whispered.

All she said was, "It's all right, don't move," (as if I could), and she kept on kissing me.

She pulled her dress around to try to cover her knees a little, but she didn't attempt to move away. She kept me inside of her and kept moving around and kissing me, while a person passed right behind us, walking a dog. I was nervous, but this girl was completely composed, like nothing was happening.

Two years before, I'd had to hold Mona in my arms because she was trembling on the pool table in the clubhouse, while someone knocked at the door. And now, here I was the one scared because someone was behind me, while she didn't even flinch. It was almost as if she was prepared to continue making love even if the person had been a cop.

We were there for about an hour, while she made me come over and over. After each time, she would slowly start moving again until she had me completely excited again, unable to move, and under her control.

I could not believe what she had learned in just a year and a half.

I'll Be Good *Tomorrow*

And it wasn't just her lovemaking that impressed me. It was also her sense of timing and her confidence in herself. We'd made love lots of times before, but that night Mona acted like she'd done it all her life. Like she'd been born for moments like this.

We finally stopped. I regained my composure, then walked her to her mother's place, and kissed her goodbye. That was the last time I saw Mona, although, I've often wondered since what could've been.

She'd been hinting about continuing together, trying to get me to go with her. I think she wanted me to move in with her, to live with her. But, I was too young then. Also, I was involved with Bernadette. So I never considered going with her.

Besides, I doubt she would have given up her prostitution. She seemed to like the life, and loved the money. So I don't know what she wanted me to do. That was the closest I ever came to going out with a prostitute, although no money was involved.

One thing we just never did, growing up in my neighborhood, was pay a girl to go to bed with us. That was bullshit. Why would anyone pay for love? If I went to bed with a girl, I had to feel she wanted to go to bed with me as much as I wanted her. To pay her cash on the line? I couldn't do it. No way! To me, making love was just that—making love—not paying for love.

After that night, although it was an unforgettable experience, Mona wasn't the same person to me anymore. Not just because she was a prostitute now, but also because I still couldn't forget her fling with The Guinea.

She had done us a favor by taking him away from us that day at Carlos's place. But because it was The Guinea, a sadistic cop, a wall came down between us. And unfortunately, Mona was on the other side.

RALPH B. LAO

CHAPTER 28

GOODBYE TECH

During my first year at Brooklyn Tech I managed to get excellent grades. Even some merit awards. But by my second year I started growing tired of the school. Tired of the hours of homework, the rich kids, and the all-boys-no-girls crap.

I started to hang out with a small group of guys who felt the same way I did about the school. Their way of coping was to cut classes they didn't like. After awhile, I joined them and started cutting classes, too.

Tech had a staircase on the first floor by the swimming pool. Behind the staircase was a door that led back to a storage room under the stairs. When they cut classes, they'd go in there and hide.

It was very dark, but in the back there was a table with a candle on it. The guys would light it, and then sit around and bullshit. Whenever they'd hear a sound outside, they'd blow the candle out, and just sit quietly until the threat was gone.

Soon, just cutting classes wasn't enough for me. I wanted to skip the entire day, so I started playing hooky.

Whenever a student missed a day from school, he had to bring a note from his parents once he returned to Tech. In my case, if I needed to be out for anything, my mother would ask me to write the note and she would sign it. She was too busy to write the whole thing; she had to go to work. The school always accepted it—my letter and her signature.

When I wanted to stay home to play hooky, I would write a note saying, "Bobby was sick yesterday," and then forge my mother's signature at the bottom. Since my mother had a very neat and clean signature, it was easy for me to match it. Especially since I'd created an almost perfect way of doing it.

I would take a lamp, put it on the floor, and then place a piece of glass over the lampshade, so that the light would go through the glass. On the glass I could trace her signature lightly in pencil. I would then take the paper to a table, go over the pencil with a pen, and then erase the pencil with a kneaded eraser, a soft, pliable eraser I had learned to use in my art class.

I had about twenty blank notes, with only her signature on them, already made out. If I was coming to school late, or if I decided to cut classes, I could always quickly write a note just above her signature, with whatever excuse I needed.

When I wasn't openly playing hooky, I had a trick that would get me sent home by the school nurse. I'd go into her office and say I didn't feel well. As soon as a student said he didn't feel well, the first thing the nurse did was take his temperature.

Knowing this, before I went into the nurse's office, I'd go into the bathroom and gargle with hot water. I would then hold the hot water in my mouths as long as possible, spit it out, and go right into her office. She'd put the thermometer in my mouth and the temperature would shoot right up. Bingo! I was then sent home "due to illness."

I had a tough second year. My marks started to go down. I did pass all my classes, but my marks weren't as good as my first year.

My third year was disastrous. That third year, I wasn't doing my homework at night. I'd get into school the next day and do it during one of my study periods. But it wasn't the same. I wasn't studying. I wasn't doing what I should have been doing.

Then one day I got into a fight with a guy named Rifkin in English class. Rifkin was a big, strong-looking kid from a fairly well to do family, in a good neighborhood. Rifkin hadn't really been in many fights, but because of his size and his muscular appearance, guys respected him, and it was enough to make him think he was tough.

One day I was sitting in class when the teacher suddenly had to leave the room. Before leaving, he asked us to copy the notes he had written on the blackboard. Although I was sitting in a front seat, I couldn't see part of the writing because Rifkin was standing right in front of the blackboard, almost daring anyone to say something. No one did.

"Come on Rifkin," I finally said. "Just move over a bit so we can see."

"Why?" he asked, with a smirk on his face.

"So we can copy what the teacher wrote down," I answered. "I don't know about the other guys here, but I can't see anything with you standing there."

He walked up to my desk, waved his finger at me, and said, " If I want to stand there, I will. So shut the fuck up. I'll move when I'm good and ready to move."

I wasn't used to this. In my neighborhood if a guy threatened someone, it meant he was ready to fight. And if they got into an argument over it, he didn't wait—he threw the first punch. It was like an unwritten law. If a guy knows he's going to fight, why wait? He makes sure he gets the first punch in, because that's half the fight.

Besides, with the rest of the class watching, I couldn't just sit there. I had to do something. I jumped up from my desk and hit Rifkin right in the face. Bam!

The sound echoed through the classroom. He reeled back and stood there, stunned, holding his cheek. That was the end of the fight.

It was a good example of our rule. Get the first punch in, and you may not have to do anything else. That's the fight—done and over.

Seconds after it happened, the teacher came in. He could see Rifkin's face was red, and I was still standing there, so he realized something was up. He wrote our names down, and for the time being, that was the extent of it.

About a month later, I was in the gym locker room and I got into an argument with a fat kid, Sylvester. It was a silly argument over my books being in his way. The next thing I knew, out of nowhere, Sylvester was charging at me. There were bolted-down benches between the rows of lockers, so I leaped up on a bench as he charged by me. I jumped on his back and he went down.

This was another rule. "If you get a guy down, make sure he stays down. If you let him get up, he might then get you down, and he might not let you get up. So you don't take any chances. You end it right there."

And that's what I did. I had Sylvester down, so I stomped him.

But, just as the fight was ending, the gym teacher came along and caught us. This time I had to go down and see Mr. Ray, my guidance counselor. Mr. Ray looked at my record, saw that I came from P.S. 43, and said, "Oh yeah, 43, uptown, in the valley." He seemed to know the school.

"Well Bob," he said, "I know what it's like there, but over here at Brooklyn Tech we don't do things that way. We don't fight. We don't act like animals."

He never once considered that maybe I hadn't started the fight. That maybe it was Sylvester who had started it. That maybe I was only defending myself.

While he was chewing me out for the fight, he reached into a folder he had, pulled out a sheet of paper, and added, "I see this isn't your first fight here. I've got a write-up from your English teacher about you and another of his students. It say's here that he caught the two of you fighting last month."

I'll Be Good *Tomorrow*

Shit! I realized he was talking about the time with Rifkin, although there really wasn't a fight, and the teacher had not caught us fighting. That had been one shot, problem solved. But seeing Rifkin holding his face, with me standing next to him, the teacher had guessed we were fighting, and he wrote out a report.

Then, to top things off, the counselor started pulling out all those notes I'd had for being absent, and for having to leave school because I was sick. After looking at them closely, he noticed that all the signatures were almost exactly the same.

So Mr. Ray called my mother at work, and told her that he wanted to see her. About forty-five minutes later, my mother showed up at the school.

The final result was…I had to leave Brooklyn Tech. The fighting was one thing. But I had been cutting classes and playing hooky on the pretense of being sick, and my marks had been going down.

Mr. Ray told my mother, "It just can't go on this way. It is bad for Bob, and it is bad for the school. I'm sorry to say this, Mrs. Lao, but he has to leave."

I'd kind of wanted out, anyway. In fact, I wanted out of Brooklyn Tech so bad that third year, I could almost taste it—but I couldn't tell my mother.

She had been so happy that I'd been accepted at Brooklyn Tech. So proud! She'd been able to go to work with the knowledge that her son was just as intelligent as her co-worker's kids, even though they all had homes in the country and in better neighborhoods.

Before that, she had been struggling so hard with me, and suddenly here was something she could be proud of, something she could brag about, along with her fellow workers, something she could point to as having made all her struggles worthwhile.

I couldn't just blurt out, "Mom, I want to get out of this goddamn school. It's too far from home. I don't like it—I hate it. I don't have any friends there. I want to go to George Washington High, which is so much closer to home."

Now, there I was, in the counselor's office with my mother. And I felt bad. But, on the other hand, it was a great relief to have it over with, to know that this would be my last trip down there.

We went home on the subway, and she didn't say a single word to me on the way. Nothing. But when we got home, she blew up. She started throwing things around, and calling me names.

"You think you're smart, but you're not. You're lazy," she yelled. "You don't want to put the effort into getting a better education, learning something new, getting a career. All you want to do is hang out with that girl, and those bums you call your friends. None of them have a future. None of them! And you want to be just like them."

The one thing she kept coming back to, repeating over and over, was, "You're no better than your father. You're both alike. Both alike!"

She didn't hit me, though, because by then I was just too big and strong. She finally said, "Do anything you want—I don't give a damn, anymore. Do whatever you want to do. Just leave me alone, and stay out of my way."

"Sure, Mom. I'll stay out of your way. Don't worry," I answered. The reality of what was happening started to set in. I was free of Brooklyn Tech. No more long subway trips. No more boring rich kids.

So, I transferred to George Washington High School where most of my friends were. It was great, and it was easy, especially after Brooklyn Tech.

During that time my mother was going out with a guy named Renaldo, who was a captain in the merchant marines. I didn't realize how close the two of them had become.

About three months after the Brooklyn Tech debacle, I came home and my mother was gone. Just gone!

My aunt Maria was there. She said, "Sit down, I've got to talk to you." She told me my mother had left, that she'd gone with Renaldo to get married.

"I'm going to take care of you from now on," she added.

I knew Maria loved me. Anything I did was all right with her. But there was also my grandmother, Sasita—the one who I never felt any love or affection from. So, as good as my aunt Maria was, it wasn't enough to keep me home.

I wanted to go out with Bernadette and the guys around the block. And before, there had always been that goddamn Brooklyn Tech homework, and my mother getting on me. Suddenly, all that was gone. Brooklyn Tech was gone. My mother was gone. All restrictions were gone—and I felt free.

Orlando and I used to talk about how great it would be to have no one to boss us around. How great it would be to be completely free. His favorite line, which haunts me to this day, was, "Never get so close to someone that you can't do without them."

He felt that the greatest thing in the world would be to have no ties at all. No ties, whatsoever. Not to have to be home at any time. Not to have to make anyone happy. To be able to do whatever the hell you wanted.

Orlando was already close to that. He was a year older than me and he could stay out late, and he could do just about anything he wanted.

Now it was my turn. Suddenly, I was free, too, and I went wild. I stayed out nights. I came home late.

I went to George Washington High School for about six more months and got my passing marks. That completed three years of high school for me and then I dropped out of G.W.

I went to my aunt and said, "Maria, I want to get a job, earn some money. I can work during the day, and finish school at night. It'll be easy. You'll see."

She couldn't believe what she was hearing. "You can't do that, Taty. You can't leave school. Not now! You're so close to finishing. So close to getting your diploma."

As long as I can remember she always called me "Taty," never Bobby. It was a form of affection. A popular child's name in Spanish. It was her way of showing me that I was always that little boy she loved.

189

"Please, don't do that. Stay in school, Taty. I have money if you need it. Just ask me. But please, Taty, don't leave school. Please!"

But her attempts to convince me that staying in school was best, didn't work. I just wanted out. I wanted to be really free. No more school. No more responsibilities. No more having to answer to anyone.

And that's when I started really running around.

I'll Be Good *Tomorrow*

CHAPTER 29

THE BIG ONE

The big score came shortly after my mother left. The one where Orlando, Manny, and I made more money in one night than we'd made in the five years we ran around together.

Carlos was also hanging around with us at the time. It was at his apartment where I'd met Carmen—my Cuban nightmare—the night he and Orlando had picked up the three girls.

A couple of years earlier, Carlos had been at Coxsackie, a juvenile detention home. That was his bid to fame: he had served time. In my neighborhood, that was enough to get you noticed, to earn you a little respect.

Now with my mother gone and only Maria and Sasita at home, money for extras, like shoes, socks and stuff, was definitely out of the question. Manny and Orlando were each in a similar situation. Manny's father worked in a factory, while Orlando's mom had a similar low-paying job.

None of us had much in the way of clothing. Certainly nothing fancy or expensive, which I had been painfully made aware of while going to Brooklyn Tech.

The four of us were looking for a clothing store to break into. One where we could get in at night, so we could spend hours rounding up enough clothes to outfit ourselves for a year or two, a store that carried pants, shirts, shoes—anything we could wear.

We found The Regal, a surplus-type store on 145th Street between Broadway and Amsterdam. It sold just about everything we were looking for, even luggage, which we figured we could pack everything into and cart off. It was on the ground floor in a two-story building, with the local Democratic Club above it. It was perfect.

We didn't want to break into a store through a rear window or jimmy the lock on the front door. We wanted to drop in from above. We wanted to break into an empty loft or room above a store, cut a large hole in the floor, and drop in. Once in, we could sort out and gather together whatever we wanted.

The Democratic Club above The Regal was tailor-made. It didn't have any alarms or heavy bolts on the door, because it didn't have anything worth stealing. It was an easy break-in. Once we were in and out of view, we could then take our time cutting a hole into The Regal below, our main target.

We picked a weeknight when we figured there wouldn't be many people on the street. We got inside the second floor club without any problem, sawed a hole in the floor, and slid down a rope that we'd tied around a beam. Perfect. We were in The Regal, all according to plan.

Unfortunately, what we didn't know was that there was an alarm wire strung out about six inches off the floor. It was a thin wire stretching from one side of the store to the other. One end was secured to an eyebolt on the wall and the other end was attached to a clip pushed into a slot on an alarm box.

Carlos walked right into the wire and kicked the clip out of the slot on the box. Bingo! The alarm went off. We scrambled up the rope to the second floor and got our asses out of there—fast.

I'll Be Good *Tomorrow*

In the excitement we left our tools behind. Although the disappointment was intense, we realized our overall plan had worked. We had managed to climb into a store in such a way that we could have easily stayed in there all night, cleaning it out.

Store windows and doors usually have locks, bars, and alarms. But who bothers to alarm a second-floor loft or a set of offices with nothing worth stealing in them? The most they might do, would be to put a couple of locks on the doors. And by now, we'd learned to break through just about any lock.

Once we broke into the unprotected second floor, we would be safe for the night. We wouldn't be out in some alley where anyone could just open a window, look down, and see us. We'd be safely indoors. Once there, all we'd have to do would be to concentrate on breaking in through the floor.

Now we were more determined than ever. We knew we had a winner. We had to do it again. So we scouted around, and finally we found a clothing store in Harlem on 125th Street. It was a cut above The Regal. This place was an upscale men's clothing store. Jackets, coats, suits, and shoes. Wow!

Above the store was an old five-story boarded-up hotel that had just been through a fire. That was beautiful! And 125th Street had a lot of activity and noise outside. There were nightclubs all around that area. It was about two blocks from the Apollo Theater. If we made a noise ripping up a floorboard, no one would hear it, because there was so much noise outside. Great!

We went out and got the tools we needed. The experience we'd gained from breaking into The Regal showed us exactly what we needed. We got ourselves two crowbars, a big screwdriver, a couple of flashlights, and a heavy rope, which we tied knots in, making it easier to climb. We also added a strong nylon rope we could use to hoist bags or suitcases up with.

Our plan was to fill the bags with as much clothing and stuff as each of us wanted and could carry, without attracting too much attention.

RALPH B. LAO

This time we planned to hit the store on a busy Saturday night. That night we headed down to 125th Street in two cabs. I went with Orlando and Manny went with Carlos. In the cab, Orlando and I joked and talked about how some girls were waiting for us, and so on, just in case the cab driver was listening. We were just two guys out for a good time down in Harlem.

We got off at 125th Street and Third Avenue. Carlos and Manny did the same thing a couple of blocks away. We all met as planned in a tenement house about five doors down from the store.

Orlando and I had already been in the store to try on a suit and check out the clothing during the day. While I was doing that, Orlando had been measuring distances by counting steps—picking a good spot to land. Where did we want to land when we climbed down into the store? We didn't want to drop in front of the door or the window. We had to pick a spot where we were protected.

This store had a big window. Part of the window was curtained off with a mannequin wearing a suit on display on the street side. That was the spot, behind that curtain. Not only would we not be seen from the outside, we would land right behind the cash register.

We stood outside the store looking in at the window display, while Orlando carefully and precisely lined the mannequin up with a store across the street. The mannequin and that store lined up perfectly. That would allow us, once inside the hotel, to look out across the street, pick out the store, and know where the mannequin was below us. We had to know exactly where to cut the hole so as to have the opening behind the curtain.

We went over this about ten times, always lining up the store across the street with the mannequin. Then we went into our targeted store and from the front of the store we counted twenty steps back into the interior. Twenty steps. Bingo. That's where we wanted our hole. Lined up with the store across the street, twenty steps back. Perfect. Once we felt confident that we knew exactly where to cut through the floor, we were ready to move forward.

I'll Be Good *Tomorrow*

So, we all met underneath the stairwell inside the tenement—one of those cheap places where you could rent an apartment for about ten to twenty dollars a month. Behind the stairs was a door that led down to the basement. We'd already checked it out.

We headed through the basement into the backyard. Behind these houses was a big wooden fence separating the 125th Street lots from the 124th Street lots.

We passed very quietly against the fence, making sure no one could see us from upstairs or across the way. We got to a bakery that was a few doors before the clothing store, but the damned baker was there, working with his back door wide open. We had to stop and wait for almost half an hour for him to finish whatever he was doing.

Finally, he walked to the front of the bakery. As soon as we saw him leave, we cut across the back door of the bakery and reached the rear of the hotel.

Earlier, when we'd gone to the store we'd checked out the back alley and the rear of the hotel. But we weren't able get into the hotel because the windows were boarded up. So, we figured we could pull off the boards at night, when we wouldn't be seen.

But now, with the baker there, it was too risky. We couldn't rip off the boards and climb in through a window without making a commotion.

Instead, we climbed up the fire escape—five stories—all the way to the roof. The entrance from the roof into the boarded-up hotel was covered with a large hatch, which, when lifted, opened to a metal ladder leading straight down. We were able to lift off the hatch with a crowbar.

Once we removed the hatch, we waited for about twenty minutes, looking down on the street and on the back yard, in case someone had seen us going up the fire escape. We found a good hiding place for the tools, so if someone had seen us and called the cops we could say we were just fooling around, exploring an empty hotel. We probably would've gotten knocked around a bit, but we were used to that.

After twenty minutes went by, we climbed down the metal ladder into one of the spookiest places I've ever been in. I don't think there's anything gloomier than an old boarded-up hotel, with its creaky floors and dark empty rooms.

As we walked down, floor-by-floor, we quietly joked with each other.

"Holy shit, Manny, it's scary in here."

"What the hell was that sound, Orlando?"

"Stop hanging onto me, Carlos."

Finally, we reached the floor just above the clothing store. We walked into the room that lined up with the store across the street, and counted off twenty steps from the front. Perfect. We had the spot we wanted. It was a large room with garbage strewn all over the place, but no rats. None that we could see, anyway.

The room had two windows, one of which had an old fireplace next to it. The fireplace had a long ledge that was wide and strong enough for one of us to lie down on, and look out the window. If we saw anyone walking by, we could say, "Cool it, quiet!" and we would just wait it out.

It was beautiful. We could check for cops or people walking by, but they couldn't see what we were doing. And now that we were inside, we were protected from view.

Outside it had started to rain lightly and there was enough activity and noise on 125th Street, that we were sure no one would hear us.

Manny took the first watch, stretched out on the ledge, nice and comfortable, looking down at the street. We waited, just in case there'd been a drunk or someone sleeping in one of the hotel rooms who could have seen or heard us.

It was about eleven o'clock, and we had a long night ahead. We could afford to just wait. After about another fifteen minutes we started working on the floorboards. This was not as difficult as the one above The Regal, because this floor was already in pretty bad shape. Once we get the floorboards loose, we were home free because, after that we only had a layer of plywood and some ceiling crap. It was no problem to get through with crowbars and screwdrivers. All we had to worry about was the noise.

We had the time, so we could take it slowly. We ripped off one board, waited, and asked, "Manny?"

He answered back, "Go."

Bam! We ripped off another one. Manny kept looking out. If he saw someone, he'd say, "Cool it." And we just sat back and waited.

We got through the boards and ended up right next to a beam. We got lucky because we needed that beam. After we'd gotten through the main floor, we hit the ceiling of the store, which was made out of tin. That was something we hadn't expected or prepared for.

Fortunately, Carlos had a pocketknife with a small can opener. We used it to cut through the tin ceiling like a can of soup. We then cut a hole large enough for each of us to fit through.

We took out the rope and looped it around the beam, tied our knot, dropped it into the store and waited, again to make sure nobody heard or saw us. A few minutes passed, and all was cool.

Manny and I were chosen to climb down first, while Orlando stayed up with Carlos. I took one of the flashlights with me, and Orlando kept one upstairs.

Manny and I climbed down and looked around. Wow! These were some pretty sharp clothes. I could already see myself looking dapper and cool, wearing the suits, ties, and shirts I'd chosen when we'd first checked out the store.

But the first thing to go for was the money. Always, the money first. So I opened up the cash register, looked inside, but there was nothing in it. Shit, where's the money? Then I looked down and saw a safe. I said, "Goddamn it, Orlando. A safe."

All of us were disappointed. Sure, we'd be able to grab the clothes and stuff, but we also wanted to get some money. At least a couple of dollars. But a goddamn safe! How were we going to break into that? That was another line entirely. We weren't safe crackers.

Then I said, "Let me try it anyway." I couldn't give up without spinning the dial a couple of times, just like I would with any lock. Anytime I saw a lock on a locker, I'd spin the dial and hope maybe the combination numbers I had in school would work here.

So I reached over, grabbed the dial to spin it, and the door opened! They hadn't locked the safe! I opened the door. Inside were stacks of dark brown envelopes.

When I was a kid, insurance men used to bring our policies in thick brown envelopes that looked just like these. I reached in the safe and grabbed an envelope. When I looked inside, all I saw were bills, packed about two inches thick. I reached in and grabbed another envelope. More bills.

I could feel Manny next to me, dumbfounded, trying to catch his breath. "Orlando," I whispered, loud enough for him to hear me upstairs. "We're rich. We're rich." I shined the flashlight on the money, flashing and flipping it so Orlando could see it from upstairs.

Manny finally caught his breath, and started laughing and banging me on the back.

But Orlando was already thinking ahead. "Quiet guys, cool it," he said. "Hurry up and put it all in a bag and send it up now. In case anything happens and we have to make it, we have the money."

As always, when it came to money, Orlando was right. Back to business. We grabbed a little valise and put all the envelopes in it. Then I started opening drawers next to the cash register. Underneath some papers there was more money. I grabbed it and said, "Holy shit, there's money all over the place."

Manny looked in the file cabinet behind us. Sure enough, more envelopes, more money. We just kept putting the envelopes in the valise.

The place must have been a bookie joint. The money had to come from taking bets, and they kept it on the premises. They didn't get this money from selling suits or they would've had it in one place, or in the bank.

I'll Be Good *Tomorrow*

After we put the money in the valise, we tied it to the other rope—the nylon rope we had to hoist suitcases and things up. If we only had one rope, and were using it to hoist something up, and a cop came along, we'd be in trouble, stuck down there without a rope. So the climbing rope always stayed put.

After we hoisted up the valise full of money, Manny and I each grabbed a suitcase and put some clothing in them. We moved quickly; we didn't take much. At that point the big thing was all that money. Our original plan of each guy grabbing two suitcases full of clothing for himself was out the window. So I threw some shirts in there, Orlando pulled our suitcases up, and Manny and I climbed out.

That's another thing. When Manny and I were down there, it was exciting. But it was also the most dangerous part of the job. Orlando and Carlos were relatively safe. If anything happened, I still had to climb up the rope to where they were. Ironically, the rope climbing skills I learned and taught at Brooklyn Tech were coming in handy, and finally paying off.

When I finally climbed the rope with Manny and got upstairs, there was a feeling of relief. I was there. I did it. I got out—at least to this point.

Then, it was Orlando's and Carlos's turn to go down. Manny got back on the ledge, replacing Carlos as the lookout on the fireplace, while they climbed down and did their thing, and then came out. But, after all was said and done, the money was the most important thing.

We headed up to the roof, down the fire escape, through the alley, and out the front. We took the same route to the street we'd used going in, in groups of two.

I walked out with Orlando. We carried the money. We hadn't known Carlos long enough or well enough to trust him, and Manny, alone, couldn't be expected to keep tabs on him. So if anyone was going to be trusted to carry this much money, it had to be Orlando and me.

Orlando and I got into a cab and headed to 155th Street. Our real destination was actually 135th Street, but we were not about to take a cab and head straight home.

We went to 155th Street, got out, paid the cab, took our suitcases, and went into a house. After the cab took off, we came out again, walked a few blocks, and took another cab. We had that cab take us to the corner of 134th Street and drop us off there, not where our clubhouse was on 135th street. We walked to the clubhouse from there.

Meanwhile, Carlos and Manny took a cab to 160th Street and went through basically the same routine. All exactly as originally planned.

We all met at the clubhouse and sat around the table counting the money. Ten, ten, ten, ten, fifty, fifty, fifty, fifty. A little over $6,000, or about $1,500 for each of us.

Being sixteen or seventeen years old, in our low-income neighborhood, and then suddenly having $1,500 apiece, all to ourselves, felt unreal. Almost as if we'd suddenly become millionaires.

At that time it was possible to buy a new home for only $16,000. A brand new car for just over $2,000, and gas for only twenty cents a gallon. If someone didn't have a car, he could ride the subway for only a nickel. We could mail a letter, first-class, for only three cents. In the early fifties, $6,000 was a ton of money. We were rich!

Carlos was with us for convenience. Orlando, Manny, and I were the real team, and now we—the team—had $4,500. Cash. And no one to spend it on but ourselves.

After we counted and split up the money, we had to go our separate ways. Carlos was going to head home, but Orlando, Manny, and I weren't going home. It was 3:30 a.m. by now, so we wanted to head to the Hamilton Place Hotel and sleep it off. Wake up in the morning, and head out for a big breakfast.

But, I felt I had to protect my money. If anything happened, I wanted to make sure my money was safe. I told them I wanted to leave my money at Bernadette's place before heading to the hotel.

Although I offered to take their money and leave it with her also,

I'll Be Good *Tomorrow*

they said, "No." They wanted to hold it, look at it, and sleep with it. So, we each hung onto our own money.

Bernadette's apartment was at the end of a long hall. The stairs leading up to the other five floors was just before her apartment. Under those stairs was a door leading to the back alley. When the door was opened, there was a single row of metal stairs going down at an incline, with a railing to protect anyone from falling off.

Bernadette's window was right next to the stairs, an arm's reach from the top of the railing, where it attached to the side of the building. So, at 3:30 in the morning, I reached over the railing and knocked on her window.

She woke up, opened her window, and asked, "Bobby, what is it?"

"Bernie," I said, "do me a favor. Just hold this for me." And I gave her the envelope with the money, and took off.

While I was inside the building, Manny and Orlando waited for me inside the hallway. Once I joined them, we carried our suitcases with the clothing, and went to the Hamilton Place Hotel. We walked up to the front desk and I said, "Hi, we just got in from upstate, and need a room for the three of us."

The night clerk asked, "Front or back?"

"Doesn't matter. Something with nice soft beds," Manny said. "As long as it's quiet, and we can get some sleep, it doesn't matter."

"Back. It's quieter," I said.

I knew the Hamilton Place Hotel, of course, because it was where Bernadette and I had stayed during our nights together. Our love nest. Any time a guy needed a room for the night, or the weekend, that was the spot. The Hamilton Place Hotel. No questions asked.

We got a room and slept the night off. Next morning, we woke up on cloud nine. We were going to have the biggest breakfast ever.

"Let me go and get my money first," I said, "and I'll meet you at the restaurant."

I went to Bernadette's and asked her for the envelope. Living in this neighborhood, and experiencing everyday life as we all did, Bernadette had become pretty slick herself. Always thinking, always planning.

When she'd seen the $1,500 in the envelope, she immediately pulled out $200 and hid it, keeping the rest in the envelope. When I asked her for the money, she got out the envelope and said, "I pulled out a little extra for us."

I started laughing and said, "What do you mean?"

"Did they count the money?" she asked. "Did they know how much it was? I got $200 hidden for us."

I said, "Bernie, all of that is mine."

"What?" She couldn't believe it. She almost passed out. She thought I was giving her the money to hold for all of us—for Orlando, Manny, and me.

We had a ball with that money. Orlando and I chipped in together and bought a used car. A 1949 Kaiser.

From then on, everyone in the neighborhood thought we were big time. Stories went around that we could just walk into a place and walk out with money. We had a '49 Kaiser, and we had spending money. We were cool. Before we knew it, we started feeling like we really had made it.

But, poor Manny. Manny took his $1,500 and kept it in his room. He didn't know what to do with it. He spent some money on food, but the bulk of it he just kept in his room.

Unfortunately, Manny was a little talkative and he happened to tell the wrong guy, Vincent, the junkie, that we'd pulled a job—and how much money he had hidden. This was Manny's mistake. You can't trust a junkie.

Manny lived on 134th Street, in the back. His window was right by the fire escape. So that bastard, Vincent climbed down the fire escape into Manny's room while he was out, and grabbed the money. But, someone saw him going in and called the police.

Just as Vincent was climbing out of Manny's room, two

detectives were waiting. The Guinea and Huntley. It was a toss up who had more larceny in their hearts—The Guinea and Huntley, or Vincent. Mysteriously, the money simply disappeared. The only ones who knew it existed were Vincent and Manny, and then The Guinea and Huntley.

They smacked Vincent around, took the money, and then let him go. Manny couldn't claim that $1,000 or more had been stolen from his room. He had to keep cool, because he figured they were going to ask him where he got this money. They never asked.

When we finally caught Vincent, he said he'd had to buy his way out. They took the money and they let him go.

But, we got Vincent one night as he was standing on the corner. We drove up in the Kaiser, shoved a shotgun in his face, and told him to get into the car. We weren't going to kill him; we weren't killers. But we got him in the car, drove down to Riverside Drive, and beat the shit out of him.

That son of a bitch not only made Manny lose his money, but also he eventually led to Carlos getting busted and going back to jail.

Trust was something that Orlando, Manny, and I never lacked among the three of us. We could always count on having each other's back. We could always count on keeping ourselves as sharp and alert as possible. Especially when it came to business.

So, one thing we never did was mess around with drugs. We smoked pot at times, but never did anything stronger. Orlando made it a point to insure that every move, every risk, had some sort of profit to it.

Drugs brought no profit unless you were a dealer. And dealing drugs meant you had to make your money from people you could never trust—junkies.

The lesson Orlando tried to get across to Manny was, "Never trust a junkie." Unfortunately, that lesson didn't stick.

RALPH B. LAO

CHAPTER 30

THE END OF OUR CLUBHOUSE

We had our clubhouse for about nine months before it came to an abrupt end. By that time, the place was really outfitted. We had great furniture, lamps, sofa, chairs, a radio, and even a rug on the floor.

The super was a pretty nice guy, never bothered us, or unexpectedly dropped by. He seemed to like us and had always been friendly with Orlando, who was one of his tenants.

But, one day he knocked on the clubhouse door and told us that two detectives had been around, wanting to see this room where we hung out. So he'd had to open up the room and they'd looked at everything. They'd looked closely at the sofa, and the desk, and the rug—everything.

They wanted to know whom the room belonged to. The super had told them, "A couple of kids," and had given them some phony names. Then the two detectives went away.

As I said, this super was all right, a pretty cool guy. And like us, and almost everyone else in our neighborhood, he was wary of the cops.

As soon as he described the detectives, we knew who they were—Huntley, with his short, bullshit, Marine-style haircut, and The Guinea.

Oh man! The Guinea and Huntley has been down in our clubhouse. Shit!

Everything there—every bit of furniture—was hot. We'd gotten it all from building lobbies all over Riverside Drive. We realized everything had to go.

It broke our hearts, because we really had a nice place. But the super thought it was time to get rid of everything. He didn't want any trouble, and he didn't want to see us get in trouble. Nor did we. So we got rid of everything.

First, we had to check to make sure The Guinea and Huntley weren't watching us. Then we took everything down to "Old Lots," the place where we'd split up the watermelon years earlier, and dumped all the furniture.

The super had told us about the detective's visit in the afternoon, and by that evening we'd emptied the place. It took us about three hours to clean out the room.

But the memories of our clubhouse still linger. Like the efforts spent on getting the sofa out of that lobby, hauling it up in the elevator and across to another building, back down that elevator, and then down the street to our clubhouse. Memories of the many trips we made carrying in the lamps, rug, desk, and other odds and ends.

Or the time some of the guys tried to get "the junkie" Vincent's sister drunk.

Vincent and his sister Elena had just moved into the neighborhood from the lower east side, and the guys got tired of hearing how tough she was, and how she could drink them all under the table. One night she showed up and Orlando and Tommy challenged her to a drinking contest. She accepted, and they bought a couple of bottles of some cheap, strong-assed whiskey.

While they were in the clubhouse drinking, Horny Felix showed up. It was amazing—Felix could smell possible pussy from a mile away. Without Elena knowing it, Felix put a mixture of crushed aspirins and fingernail-fillings into her bottle.

"This'll get a girl high and hot," Felix whispered to them. "It's just like Spanish Fly, only stronger."

They'd all heard of Spanish Fly, but none of them had ever seen it.

"In my hometown in Cuba, this mixture was one of the things we did to get girls horny," Felix told them. "It'll work. You'll see," he added.

Unfortunately, after drinking some, poor Elena turned around, said, "I don't feel well," and threw up.

It didn't seem to have the effect Felix said it would. Or maybe this "mixture" only worked on Cuban girls—or only in tropical countries, or something.

When Elena threw up, most of it got on Orlando, some of it on Felix, and some on our nice sofa. They had to clean it up, and although they tried to get Felix to help, he didn't go for it. Cleaning up vomit, ugh, not his thing. Felix was a lover, not a janitor. And obviously, he was not a chemist.

Then there was Mona and the pool table. Good times; great memories. But that was the end of our clubhouse.

RALPH B. LAO

I'll Be Good *Tomorrow*

CHAPTER 31

MIAMI

The three of us—Orlando, Manny and I—had cased a jewelry store months before the $6,000 robbery. We'd noticed that, from the alley in back, it had a window that could be climbed up on. There were bars on it, but we could easily bend and remove the bars, and the window didn't seem to have an alarm. But, it seemed too risky, too exposed, so we'd decided against it. Instead, we'd broken into The Regal. And then—Bingo!—the $6,000 score.

After the $6,000 robbery I always had some cash on me. Orlando and I were fairly thrifty with our money. We went 50/50 on the Kaiser and nursed the rest, so we could made it last. I kept my share at Bernadette's place and would take out small amounts when I needed some. I told my aunt that I did odd jobs, and I always paid her some amount of rent. But, I made sure to always have spending money on me, as did Orlando.

Unfortunately, Carlos was not used to having money and went through his share quickly. Manny, of course, lost his to Vincent the junkie—or rather, to a couple of crooked cops. Manny had nothing.

We'd treat him to malteds, sandwiches, and stuff at times, even give him a couple of dollars here and there, but it wasn't the same thing. It's difficult for a guy to see all that money in his hands one day and not have anything the next. He'd gotten spoiled. Now he was hungry, and he wanted it back.

A month or two after our big score, news came that Manny and Carlos had been busted. They'd both been caught trying to break into a jewelry store on Amsterdam Avenue and 133rd Street.

The story hit Orlando and me like a ton of bricks. We couldn't believe it. On his own, Manny wouldn't do anything like that. He would never try to break into a place without us. Not Manny.

Then we remembered that Manny could get himself talked into anything. It was all right when he was with Orlando and me, because we were fairly sharp and we did the planning. But now he'd let Carlos talk him into breaking into the jewelry store we'd given up on as being too risky. Carlos was sure they could get away with it, and Manny had believed him.

Since Manny no longer had his share of our $6,000 score, it wasn't difficult for Carlos to talk Manny into hitting the jewelry store. Unfortunately, they didn't notice that the window was wired. The alarm alerted the cops, and they were both caught before they even got inside.

Manny's bail was set low because it was his first offense, and he was still a minor at seventeen. Along with Carlos, he was only booked on "attempted burglary" since they never got inside. Manny's family got him out on bail.

Carlos, however, had done time before for the same charge of attempted burglary, so his bail was high and he didn't get out. After the trial, Carlos was sent to Elmira for three years, and Manny was put on probation.

With a probation officer checking on him, Manny had to be home early and stay out of trouble. The heat was on him, so we couldn't do anything together. With Manny on probation, The Guinea and Huntley had their eyes on Orlando and me. They figured we couldn't be far behind; we just hadn't been caught yet.

I'll Be Good *Tomorrow*

So, Orlando and I had to cool it. Because of the heat on Manny, everything had to be toned down.

Actually, this was like a blessing to me. I'd started to feel caught between Bernadette and Orlando. Orlando didn't have a girl. He didn't want ties with anyone. He felt that was the best way to be, so he resented Bernadette.

With my mother leaving, I was able to stay out nights, and Bernie and I started spending more time together, more nights at the hotel. Orlando and Manny resented this. They'd wanted me to go along with them, to continue our ways, but now there was always Bernadette. She was pulling me one way, while they pulled me the other way. I felt caught in the middle.

This allowed me to spend more time with Bernadette. It became an idyllic time for both of us. Our romance blossomed; we really got close. I had turned seventeen, and the topic of marriage started cropping up more and more. I loved Bernadette, and she loved me, so we felt that the next logical step for both of us was marriage.

But, I knew I couldn't marry a girl and not have a job, or any money, or any future. And Orlando hated the fact that without us pulling any jobs now, his private money reserve was dwindling.

So, we decided to look for a job. A real job.

One day Orlando and I walked into the offices of the Otis Elevator Company. We'd chosen them at random. We told them we wanted to start as trainees, the lowest level, and work our way up. It never scared me to have to work my way up. I knew I could do it.

We had to take a test. That was a jolt for Orlando. He didn't do well at all, while I scored high on the exam. They checked our test papers, then called Orlando in and told him they weren't interested in hiring him.

The interviewer then called me in and she said, "You did very well on the written test. Very impressive. But why do you only have three years of high school listed? Are you still in school?"

"No, I'm not in school now. I live with my aunt and she has money problems," I answered. "I thought I could help by quitting school during the day and getting a job. But since I've only got a few subjects left to complete in order to get my diploma, I'm going to finish at night."

The interviewer seemed to understand, saying, "Let me call upstairs and speak to the head of training. Just wait outside, and I'll call you back in as soon as I'm finished—okay?"

"Sure," I answered, and I stepped out, sat, and waited.

After a brief conversation with someone, she called me back in and said, "I talked to Miss Turncliff, head of our training department, and she wants to speak to you. Take the elevator up to the third floor and you'll see her office as soon as you get off. You can't miss it."

When I got to her office, Miss Turncliff asked me to sit down, and then said, "I understand that with only a year to go before graduating, you quit school. Why?"

I told her the same thing I'd told the interviewer. "I live alone with my aunt, and money is a little tight, so I thought I should help out. If I can get a job, the extra paycheck will help at home, and I can finish school and get my diploma at night."

She seemed impressed, both with my story of having to leave school because of financial obligations, and with my test score. But getting my high school diploma was something she thought was very important.

"It would be a shame to waste such potential because you lacked a diploma," she said. "Normally I don't hire anyone without a high school diploma. But because of your high test score, I'll make an exception." She then added, "You've got the job if you want it, but only if you promise to finish high school at night."

"I will! I promise! I'll enroll in night school, finish my last year of high school, and get my diploma," I said.

She smiled. "Okay, the job is yours. Go back to the personnel office and they'll fill you in on when and where to start."

I thanked her and left.

Going home with Orlando was a bit awkward, but he seemed to take it in stride, saying he was happy for me. Especially since I was the one who really wanted the job.

I was now an employee of the Otis Elevator Company. I wasn't making much, but it was a start. As a trainee, I had to work for three months in the mailroom. After that I would spend three more months in the machine room, which consisted of working on an Ozalid blueprint machine making copies, as well as operating various other machines.

After six months, I would then be assigned to whatever department I was best suited for. The drafting department was the one that caught my eye, and interested me the most.

While I worked in the mailroom, my love of drawing was reawakened in me whenever I had to deliver mail to that floor.

The guys in both the mailroom and the machine room were all college kids. They mostly talked about their studies and what it was like at school — NYU, City College, or wherever.

Since I hadn't even finished high school, it was difficult for me to communicate with them. I made friends (I always made friends), but I didn't feel comfortable around them. It was the same feeling I'd had at Brooklyn Tech.

While I was working at the Otis Elevator Company, Bernadette and I continued talking about, and making plans for our marriage. In another year she'd finish school and we'd get married, or maybe even sooner than that. Things were moving pretty fast.

Then, it all started to change. While I was working, Bernadette was coming home from school and having little parties in her apartment. The guys and some of the girls would get together with Bernadette, play records, and dance. Since Bernie's mother and father were both working and she was alone during the day, her home was a perfect place. And it was a central location.

I started resenting this. I'd get home from work, go around the block, and one of the guys would say, "Damn Bobby, you missed a great jump at Bernie's place." Or "You should've been there today, Bobby. Richard just got the new record by the Penguins, *Earth Angel*. It's really a cool side. You've got to hear it."

I didn't like it. One day I got angry and said, "Damn, Bernie, you could get a job or something after school, and help me save money for our marriage. Instead, all you do is have everyone over for a party, day after day, while I'm working. What the hell?"

She threw her arms around me and said, "Oh, honey, I'm sorry. I'm sorry. You're right, Bobby, you're right. I'll start looking on Monday. I'll look for something part time up at the Five & Dime, or the A&P. You'll see. I'll get something. No more parties, I promise."

She stopped for a short time, inquired at a few stores, places that might be hiring after-school kids. But then, unfortunately, the parties started all over again. This same scene happened a few times.

One day I came home from work and found that she'd had one of her parties. I blew up. "Stop bullshitting me!" I yelled. "You keep telling me you want to get married and for us to be together forever, but it's all bullshit. Crap. I don't believe you anymore." I continued, "You're not taking our marriage plans seriously."

"I do, Bobby. I swear. I do take them seriously. I want us to get married. I love you," she answered.

"You say you love me, but you don't show it. You don't mean it, and you keep acting like a tramp," I retorted. "You keep having parties while I'm out working. While I'm saving money for our wedding. You're not holding up your part of the deal."

She started to cry. "I do love you Bobby, I do. I come home and some of the girls always seem to drop by and before I know it, they're playing records and everyone's dancing. I can't help it. I'm trying, Bobby, I really am."

"Bullshit! You've let me down for the last time. It's over! It's over for good this time," I said. "I'm not going through this crap anymore. I don't want to ever see you again. I don't want anything to do with you anymore." I walked out.

Honestly, I felt terrible about breaking up with Bernadette. Pain set in as I realized that all our plans were out the window. I felt so bad about ending it. I needed to get away from everything. I needed to think. I needed space…distance.

On top of breaking up with Bernadette, Orlando and I had also drifted apart during those months. I'd gotten the job at Otis Elevator, and all my free time had been spent with Bernadette. He and I weren't hanging out together the way we used to, and he resented that. He resented Bernadette. He blamed her, instead of Manny, for everything coming apart.

I'll Be Good *Tomorrow*

Now, I started to fully understand what Orlando had repeated over and over to me, "Never get so close to someone that you can't do without them."

The day I turned eighteen years old, February 24, I quit my job at Otis Elevator Company and collected my final paycheck.

Unfortunately, I also had to break my promise to Miss Turncliff about finishing high school at night. I hated doing it, but I just wanted — and needed — to get away.

How to go about leaving, was a problem. The Kaiser wasn't an option, because, unfortunately, Orlando and I had wrecked it a few weeks earlier, while going down an icy hill.

My best bet for getting away was a ticket on a Trailways bus. So on the way home from work, I stopped at the bus station and bought a one-way ticket to Miami, Florida.

When I got home that night, I sat down with my aunt, and said, "Maria, I'm going to leave here for a while. I bought a bus ticket today, and I'm heading down to Florida, to Miami, and see what it's like down there."

"Oh no, Taty" she said. "You can't do that. That's crazy. Why would you want to leave everyone you know? Leave everyone who cares for you? Why?" she asked.

"I just have to get away for a while, Maria. I need some time away from the neighborhood. Away from the guys," I answered.

"First it was school, and now me," Maria said. "You're like my son. I love you just as if you were my son. You know that, Taty. Please don't leave. Stay here. Please."

"Maria, I know you've always treated me as if you were my own mother. Better. I know that. It's not because of you. It has nothing to do with you. I know you love me, and I love you. But I have to leave. I have to try something different. I've spent my entire life here, in this damned city, and I just don't want to be here anymore. I want to see something different. See the world."

My aunt cried and continued pleading with me to stay. But, I had my mind made up. There was no stopping me. I had my bus ticket, and I was leaving.

"If my own mother could leave so easily, why can't I?" I said. "It's not you, Maria, I swear. I'll call and write almost every day. You'll always know where I am. I just have to go. I have to leave New York."

Finally, things settled down. Maria stopped crying, and I started packing a few things. I didn't want to spend any more time than necessary, packing, or crying. I'd made up my mind and nothing was going to change it. I left early the next morning, boarded the Trailways bus, and headed to a new world.

Before I knew it, I saw palm trees waving in the wind, and I could smell the ocean. I had arrived at my new life. I was in Miami.

My first night in the city I was able to get a room in a hotel for about six dollars a day. That was cheap for Miami Beach. It was the kind of place where I was sure someone was going to come in and steal my clothing in the middle of the night.

I propped a chair against the door and balanced a little dish on it against the doorknob. If anyone tried to open the door, the dish would fall off, break, and wake me up. That's how much confidence I had in that hotel room.

The next day I went out to look for a job. Although I still had money on me from the clothing store break-in, I didn't want to risk using it all up.

In Miami Beach, the main industry is tourism, so there are hotels everywhere. They line the beach for miles, one after another. Lots of tourist. Lots of money. So that's where I started.

I tried the Fontainebleau Hotel, which had just opened that year. Bingo! I got a job as a bellboy, just like that.

Because it was new, and a prestigious hotel, it had lots of celebrity guests. I got to carry bags for Tony Martin, Cyd Charisse, and other big name stars. And, once I saw Esther Williams—wearing bright glowing makeup—swimming underwater in the pool.

But I didn't really like this kind of life. I wasn't a bellboy. I didn't like carrying other people's suitcases and crap, feeling like a flunky.

The Fontainebleau Hotel was building cabanas along the beach, and they were still empty because they were under construction. One day I brought a bathing suit, a pair of sunglasses, and a towel, in a little bag. In the morning when I got to work I hid it in one of the cabanas.

Later that day, I slipped out to the cabanas, took off my bellhop's uniform, and put on my bathing suit. I put my sunglasses on, draped the towel around my neck, and came out looking like one of the guests. I told myself that after carrying people's suitcases up to their rooms and acting like a servant for them while they sat around the pool, I was going to swim with them.

The swimming pool was on the raised level. It had a glass bottom with a bar on the lower level where guests could sit and watch people swimming from the underwater side.

I'd made up my mind I was going to swim in that pool. I boldly strode up to the swimming pool and sat at a table.

Philip, one of the waiters who had become my friend, cracked up when he saw me. He couldn't believe it. "What are you doing? What are you doing here?" he whispered, with a big grin, and a look of disbelief on his face.

I looked up at him and said in a normal voice, "I'm just going for a swim. But I could sure use a drink first. Will you bring me a Tom Collins, please?"

Philip laughed, then disappeared, and came back with my drink, which he'd paid for. This was too much for him, but he loved every minute of it. I sat there and sipped the Tom Collins, while Philip hovered around the pool. Then I took off my sunglasses, and dove into the pool. He still hadn't believed I was really going to do it.

I swam around a bit, and that was it; the thrill was over. So I got out, dried myself off, and walked away. I went back to the cabanas, put on my bellhop's uniform, and finished the day.

That was the last day I worked there. That was it. I'd worked there for a little over two weeks. Although I was doing very well on tips, I didn't make it through the month.

I was beginning to get homesick. I started to think about the guys at home, the neighborhood, my aunt. So I decided to leave—to head back home.

Earlier, knowing I was going to leave, I had connected with an agency that shuttled cars between New York City and Miami. They put me together with two guys who were heading to New York in a couple of days. Since they'd made the original deal, my part was just to chip in on food and extras.

When we got to New York, they dropped me off at 143rd Street, just off Broadway, where there was a boarding house. I knew I could get a room there. They rented both single and double rooms, some with outside kitchens. The bathrooms were at the end of each hall. I got a room on the top floor, by the elevator.

That first morning I slept in late. I didn't want to go to 135th Street. I didn't want to see Bernadette, or Orlando. I wanted to have some time to get myself together. But, I was glad to be back in the neighborhood. I had to be in the neighborhood. This neighborhood had been my life for over fifteen years.

Later, when I finally got up and headed out to get something to eat, I heard someone calling, "Bobby."

I turned around, and it was Angelo. "Angelo! How are you doing?" I asked. "What are you up to these days?"

"I'm okay," he said. "I'm working at Al's dinette, just down the block here, on Broadway between 143rd and 144th Street."

"Al's dinette? I don't know the place. I've never heard of it," I said.

"It's kind of the local hangout around here," he answered. "It's pretty cool. There are always a couple of guys and girls in the place. Come on down and get something to eat. I run the place, so it's on me today."

"Great! Let's go," I said.

We kept talking as I followed him down to the luncheonette. Just as he'd said, there were a couple of girls and a guy sitting at the counter, talking, and laughing. It was a long counter with seven or eight stools, and served sandwiches and things — just like a malt shop.

That first day Angelo introduced me to Victor. A couple of days later I met Lou. Shortly after that, the three of us — Victor, Lou, and I — started hanging around together. And for the next four months, it was a wild time.

I'll Be Good *Tomorrow*

CHAPTER 32

NEW NEIGHBORHOOD, NEW ACTION

I ran into some of the guys from 135th Street now and then, but it wasn't the same anymore. The Gladiators had broken up months before. Orlando was still mad at me because of Bernadette. Tommy told me she was going out with Hector, the guy from the Jacobins on 176th Street, who'd got into the fight at the Gay Blades for laughing at one of the Italian guys.

I didn't like Hector. A few times when Bernie and I had broken up, he'd tried to get her to go out with him, to a movie or something. He liked Bernadette. But, lots of guys liked her, since she was one of the prettiest girls in the neighborhood.

Now, none of that mattered to me anymore. I'd made up my mind I wasn't going to see her again. Although I couldn't get her out of my head, I'd sworn to myself that I would stay away from her. It had ended. It was over.

One day, while I was having a malted at the luncheonette, Angelo said, "You know, Bobby, I ran into Bernadette on my way in to work, and she asked about you. She knows you're back."

"What did you tell her?" I asked.

"Nothing much," he answered. "I didn't know what you wanted her to know, so I just said I'd seen you once or twice, but that you and I hadn't talked much. Nothing else. She said she misses you, and to let you know she asked."

But, for some reason that just made me even more determined to not see her. I knew that if it was hard for me, it had to be harder for her, knowing I was back, but not knowing where I was or what I was doing. Although it still hurt, the satisfaction I felt over her pain, allowed me to stay away. To not give in.

I'd learned well the lessons of my father in my childhood, and they held true. "Men don't cry; men don't cry." I'd learned well to lick my wounds and cry in secret.

Spending my time at the diner on 143rd Street was fine. I started hanging out with Victor and Lou, and had met some other people there I liked.

Also, while working at the diner, Angelo was spreading the word, building me up. He'd tell people, "You know, this guy, Bobby's a pretty cool guy. He can just walk into a place and walk out with money. He's always got something going."

Angelo was the guy who had told Orlando and me about the '49 Kaiser. He'd been working at a gas station when the owner put it up for sale. He told us it was a good deal and remembered that we looked at the car, liked it, and paid cash for it. Cash on the spot. That had impressed him a lot, and now he was telling everyone about it.

Guys also heard about the fight with Abrams, and they wanted details from me about it. Suddenly I was getting a lot of attention. It nurtured my ego and I liked it.

Lou and Victor were as different as night and day. Lou was seventeen, fairly tall, a Spaniard, well spoken, but a little on the too-quick-to-anger side. Bordering on crazy. His parents often took trips to Spain and left him alone for months on end. I'd heard that they had first done this when he was fourteen, and the only person he had taking care of him was an aunt who'd come by their apartment and cook for him.

I'll Be Good *Tomorrow*

That may have affected Lou, because he would fly into a rage over the slightest thing. If someone got him mad, or made fun of him for something, he'd want to kill that person. No thought whatsoever— just pure rage. Otherwise, he was a fairly quiet guy. I found him interesting to talk to, although Angelo referred to him—but, never to his face—as "Crazy Lou."

Victor was twenty-two, lived with his aunt, and was a happy-go-lucky type. He was from Puerto Rico, about five feet six inches tall, and bordered on dumb.

Whenever Victor needed a few bucks, he'd either pull a job or he'd go down to the neighborhood gym and pick up a few dollars, boxing. He was good enough to be a sparring partner, but not good enough to turn pro and be a professional boxer.

Victor was always joking; I rarely saw him in a bad mood. He'd laugh at anything. He had an almost uncontrollable laughter that, once started, he couldn't stop. Although, this often got him into trouble with Lou.

Victor loved teasing Lou until Lou lost his temper and wanted to fight. That just made Victor laugh, even harder. But, even Victor never called him "Crazy Lou" to his face. They were an odd couple.

Angelo also introduced me to Maureen. She was twenty years old, and, like Bernadette, she was Irish. She was a bit of a lush; she liked to drink. I'd seen her around the neighborhood before, and I was slightly in awe of her.

She was a tough looking girl, something along the lines of Joan Crawford, with high cheekbones, and a very square-cut face. Hard looking, but pretty. And, very sexy. I'd always thought of her as an older woman, a bit above me.

When Angelo introduced me to Maureen, I got the impression she liked me. I could usually tell when a girl was interested in me, especially if she wanted me to know it. And Maureen made it her business to let me know she was interested.

The first time we met, Maureen, who was two years older than me, said, "You're Bobby Lao? After listening to Angelo talking about how cool you are and all that crap, I expected an older guy. You're just a baby. What are you, fifteen, sixteen?"

I laughed, and said, "I'm eighteen."

"Well, you barely look sixteen," she said. "How bout I call you 'Young Bob' instead of Bobby. Is that okay?"

"Sure," I laughed. "Young Bob's fine."

I got the feeling she was teasing me. That she was older and more experienced, while I was just a kid. But, that was okay. I was still a little in awe of her.

I had been on 143rd Street for about three weeks, when one day Lou, Victor, Maureen, and I were sitting around talking in my room at the boarding house. It was starting to become a little hangout for us. We'd meet at either the dinette, or at O'Shaughnessy's Bar across the street from the dinette.

That was something new to me. I'd never hung around bars. But Maureen and Victor were both used to going there a lot. So, I started meeting them there, having a couple of beers, and listening to music on the jukebox. When we got tired of that, we'd go up to my room, sit around, and talk.

One day I was telling them about Johnny Loco running out of the Chinese restaurant, and about Manny getting busted breaking into the jewelry store.

At that point, Victor brought up the fact that O'Shaughnessy's Bar had a window in the men's room, facing the back alley, that wasn't wired. He and Lou had been checking it out and they knew it didn't have an alarm.

They had opened the window and found four iron bars set in concrete on the sill. They'd checked the bars, Victor loosened one of them, and he knew he could easily snap them off. The window was just high enough that, while standing in the back alley, Lou could boost Victor up to the window ledge, where Victor could lift himself up, grab each of the bars, and snap them off.

I never understood why all the stores in our neighborhood put bars on their windows that could be ripped off so easily. It was the same thing at the jewelry store where Carlos and Manny had gotten caught.

As it turned out, the place was wired, but the bars on the windows were old ones, and they just snapped off. It was the same at Armando's grocery store. The whole neighborhood had these bars in the back that were easily popped off.

So, Maureen and I listened while Lou and Victor explained how they were planning to pull this off. They wanted the cash, but it was the bottles of liquor they were really after.

Everything sounded plausible, except something was holding them back. They didn't seem to have enough confidence in their plan to go ahead.

When I asked them to explain their plan, they told me that once they got in the back of the bar, Victor would then drop bottles of whiskey down to Lou, one at a time.

"Drop them one at a time, bottle by bottle?" I asked. "That sounds kinda risky to me. Not too cool. All you have to do is drop one bottle and there goes the whole thing. Someone hears the crash, and Bingo! You're both busted."

They looked at each other with a look that said, "He's right. How stupid of us."

Maureen laughed. I looked at Victor and said, "Why not get a bag, fill it with bottles, and then slowly lower it to Lou? It's a lot faster, and a lot safer than having Lou trying to catch one bottle at a time."

They loved it. It seemed to be the missing piece in their plan.

"That's a great idea, Bobby. Would you be interested?" they asked. "Would you help us pull it off?"

I'd been missing the excitement I'd had with Orlando and Manny, so even though their original plan sounded risky to me, getting involved in this seemed like fun.

"Okay," I answered. "Count me in."

Lou and Victor's plan was to enter the bathroom just before closing time and unlock the window, leaving it closed but not locked. After the bar closed, they'd get in through the window and start lowering bottles.

It sounded good, but if I was going to be involved, the first thing I wanted to do was check out all the alleys. One of my rules was to always make sure we had a getaway, an escape route. If something went wrong, I wanted to make sure I knew where I was going.

While we were discussing it, I was surprised, and even a little amused, to see that Maureen seemed very interested and excited. She loved this. Especially the idea of getting all that liquor. She also wanted in.

That surprised me. Even though I'd seen Maureen around the neighborhood, and she was a tough-looking woman, I'd never pictured her involved in something like this. But, great! A woman walking with a guy at night made him look less suspicious.

We decided to break in on a Saturday night, because that would be the busiest night and the best chance of money being left overnight in the cash register. We were going to use the suitcase I'd taken with me to Miami to transport the bottles from the back alley to my room, which was going to be the storage place for everything we took out of the bar.

That Saturday night the four of us went into the bar and sat around drinking. About half an hour before closing time Lou went into the bathroom and unlocked the window. Everything was cool.

We had a crowbar with us. Victor was sure that once we got the bars off, even if the bartender had locked the window, he could force it open.

The bar closed and we left. We cut over to my room and got my suitcase. We had two cloth shopping bags, one inside the other, to make sure they could hold the bottles without the bags tearing. We then took a long rope strong enough to hold the bags, and tied it around the handles of both bags. Then we put the bags, rope, and crowbar into the suitcase.

Victor and Lou took off ahead of us to the alley behind the bar, while Maureen and I started walking down the street. It was 3:30 in the morning. If the cops drove by, Maureen and I just looked like a couple with a suitcase, going somewhere. Very natural.

We walked into a building we'd checked out beforehand,

and headed down to the basement. There was a staircase going down from the back of the first floor of that building to the alley. Each building on the block had its own basement, facing a rear alley, which they all shared. The bar was on the street level of one of the apartment buildings.

Our plan was to take the bottles in the shopping bag, go up the stairs, and unload the shopping bag underneath the first floor staircase where people kept carriages and things. We could put all the bottles in the carriages and go back for another load. When it was all transported, we'd take everything in the suitcase up to my room.

When we got to the alley, I left Maureen underneath the staircase in the building where the carriages were. Her job was just to make sure nobody came and saw anything from inside the building. Then I went to the back alley where Lou and I boosted Victor up.

Victor got picked to do this because even though he was small, he was very strong. As a boxer, he always kept himself in good shape.

We quietly boosted him up, listening to make sure no one opened a window, no heads stuck out. It took about five minutes before he was able to pull the bars off and slip in. The window was open, just like we'd planned. Victor dropped the bars, one by one, down to us and went inside.

Victor is like another Manny, I thought to myself. I wasn't going to get caught inside there. I'd done this already. If I was going to break into a place, it was going to be from a hole in the ceiling overhead, climbing in. Not through a back alley, or anything like that. I didn't like it. If anything happened, I was outside, and that was cool. I could get out of there.

First thing Victor did was hit the cash register. Then he checked around to make sure there weren't any little cigar boxes with money in them. After Victor put the money in his pockets, he got the bags and started loading up with liquor. He loaded up the bags with bottles and lowered down the first shipment. In all, he must have lowered the full bag down about ten times.

I was thinking, *What's to stop Victor from taking half of that money and putting it in his shoe or another pocket?* But I really didn't care. I was looking only for the liquor. Besides, Victor was really taking the biggest risk. He was the one who was inside. If anything happened and we had to take off, he was the last one out, and he could get caught. Lou would wait in the dark alley while I was running up the stairs.

Maureen was inside guarding the bottles of whiskey. But on one trip, I came up and found Maureen guzzling on a bottle. She was such a lush she'd already opened one up. She couldn't wait.

Although I'd been a little awed by her because of her age, when I saw this, I got pissed off. I walked up and said, "What the fuck?" and took the thing out of her hands. I just looked at her. I didn't go for that shit. We were pulling a job, this was business, and she was drinking. I didn't care to work with anyone who was drunk.

"None of this bullshit," I said. "What are you? Crazy?"

The reaction I got surprised me. Maureen had been sitting underneath the staircase drinking, and now she got up and came over to me as if she wanted to put her arms around me. "I'm so sorry, hon. It was stupid of me. I just wasn't thinking," she said. "All this free booze…"

"Okay, okay. But just remember, this is business. If something happens, we have to be alert. We have to be ready for anything," I said.

She really was sorry. My anger seemed to impress her, apparently asserting me in her eyes. She realized I was in charge. It was almost as if she wanted to hear my words.

When I went down with the shopping bag, I thought about it and it made me feel good. Here was this girl, twenty years old, a hard, tough neighborhood girl, almost putting her arms around me, telling me she was sorry. And she'd called me "hon." That was really the beginning of the romance between Maureen and me.

Finally we finished our job. Victor had been inside for almost an hour. The sun was going to start coming up soon, so it was time for him to get out of there. We had enough liquor.

Victor got ready to jump. He held himself on the ledge and Lou and I cupped our hands. He was supposed to land on our hands, but he

I'll Be Good *Tomorrow*

jumped down so hard he broke our grasp and hit the ground, making a lot of noise. We all froze. But, everything was cool; nobody heard it.

All in all, we only got about $300 in cash. It wasn't much, but the liquor was the big thing. I don't know if he ever kept any money to himself, but I doubt it; he wasn't that clever. We split the money afterwards.

The three of us then went into the building, and loaded the suitcase full. Getting the bottles out of the bar was one thing. Now we had to get them from the building to my room, and that wasn't going to be easy. It would take four or five trips, and we had to allow some time for that.

The next step was for Maureen and me to head to my room with a suitcase full of whiskey, while Lou and Victor stayed behind. We didn't want to risk all of us walking down the street together—four people with bags full of whiskey. We could've loaded up the bags and the suitcase and made it in one or two trips, but that was too risky.

I said, "You wait here. Maureen and I will go." She and I would look like husband and wife coming back from a trip.

We had to go a block and a half from O'Shaughnessy's Bar to my room. We made three trips, and each suitcase full was heavy as hell. We unloaded each one on the bed in my room, and headed back.

Every trip we made, Maureen made it a point of saying, "I'm really sorry, hon. I'm so sorry. I realize now how stupid it was of me to open that bottle. To be drinking while we were working. I feel like such an ass."

"It's okay. Forget about it and let's get through this," I said. But I realized that she'd liked my getting mad at her. I could see it, and hear it in her voice.

Finally, we'd made all our trips, got to my room, and everything was cool. The four of us sat around the bed splitting up bottles, just the way Orlando, Carlos, Manny, and I had split up our money after the $6,000 robbery. "One for you, one for you, one for you, and one for me."

We grouped all the bottles by type: rum, gin, bourbon, scotch. But everybody wanted rum, although Maureen didn't really care what she got. Lou, Victor, and I preferred rum so we could mix it with Coke and have a "Cuba Libre," the tropical name for Rum and Coke.

We divided everything equally. But since Maureen lived with her mother, and her mother was always on her back, she couldn't take her share to her place. So she asked, "Can I leave mine here with you?"

"Sure," I said. "Leave them right there." I pointed to a corner of the room.

She trusted me. She knew I wasn't going to drink her bottles. And after the incident under the staircase, she wanted me to trust her.

Lou and Victor didn't take their bottles home that night, either. They left them there and took them home the next night.

Now I had a room that looked like a bar. I put bottles of whiskey on my bureau, on a little table, and along the walls. With Maureen's share, I had about forty bottles of liquor. It looked great.

After that, some of the guys from the luncheonette would come up to my room to have a drink, see all the bottles, and say, "Holy shit!" Everything they'd heard about Bobby Lao was true.

I wasn't there a month before all of us were swimming in whiskey. It was amazing to them. Victor and Lou would have never done that by themselves. They had planned it, but there was something holding them back. It had taken me to come along to make everything fall into place.

So, I fit in very nicely. I became the leader of the little group. I liked it. I was starting to really enjoy it.

And, Maureen and I were really getting involved. The little incident under the staircase had done the trick. She always kidded and teased me about my young looks, but when it came to business, she respected me—and nurtured my ego.

But, as I learned later, however, too much of an ego can be a dangerous thing.

CHAPTER 33

MAUREEN

Having my own place was great. When I'd been living with my aunt and grandmother, before going to Miami, I was pretty free. I could stay out late. My mother wasn't around, so I could do just about anything I wanted to. But I couldn't bring friends over—girls or anyone.

Now, I had my own place. I paid rent. It was mine. I could bring anyone I wanted up there. That was a new experience for me, and I liked it. It was fun.

A couple of nights after the bar robbery, the four of us went up to my room and started drinking and talking about earlier times. Lou and Victor told me things they'd done before I'd come along, and I told them a couple of my experiences.

They were sitting in some chairs while I was lying on my bed. Suddenly, Maureen got up, moved to the bed, and started inching closer to me. As I was talking with Victor and Lou, she lay there with her shoes off, tickling me with her feet—right in front of them. She was starting to get me excited.

It was about one o'clock in the morning, and she wanted them to leave. They got the hint and left. I was also glad to see them go. Nothing was said. They left, and she didn't make a move to follow. She just lay there on the bed, her shoes off, drinking and talking with me, while I sat next to her.

Suddenly we just looked at each other, staring as if frozen in time. Then she leaned over and kissed me. The next thing I knew, the lights were out and we were lying in each other's arms, kissing, and making love. That night she stayed.

After that, Maureen moved in. She brought some of her clothes to my place—shoes, jacket, blouses, pants, and things. She still lived at home, technically, but she spent three or four nights every week with me. She'd sleep a night or two with me, go home for a few nights, and then come back to my place.

This was all right with me, because after having been with Bernadette for so long, it was good to have a girl around again. To have the smell of her things there. The touch of her. To have the taste of her in my system—in my brain.

Maureen fit right in. She was almost always there, and she took care of me.

Before, when my clothes got dirty, I'd take them to a laundry to have them cleaned. But Maureen didn't see the advantage of spending money at a laundry when she could just put the clothes in the washing machine in the basement for only twenty-five cents. Maureen took care of it.

But once, when my money was starting to get low, I looked at Maureen and said, "Damn, I've only got about fifty dollars left on me. I'm going to have to start looking for a job or something, anything, to make some money."

Hearing me say that, Maureen immediately stepped in. "Fifty dollars?" she said. "No problem. Don't worry about it." Then after a minute, she added, "You don't have to look for a job, hon. That's plenty for us. We'll just start saving our money."

I'll Be Good *Tomorrow*

She started making a budget. She just took over. She wasn't bossy or anything, but this seemed to bring the maternal side of her out. It was an area she felt comfortable in, one she could help with.

I got a kick out of it, so I let her do it. I could see it made her feel good to budget us. She bought bread, ham, cheese, and stuff, and we started eating in. Or, we'd go to her place when her mother wasn't home, and eat there. Anything, so we wouldn't have to spend money. By not spending money on breakfast or lunch, she felt our money would last longer. And it did.

Maureen had a lot of friends and she knew how to hustle things out of people. She didn't sleep with anyone else. She spent most of her time with me, and when she wasn't with me, she was home. But, she could go out and come back with a couple of dollars she'd gotten from one friend or another.

Once she hustled a package of ham and a loaf of bread from Angelo at the restaurant. She just went in and said, "Come on Angelo, how about letting me have some bread and stuff?"

She had a way about her and she'd get things. I could never do that. I'd prefer to buy it than hustle off friends.

Maureen started taking care of us. Making sure our clothes were clean, the bed was fixed, and the room was tidy. Her maternal side really came out. She'd always felt this way towards me, I think, because she was older.

She would kid around and say, "You need a woman to take care of you. But don't worry, Momma will do it." That kind of thing. She was always a lot of fun—and always a lot of woman.

We spent two months together, almost like husband and wife. If I was out with Victor and Lou, I'd come back, and Maureen would be waiting for me. No problems, no questions asked. She just wanted to have me there. We never mentioned my having to get a job again.

I think it had bothered her when I'd first said I needed to get a job, because it would've meant less time together. Neither of us was working. We didn't have any responsibilities, other than looking out for each other. So, we were always together. Maureen filled in very nicely during the period when I was trying to get over Bernadette.

One day I bumped into Bernadette while she was shopping with her mother up around 145th Street. I was with Maureen, who knew about Bernadette. Maureen looked good that day. She always knew how to handle herself, so she made it a point to get very cuddly with me. She put her arm around me, making sure she was very close to me. That was good, because I wanted Bernadette to see I wasn't just sitting around thinking of her. It had gotten so that now everyone started associating me with Maureen.

Being seen with Maureen wasn't just like being seen with any other girl. She was striking. She could intimidate guys just by looking at them. She was as tall as me when she had high heels on. And, she had this hard look about her, while still looking very pretty. She also looked older. Not worn out or anything, just older. Anyone could look at her and instantly see this was no girl; this was a woman.

It made me feel good to have Maureen next to me the day I bumped into Bernadette. Seeing Maureen holding onto me seemed to rattle Bernie a bit. She smiled, but then stumbled, almost tripping, as we passed each other.

As always, Maureen looked in control, and made a great appearance.

Making love with Maureen was also quite an experience. She never stopped moving. Her hands were constantly moving, slowly, all over me. She loved to put her nails in me, or gently bite and kiss me. She would wear me out. If she didn't feel every part of me on every part of her, it wasn't right for her.

Once I almost yelled out, "Maureen, you're killing me!" Instead I started kidding around while we were making love, and I said teasingly, "You're wearing me out, beautiful."

Right away her maternal side kicked in. "Oh, poor baby," she said. She became very gentle and started petting and caressing me. "Ah, I won't wear my little boy out. Don't worry, momma will take care of you."

I'll Be Good *Tomorrow*

After that, whenever we started making love she would make it a point to say, "Am I wearing you out, honey?"

I would say, "Well, yeah, maybe a little," because then she'd start petting and caressing me. She enjoyed being motherly, saying, "Come to momma." And I loved every minute of it. We really had a good relationship.

Being seen with Maureen, going around with her, not only made me feel good, it made me feel older. It also made it easier for me to break away from the group on 135th Street—Orlando, Manny, and the guys.

I felt I had grown up and was in another world—an older, grown-up world. Victor was twenty-two, Maureen was twenty, and even Angelo was older. In that way I made the transition from one group to the other. And from the girl to the woman.

Besides breaking into the bar, Maureen was in on another burglary with me. A much simpler one. One night, because she didn't believe in spending money on a cab or a subway, we were walking home from a movie on 160th Street. We came across a candy store. It was in a dark area, which was what attracted us to it.

Maureen had run out of cigarettes, and she said, "There's a candy store. Why don't we just break the glass, grab some cigarettes, and run?"

I looked around carefully, and answered, "It's quiet and dark enough here so I think we can do this without having to run. Just stand there and make sure no one is coming."

I wrapped my jacket around my arm, and walked up to the door of the candy store and hit the glass. I had to hit it a few times before it shattered, because I was trying to be as quiet as possible.

Then, we kept on walking for about a block and a half, up a slight hill, where we stopped. From there we could see the door of the candy store. We went into a hallway and stayed there for about twenty minutes, just watching, looking around.

When we were sure the cops weren't coming and no one had

seen or heard us, we went back. Maureen became my lookout, leaning against a car, right in front of the candy store.

The store had a police lock inside, which was a steel bar that went from the edge of the door down to a small bracket-like hole in the floor, making it difficult to push the door open without having the key to slide the bar over. But, with the glass of the door broken, I was able to reach in and easily move the bar over and unlatch it.

I went inside and got about twenty-seven dollars out of the cash register. I then filled some paper bags with ten or fifteen cartons of cigarettes. Camels, Kools, Pall Malls, everything I could grab.

We kept our brand, and sold the others to Angelo for half price, about a dollar a carton. He sold them through the dinette and kept the money for himself. That was his own little business deal, so he never told the owner what he was doing.

This little job gave us all the cigarettes we needed for some time to come, and some extra cash. It also meant I didn't have to worry about getting a job for a little longer.

I'll Be Good *Tomorrow*

CHAPTER 34

DEAD LOSS EVENING

Right after breaking into the candy store with Maureen, I tried the same thing in a grocery store with Lou and Victor. But that time it didn't work out as well.

Lou had a friend who'd offered him his car with the idea of having Lou take it and dump it somewhere. The river, a lake, anywhere it couldn't be found, so that he could report it stolen and collect the insurance on it.

Lou told Victor and me about the car and we said, "Sure, why not? We'll do it." It would give us a car to drive around for the evening, and when we got low on gas, we'd just dump it somewhere.

That night we got the keys to the car from Lou's friend, and the three of us drove off. It was a rainy night, which we thought made good conditions for dumping a car off a cliff or into the river.

The car was an old Chevrolet, but it was in excellent condition. We headed downtown on the Westside Highway, with the intention of driving around lower Manhattan for a while, and then heading back up and ditching it somewhere along the Henry Hudson Parkway.

I was at the wheel, and we were driving down the Westside Highway around midnight when a car pulled up alongside of us with a couple of guys in it. Before I knew it, we were racing each other down the highway.

We'd move ahead, and then they'd move ahead. Neither of us wanted to lose ground to the other. We sped by 34th Street, and approached the 19th Street exit. But, I'd forgotten that, besides having a very sharp curve, 19th Street also had a cobblestone surface. It wasn't like the rest of the Westside Highway. And, when it rained, the cobblestone got very slippery.

I had my foot on the gas, almost to the floorboard, and I didn't want to let up. When I was in a race, all I could think of was not losing. Suddenly, the 19th Street curve was up ahead, so I started easing up on the gas to get ready for the turn. But it was too late to slow down, and the car went into a slide.

I could feel I was losing control of the steering, as the car started to shimmy from side to side, and I pictured us slamming into the abutment, the wall. As we got nearer to the curve, I tried easing down on the brake. It didn't do any good.

At this point, I figured, *The hell with it. It's either hit the brake and try to keep this thing steady, or we're going right into that abutment.* So, I hit the brake and the car spun sideways.

The 19th Street exit had a concrete strip, about a foot high, dividing it from the road for about half a block. The car went sideways, Boom! right over the divider. I could feel it tearing up the underside of the car. I managed to stop the car when we drove completely over the divider, and were facing the exit side of the highway. The car we were racing just kept going.

The three of us were all right; none of us was hurt. But, now the foremost thing running through our minds was not getting caught by the cops.

I was able to quickly straighten the car out and drive down the exit. But the 19th Street exit was very narrow, so the car kept bouncing from one side to the other, because the front wheel was bent from going over the abutment.

I'll Be Good *Tomorrow*

We got to the bottom, went another half block, and parked it under the Westside Highway. Lou looked up and down to make sure no one was coming, while Victor and I got the plates off the car. Then we ran off.

We made it down to 14th Street by the river. There we came across a grocery store in an area that was pitch black, and without a soul around. We figured, "Shit, why don't we break the glass, get in there, grab a couple of dollars, and take off?"

That way our whole evening wouldn't be a loss. It always bothered us when our plans got screwed up. Besides, if we got into the place and got a little cash, we could take a cab home instead of going on the subway.

So, we went up to the grocery store and, just as I'd done at the candy store, I wrapped my jacket around my arm, and Bam! hit the glass door. It was dark and the door was recessed, which is what made it look like an easy setup.

But when I hit the glass, an alarm went off. That son of a bitch rang up and down 14th Street. I was sure every police station around was going to hear the alarm.

The three of us started running, but we didn't know the area— 14th, 15th Street. Manny, Orlando, and I always used to run as a group. We always knew which way each of us was going.

It wasn't the same with Victor and Lou. We ran into the alleys, but we got split up. They went in one direction and I headed in another one. I made a turn, figuring I'd be able to get into another building and come out on another street. But it was a dead end. I ran right into a boxed-in area. *Shit.*

When a guy is running, if he can keep his cool he'll be all right. But if he starts to panic, then he imagines police all around him. It's like every cop in the world is after him. *I have to calm down. I have to stop.*

There were a lot of garbage cans in the dead end. I hid in the corner behind the garbage cans, and buried myself in garbage. I lay there in the dark and cold—in a strange neighborhood—with garbage all over me.

I kept thinking of Maureen and getting back home. That night she had wanted me to stay home with her. Now I felt stupid. I should have listened to her.

I had to figure a way out of there. I knew if the cops came down this alley they would look behind these garbage cans right away. I realized I wasn't safe there.

I looked up. There was a drainpipe in the corner of the three-story building. I tested it and it felt sturdy. I figured I'd climb up the drainpipe until I hit the roof. But, then I realized that, even though the pipe might be strong down here, what if, when I was halfway up, the damn thing came loose from the wall? I'd be dead. That was no good.

So my final plan was that if I heard the cops coming, I would climb up the drainpipe to the first floor. Then, as soon as I got to the first set of windows in the apartments there, I would open one and climb in. There might be people inside the apartment, but I could just push them aside, head for the door, and take off. I figured I had a better chance fighting with whoever was in there, than being caught down here by the cops.

I realized later what a stupid plan that was. I probably would've gotten killed climbing up the drainpipe, or shot by someone inside the apartment. They would've thought I was a burglar.

So, I lay in the alley for about an hour, praying to my dead grandmother. "Abuelita, please let me get out of this. Let me get out of this, Abuelita. Don't let me get caught. Please don't let me get caught. I'll never do this again. I'll be good. Tomorrow!"

How stupid to try something in a neighborhood I didn't know. I could hear Orlando in my head, saying, "Always make sure you know the way out." What a dumb mistake.

I must have prayed to my grandmother for about an hour. Finally, when I was almost sure there were no cops around, I got up and quietly walked out. As soon as I hit the street, I started walking, just like I was some guy who lived around there, on his way to work. I finally reached the subway and headed home.

I'll Be Good *Tomorrow*

Earlier, when I'd told Maureen I was going on this ride, she had wanted me to stay with her. "Why are you going to go with these guys?" she'd asked.

But foolishly, I'd wanted to take care of this car. So, rather than wait around for me, she'd decided to sleep at her own place. When I got to my room, I was alone, and I passed out.

I didn't know what happened to Lou or Victor. And I didn't care. I just wanted to sleep. To forget how stupid I'd been—to forget what a complete loss the evening had been.

German Luger and bullets

CHAPTER 35

POOLROOM STICKUPS

A couple of days after the grocery store incident, Lou came around the neighborhood acting all excited, like a kid. "Oh man, come over here, let me show you this," he said to Victor and me. "Wait till you see it."

Lou often acted kind of weird. Victor and I looked at each other and started laughing. Lou took us over to one side and opened his jacket. The handle of a gun was sticking out of his belt.

He closed his jacket, still excited. "Man, I just got me a gun. I bought it from a friend of mine. He can get guns and whatever else a guy needs from Chinatown."

Victor and I took a look at the gun and decided we'd better go up to my room to inspect the thing.

Once in my room, Lou pulled out the gun, a German Luger, and held it like a baby. It really was a beautiful gun. He carefully showed us how it worked, and said, "I only have four bullets now, but I'll get more."

While Victor and I were handling the gun, he didn't take his eyes off us. It was all he could do to let us just touch it. He couldn't wait to get it back in his hands. He acted as if he wanted to pet it.

Now, thanks to Lou, we had a gun.

Victor and Lou were like two Mannys. They were willing to do anything, the same way that Manny would always go along with anything Orlando and I came up with. But, Orlando and I had a lot of success, and Manny knew he was fairly safe with us. He wasn't smart, but Orlando and I were, and Manny knew it. So, back then everything was cool with the three of us.

But Lou was bordering on crazy, and Victor was just dumb; he had already done time. Now, here was Lou with a gun, and all he could think about was stickups. He kept saying, "Now we can go out, stick up a place, and get some real money." It didn't seem to occur to him that this was a pretty big, and dangerous, step. That someone could actually get shot—or killed.

Victor, like Lou, kept repeating, "Yeah, we've got a gun. Now we can stick up a place." As if that made all the difference. With a gun, we could really make some money. Before, it was burglary, but now these two guys—with a gun—pictured the whole world opening up for them.

I'd never done this shit before. Orlando, Manny, and I had mugged a guy once by putting a comb in his back. But, mostly whatever we did we did on muscle. We'd never pulled a stickup with a loaded gun in our hands.

I couldn't believe how happy both of them were. To me, a stick up was a big jump. But to these two, it didn't seem any more difficult or dangerous than a walk in the park.

Back when Orlando and I were hanging out together, we would sit back and plan all kinds of robberies. We used to plan breaking into dry-cleaning places, clothing stores, anything, even sticking up places. We'd enjoyed trying to come up with the best way to do those things, even though we didn't really do them. Like the jewelry store that Manny and Carlos got caught trying to break into. Orlando and I were always planning something. It became like a game for us.

I'll Be Good *Tomorrow*

During that time we'd hit on the idea that poolrooms would be the easiest and safest places to stick up. Poolrooms close at one o'clock in the morning. When the place was closing, we'd have to make sure we were the last ones there. As the guy went to lock the door, Boom! we'd shove something in his back, and make him think it was a gun.

That would be as good to us as breaking into a place through a hole in the ceiling. And the poolrooms we talked about were all on the second floor, upstairs. Once we were in there and all alone with the guy, no one could see us from the street.

We had gone over this and planned it in our minds. We hadn't thought of it in terms of pulling a gun on a guy. We'd thought of it in terms of mugging a poolroom owner. We'd grab the guy, put a comb in his back, and tell him it was a gun.

But, we never got around to it. One thing had led to another, we did the $6,000 robbery, then Manny got caught, and that had been the end of our plans.

I got the feeling that these two guys, Lou and Victor, thought they could pull off any job as long as I was there. Any planning that had to be done, I could do it. They never thought anything out. To them, it was just walk in, stick a guy up, and take off.

"Wait a minute, there's more to it than that," I said "We need a plan."

I guess that, because the burglary at O'Shaughnessy's had gone so smoothly, they both felt confident I would take care of any planning needed.

"So think about it, Bobby. You can come up with something," Lou said.

"Yeah, just like before," Victor added. "You figured out the best way to handle the bar. Now with a gun to work with, this should be easier for you."

My ego was getting stroked. That damn ego again. Before I knew it, I said "Okay, let's do this."

Now, here I was with these two guys and they were all excited, talking guns and stickups. I was on the spot. They expected me to come up with something.

Then, I remembered the poolrooms idea. That would be a great way to start. I had just never imagined actually having to shoot anyone. When Orlando, Manny, and I had talked about it, we were going to do it on pure muscle.

I said, "We'll hit a poolroom." I explained the idea to Lou and Victor, and how it worked. I told them that if the guy didn't react to the gun, then Bam! we hit him with the butt of the gun.

But, Lou wanted to have a bullet in the gun. "Just in case," he said. "I've got to have a bullet in the gun. If the guy goes for his own gun, I'll shoot him in the leg." Lou was going to shoot at the guy's leg, just like in the movies!

I said, "Okay, okay."

Lou was too weird to argue with. When he got off on something, it was better to just let him go. Besides, I figured it would never come to that, and if it did, I could handle the matter.

We started visiting poolrooms until we found the right one. It was on 113th Street and Broadway, and was a beautiful setup. It was a fairly large poolroom, so there was going to be a lot of money. It was upstairs, and the owner was a skinny little guy about forty years old. If the gun didn't make him behave, Victor could easily knock him out. This was great.

We walked in around midnight, rented a table, and started playing. After about an hour, the guy said, "Start racking up."

We ignored him, acting like we didn't hear him.

The owner then came over and said, "Look, I have to close."

We said, "Okay, we're just going to finish this game."

Meanwhile everyone else was drifting out. We'd already made up our minds that this was the place. We weren't going to leave.

But there was another table playing, and those goddamn guys wouldn't leave.

We took our time racking up. I told Lou and Victor, "Cool it, don't worry. Just wait for me." I took a dime, went over to the pay phone, pretended to dial up someone, and started talking.

The man saw me on the phone and he apparently figured, "All

right." At least we'd cleaned up the table. The other guys were still playing, so he started rushing them so he could close up.

Meanwhile, I kept talking on the phone. Victor and Lou hung around waiting for me, laughing, and talking to each other. Acting natural. They didn't want the guy to get suspicious. In a situation like this, if we'd looked too hard or too tough, he would sense something right away. But if we were just laughing and kidding, he wouldn't. Victor was great at laughing. He could laugh at anything. And he was into his act.

Finally, the other guys left. I hung up the phone, and the man said, "Okay, you've got to go."

We started heading towards the door. Lou had the gun, and it was up to him to pull the gun out and make a move.

The plan was that once he got the gun out, we'd get on each side of the guy and make sure he obeyed. But, fuckin' Lou waited until the guy walked with us all the way to the door. That wasn't necessary. Lou could have done it right in the middle of the poolroom.

I started getting the feeling we were going to go outside and Lou still wasn't going to pull the gun. So, just as we got near the door, I turned around and grabbed the guy's arm and kind of lifted him up a bit and said, "Son of a bitch, turn around. This is a stickup."

When I did that, Victor grabbed him and Lou pulled the gun out. From then on, everything went smoothly. We locked the door and took the man back inside.

We had clothesline rope, so we tied up his hands and feet, and rifled the cash register. I think we got about $160 each. After we got the money, we took off. We didn't fool around with Coke machines or anything else, like we would do later.

This night—our first time—we were a little nervous. We left the door open so someone could come in and find him and release him. Then we took off.

That job went so easy we didn't stop. We kept pulling this kind of stickup, but always in a different neighborhood. It was like, once a week we'd go to work. Just like anyone else going to work and then getting a paycheck. We ran this thing for about a month and a half, hitting poolrooms downtown, uptown, Brooklyn, all over the place.

That was a good time for me because I was getting steady cash. I didn't have to stay on the budget Maureen had set up for us. We were able to eat out again. Maureen and I were going to a lot of movies; Maureen loved to go to movies.

She knew what I was doing, and she didn't care. She would only tell me, "Be careful with Lou."

Victor she didn't mind. Everyone liked Victor because he was a fun guy, always laughing.

But she kept warning me about Lou. "Be careful with that guy, he's kind of weird, even crazy. So be careful."

Realizing she was right, I told Maureen, "If I ever get into trouble, please don't let my folks know."

"What do you mean, 'don't let them know'? What if something happens to you? Won't your aunt be expecting you for dinner? Won't she be worried if you don't show up?" she asked.

Maureen knew my aunt since she'd joined us for dinner a couple of times. They got along well, and my aunt seemed to like her.

"If anything happens to me, if I get caught or something, just call my aunt and tell her that I went back to Miami," I said. "Tell her I got on a bus, went back, and I'll call or write to her later."

"Okay. But what about you? What if you need help or something? Money, or whatever?" she asked. "What should I do then?"

"Don't worry about me. I'll be fine," I said. "As for money, you know where it's hidden in the room. Just head up there and grab it before the cops or the manager find it. Keep some for yourself, then get some to me for cigarettes and stuff, wherever I am."

"Okay, hon," she said. "I'll take care of it. I promise."

That was the plan if I ever got caught.

I'll Be Good *Tomorrow*

CHAPTER 36

JOB IN THE BRONX

We'd held up a few poolrooms here and there, but now we wanted to stick up a store where we could get some clothes and some shoes. To have two pairs of shoes at one time, that alone seemed like a treat to us. But, it also meant doing something we hadn't done before. Until now, all of the stickups had been done at night. This one would have to be done in broad daylight. A first for us.

When we were trying to figure out where to pull this daylight job, Victor suggested the Bronx. His sister lived there and he knew her neighborhood.

"Let's go to my sister's area," he said. "We'll pick out a store, hit it, and then hide at her place. Come nighttime, we'll get a cab and head back home."

Cool. We knew we couldn't do anything around our own neighborhood because we were too well known there. So, even though Lou and I didn't know the Bronx well—didn't even like the Bronx— we agreed.

We walked around until we found a small store on Bruckner

RALPH B. LAO

Boulevard, near Victor's sister's place in the Bronx. We looked in the window and noticed only one guy was inside, all by himself. He was about five feet nine, 150 pounds, fragile looking. No problem.

When someone's pulling a job, he never picks a place where there's a big, strong guy. Not that we couldn't have taken a big guy, but at what cost? Rolling around on the floor, fighting, and yelling? Not good. The last thing anyone wants when he's sticking up a place is publicity. He wants to walk in—hit—then walk out. So he makes sure he's picked someone he can intimidate.

I was the best talker and could act natural, so it was my job to go inside first. The plan was for me to go in, check around, and pretend I wanted to buy something. After a few minutes, if everything looked safe, Victor and Lou would come in. If I noticed something wrong or heard anyone in the back, I'd walk out and warn them, "The thing's off."

The store looked good, because we could see a hall leading to the back. If there was a hall, there had to be a bathroom or a storeroom. We could take the guy back there, tie him up, and clean out the store. Great!

It had a counter that started on the left at the front and ran straight back about twenty feet. There were two steps in the back leading up to the hall, which ran about another ten feet. The rest of the store was just a lot of boxes and junk.

This was no fancy place. It was one of those stores where you'd never find something by yourself, no browsing around, but the owner knew exactly where everything was. That was just what we wanted—a little place, not too much activity, not too many people around. Hit, grab a few things, and leave.

I asked the man for a pair of shoes I had seen in the window, and sat down to have my feet measured. When he went to look for the shoes, I checked for signs of trouble. Nothing. I waited. A few minutes later, while the guy was sitting on a stool, measuring my foot, Victor and Lou strolled in.

Victor turned around to lock the door behind him. The lock went CLICK! It sounded like an explosion. Our plan had been to walk in, get the jump on the guy, and get the money. Then if we had time, we could get some shoes and stuff. But the noise Victor made with the lock startled the man, and he turned around.

Pulling the gun out fast, Lou stood right behind him. The guy turned around and looked straight into the gun. The expression on his face was unforgettable. It was a look that made me feel like I didn't really have the stomach for this kind of thing. He looked as if everything in the world had just come to a stop.

Lou said, "All right you son of a bitch, get your ass in the back or I'll blow your head off."

In real life a guy would never put a gun to a man's head and say something like, "Stick 'em up or I'm gonna shoot you."

"Shoot you"? That's crap. They show it that way in movies and television but it doesn't really work that way.

The guy pulling the job must always come on strong. Say something like, "I'm gonna blow your head off." Bingo! The message gets through immediately.

The man turned and looked at me, a gleam of hope in his eyes. He had a gun at his head, but he still had a chance. He wasn't alone. He had me—his customer. He looked over at me with fear in his eyes, as if to say, "What do we do? What are we going to do?" He was waiting for me to help him.

I got up, looked down at him, and said, "You heard him. Get your ass in the back."

Now, the look on his face was one of complete defeat. That little psychological twist was just what we needed. Even his own customer was against him.

Now he was willing to do anything. "All right," he said, and he got up.

Victor grabbed him, and the three of them marched to the back while I headed for the cash register. If anyone looked in the window my plan was to just wave him off. I'd act as if I were the owner and had closed up while I counted my receipts.

But, Lou and Victor were running into problems. It turned out that the store didn't have a back room. It didn't even have a goddamn bathroom. There was nothing but the hall with shelves full of shoeboxes on both sides. And the hall was directly in the line of vision of anybody looking in the window.

Lou and Victor were trying to keep the guy out of sight while they tied him up, but there was no place to put him. Lou was losing it. "Goddamn it, where's the bathroom?" he screamed at the guy. "The bathroom! There's gotta be a bathroom."

The terrified man kept repeating that there wasn't any bathroom. "I have to go next door to use the bathroom. I swear," he cried to Lou, who looked like he was getting ready to kill him. "Look around you, there's no bathroom here!"

Victor had to step in to try to calm Lou down so he wouldn't shoot the guy. "Cool it, man. Calm down. He's telling the truth. There's no bathroom back here," Victor said, adding, "There's nothing back here, only this hallway."

Realizing that we weren't going to have time to also take shoes and clothes, I concentrated on the money from the cash register. I was hurrying, trying to get every dollar out of it.

Suddenly I looked up. A girl of about twenty, and someone who looked to be her mother, were standing outside, knocking, trying to open the door, and peering in.

I did my owner act, counting the receipts, and waving them off. I whispered to the guys, "Cool it, there's two broads out there!"

Victor and Lou froze, trying to press themselves back against the shelves.

"Store's closed!" I yelled to the women, checking my cash receipts. But the bitches wouldn't go away.

Suddenly I heard one of them say to the other in Spanish, "Something's wrong in there. I know the owner of the store and that's not him."

Fortunately for me, she was too excited to keep her voice down, and I heard her. I had to do something quickly. I walked to the door, all the while trying to block their view so they couldn't see the hall.

I shouted through the glass, "The man's not here. He went down the street and he'll be back in ten minutes. I'm just holding the store for him. Come back later." I turned around slowly, still trying to shield the hall from their view.

"*Es un robo, es un robo*," one of them said. "It's a robbery, a robbery."

"Lou, Victor," I shouted. "Let's make it!"

They both came charging out of the back toward the door. When they saw us run toward them, the women jumped back. If they'd started yelling as soon as they got suspicious, we might have gotten caught. But, they may not have wanted to commit themselves until they were absolutely sure.

That gave us the few extra seconds we needed to get away. We took off past them and ran down the street. By that time they knew they were right.

"*Pillos, pillos, pillos*," they screamed. "Thieves, thieves, thieves."

When a guy is on the run, every little sound is magnified. Nothing seems real. A person talks, and it sounds like a scream. Half a block is like a mile. People are faceless, and they are all after him.

I was in good shape and a fast runner. But goddamn it! I didn't know this neighborhood. Like ignorant assholes, Lou and I hadn't bothered to find out where Victor's sister lived before we pulled the robbery. We had to wait for Victor — not the fastest runner — to catch up. He was a little guy, and although he was in great shape, he just couldn't go any faster.

Finally, after Lou and I slowed down, Victor caught up to us and yelled, "This way!"

We turned the corner and ran a few more blocks. Then Victor said, "Cool it, we're getting near the building." We started walking, so we wouldn't look so suspicious.

His sister lived in the back on the first floor of a six-story tenement. As we went into the building I was praying, "Oh God, please let her be there." Foolishly, we'd taken for granted that she would be at home. We hadn't even bothered to call first and check.

Victor knocked for what seemed like an eternity. Finally, his sister answered and we all went inside fast. She took one look at our sweaty faces and heavy breathing and said, "Victor, what's wrong?"

Victor laughed. "Nothing, Carmen. Relax. We just got into a little fight with some Irish guys." His sister's neighborhood had an Irish section and a Puerto Rican section side by side, and they were always fighting.

"I haven't been here in awhile, Carmen. I forgot that some bars don't want Puerto Ricans in them," Victor told her. "We just wanted a few beers before stopping by to say hello to you, and a bunch of Irish guys wanted to kick us out of the bar. And you know me, Carmen. I don't hesitate," he added. "I just swung out and knocked one of them through the front window."

"Yeah, we had to run out of there before the police came. That's why we're sweating and out of breath," I said. "Victor hit him pretty hard—hard enough to send him flying through the window. So if you hear police cars, they're probably looking for the guys who did it."

Carmen was pleased to hear Victor had beat up an Irish guy. In those days it was good news when Irish guys got beat up; they were always giving Puerto Ricans a hard time. Victor had managed to make us look like heroes in her eyes. Thank God for the Irish—and their dislike of Puerto Ricans.

Carmen was between marriages and lived alone with her daughter. That was a normal thing. In these neighborhoods people were always going from one marriage to another, lots of divorces, broken homes, little kids.

Carmen told us she was on her way out, and it was okay to stay at her place. She was taking her four-year-old daughter to a doctor's appointment. "I'll be back in a couple of hours. If you leave before I return, just make sure to lock the door," she said.

As soon as Carmen left, Victor and Lou started joking about how close we'd come to getting caught, and how things had turned out fine, anyway. We got some money after all, and now here we were, safe and sound.

I didn't feel that way. I didn't like the situation at all. We were still in a strange neighborhood—one of the last places you want to be when you're running from the police—and I didn't like it. I wanted to get home. I wasn't going to be comfortable until I was home in bed, in familiar surroundings.

Just as soon as we sat down to split up the money, police sirens sounded outside, and seemed to stop right in front of the building. Someone must have seen us run down the street and go into the building. There's always some nosey bitch or some guy who can't keep his mouth shut, who'll run up to the police yelling, "They ran in there, they ran in there!"

Shit! Now what? We ran into the bedroom, the furthest room from the front door, and stood there in dead silence. We could hear voices coming from the backyard, just outside Carmen's back window. We couldn't hear what they were saying, but I couldn't just stand around, hearing the commotion outside, without knowing if it was the police or not.

"Wait here," I whispered to Lou and Victor. "I'm going to the kitchen to check it out."

I headed for the kitchen window that overlooked the backyard and looked out. My heart almost stopped. Right outside the window I saw a person wearing dark blue pants, moving around. It was a cop, standing on the fire escape by the kitchen window, leaning over the railing.

I was too close to risk going back. I spun myself against the wall by the window and held my breath. There was no room to hide because the kitchen sink was almost right alongside the window.

Pressing up against the wall as flat as I could, I prayed, "Please Abuelita, don't let him see me. Don't let him see me. I just want to get out of here." Always praying to my dead grandmother for help.

Meanwhile, the cop on the fire escape said to the cop below, "I don't see anything up here. Why don't we try some of the doors?"

"Okay," answered the other cop. "But, first let's check around a little more down here."

I stayed flattened against the wall between the window and the sink for another ten minutes before I dared to look out again. The fire escape was empty, so I quickly headed back to the bedroom.

Thank God the guys hadn't come into the kitchen to see what

was keeping me. With the cops so close, I had no way to warn them. If they'd come to the kitchen, the cop would've seen them and we'd have been busted.

"The cops are all over the place," I told Lou and Victor. "Where can we hide in here?"

We decided under the bed was best. When a guy is trying to hide, just hiding in a room isn't enough. If he's in a closet, and there's a little space in the corner, that's where he'd hide—the furthest corner. He wants to crawl into a hole. The only "hole" we could imagine was under the bed, which was silly. If the cops came into the room, they'd certainly look under the bed.

But we had to do something, and there was always the chance they might just look through the window, or do a quick check, and not see us hiding there.

I lay under the bed next to Lou and Victor, sweating and praying. Suddenly, a loud knocking came on the front door of Carmen's apartment. "Open up, police!" We could hear them trying the door to see if it was open. Fortunately, we had locked it after Carmen left—although for a few seconds we weren't sure we had.

The police kept knocking. I figured by now they'd checked around, checked the alleys, checked the apartments door to door, and this was the only place they couldn't get into. Now they were trying to force the door open. I was sure they were going to break the door down and come in. *Shit!*

Lou was starting to panic. This had all been too much for him—running from the store, police in the backyard, now them knocking on the door.

Out loud he said, "They're not going to get us!"

I put my hand over his mouth. "Cool it, man!" I whispered. "Do you want them to hear us?"

He pulled away. His now all-too-familiar look of rage had appeared. "The first fuckin' cop that comes through that door, I'm going to shoot him. We'll shoot our way out of here."

I couldn't believe my ears. *Shit, he's going to get the three of us*

I'll Be Good *Tomorrow*

killed for sure, I thought.

I wanted to take the gun away from him—fight him for it if I had to. But I couldn't. The cops were right outside the front door and I didn't want them to hear us.

Then Victor started laughing and couldn't stop. He tried to muffle himself, but he couldn't. His laughter was out of control "Ha, ha, ha, this idiot thinks he's Dillinger, he thinks he's Dillinger!"

I prayed silently to my dead grandmother, "Abuelita, please, let me get out of here. I'll be good. I'll be good. Tomorrow. I promise."

But, it wasn't doing me any good. This dumb bastard, Lou, wanted to shoot it out.

I knew that if the police broke in and heard a shot come out of this room, they'd spray the place with bullets. They wouldn't know there was only one crazy guy in here with a gun. They'd think we all had guns and were trying to shoot our way out. They weren't going to take any chances on getting shot; they'd kill us all. I knew we were going to die.

But the Bronx? Why the Bronx? Why die here? I hated the Bronx. I always hated the Bronx. I asked myself, *How the hell did I end up here?*

I'd always heard that when you're dying, your entire life flashes before your eyes. But lying here, all I could think of was the events of the past ten years—the time after my father left. Everything before that, the time spent growing up in what then seemed like a normal household, was just a blur. A distant memory.

Yes, I knew how I got here. Ten years of slowly progressing from games, gangs, and girls, to burglaries and stickups. And now it was all coming to an end. I was going to die.

Suddenly, a woman's voice came from outside. "Nobody's home. I saw the lady who lives there leave a little while ago with her daughter. They live alone."

Silence. Blessed silence. And then the cops went away. They went away!

I realized then that it wasn't some neighbor's voice. It was the voice of an angel that my grandmother had sent down to save me.

She'd heard me praying, and she figured, "Okay, you said you'd be good tomorrow. I'm going to give you another chance, just one more time." And she'd sent an angel.

As soon as it sunk in that my life had been spared—that I wasn't going to die—I said in my heart, "Thank you, Abuelita. I'll never do that again."

Of course, as always, that promise was only good until tomorrow.

I'll Be Good *Tomorrow*

CHAPTER 37

A BULLET FOR LOU

After the close call at the shoe store in the Bronx, we decided to limit ourselves exclusively to sticking up poolrooms. It was a good business. We would hit a poolroom a week, and have enough money to take care of all of our financial needs. For me that included a little money to my aunt, rent for my room, food, and movies for Maureen and me we both loved going to. I was happy.

However, during all that time, we had been using the German Luger with only two bullets in it. We'd used up two bullets the first couple of days testing it, and had left two in the clip. That was fine with Victor and me. We didn't need bullets in the gun.

But it was Lou's gun, and Lou wanted more bullets for it. He wasn't happy not having a fully loaded gun.

One day I was having lunch with Victor at the dinette, when Lou walked in with an old acquaintance of ours, Johnny Loco. Everyone in the neighborhood knew Johnny because of all his bullshitting and bravado. Lou had run into him that morning, they'd started talking, and Lou had told him about the German Luger.

257

One of Johnny's favorite bullshitting topics was about all of the connections he had. Lou fell for it, and he asked Johnny if he could get some bullets for the Luger. Right away Johnny said, "Yeah man, I get you bullets. I get anything you want."

So, all excited, Lou brought him over to see Victor and me. I hadn't seen Johnny since the days of running out of restaurants without paying. He was always good for a few laughs, so we all went up to my room to talk and joke around. I still had a lot of whiskey from the bar break-in. That really impressed Johnny. He was impressed with that and the German Luger when Lou showed it to him.

We made a deal with Johnny that he would get Lou some bullets for the gun. But, Johnny said he needed a sample to give his connection downtown so the guy could match it. Being a German Luger, it needed special bullets. We figured 9mm shells were okay, but Johnny convinced Lou that the Luger might need special shells, special 9mm's.

So Lou gave him one of the two bullets he had left. Johnny took the bullet and said he'd get us a box of shells in a week or two. After we had a few drinks, talked and bullshitted some more, Johnny took off with the bullet. And, that was the last we saw of Johnny Loco.

That same week we needed some money. We were trying to figure out where to go next. We had hit a couple of poolrooms in Brooklyn, some in Manhattan, and we were looking for a new one.

I remembered there was a poolroom on 160th Street that we hadn't hit. Beautiful place. Big, second floor, and it really wasn't in our immediate neighborhood. I'd played eight ball there a few years earlier with Orlando and Manny.

But I hadn't been in that poolroom in a long time, so they didn't know me. Lou and Victor hadn't been up there at all. So we figured, "That's it. We'll go up there and pick up a couple quick bucks." It was close to home and yet not so close we had to worry.

We went to the poolroom on 160th Street around midnight and went through our usual routine. We looked in each room, made sure the guy who worked there looked like he could be taken without any trouble, and checked the bathroom. Everything was cool.

I'll Be Good *Tomorrow*

As usual, we were the last ones there. By this time we'd gotten to be old hands at this. If we saw someone else still hanging around the place, we'd hit the telephone. Or go into the bathroom. Or we'd buy a Coke from the Coke machine. Anything to stall.

By this time Lou was getting used to the routine. As the guy working there got ready to close up and head to the door, right away Lou would pull the gun out. He was fast.

Victor and I would make sure we were right behind and we'd grab the guy before he could make a move, put him down, and tie him up.

After we'd tie him up, I would always try to let the man understand he was not going to be hurt. That was my job. I figured the best thing we could do was make sure the guy kept quiet—wouldn't yell or panic. And the best way to do that was to reassure him.

I'd say, "We don't want to hurt you. We just want the money. We're going to tie you so you can't chase us. If we wanted to hurt you, we wouldn't tie you up."

We took screwdrivers with us now, to open up the vending machines. A Coke or candy machine was always good for ten or fifteen dollars. While Lou had the gun on the guy, Victor would pry open the vending machines.

So, this time, just as before, when the guy headed for the door to close up, Lou was ready with the gun. He was used to this now. This time the man on the floor seemed like a pretty nice guy. He said, "All right, don't hurt me."

But, Lou noticed he was wearing an expensive looking watch, and he reached down to take it.

Right away the man started complaining. "Don't take my watch," he said. "My daughter gave it to me. Take the money, take everything. It doesn't belong to me, I don't care about it. But, please, the watch is mine."

Victor and I both jumped on Lou for that. "Leave the man alone. Don't take his watch."

Lou said, "All right, all right." We finished up the job, left the man tied there, and took off.

RALPH B. LAO

We got to my room around 2:00 a.m. The way the building was laid out, when you got to the top floor and got off the elevator, you made a right turn past a big metal door that led to a corridor. The metal door was always closed, because it was big and heavy. After that, the first door you saw was my room.

We went to my room to split up the money. We'd only gotten seventy-seven dollars from that poolroom, far less than we'd expected for such a big place. I suspect the man must have had some money hidden somewhere else.

We split the money between the three of us, washed up, and then went to eat, leaving the German Luger on my dresser. We were hungry. On the way down from the poolroom we'd been talking about the roast pig we were going to eat at a Spanish restaurant that was open late. Then I figured we'd come back after we ate, Lou would take his gun, and I'd get some sleep.

After a good meal at the restaurant, Lou and I started back to my room. As soon as Lou and I got off the elevator, I made the right turn towards my room. Something clicked in my mind. Somehow, things didn't look right. The metal door was open, being held that way with a can opener. That was strange at three o'clock in the morning. We'd been there at two o'clock and the door had been closed when we left.

Yet, I kept walking towards my room, thinking about it. Wondering what this meant. Then, as I went to reach for my door, I saw that it was ajar about two inches. I started to pull back, but it was too late.

I heard a stern voice behind me. "Put your hands up, don't move."

We turned around to face a guy coming down from the roof landing. He'd been waiting up there. We turned back toward my door, and another guy came out from inside my room. They both had guns pointed at us.

They were detectives. They weren't The Guinea and Huntley. They were Lieutenant Kavanaugh and another guy. They marched us into my room, showed us the Luger, and asked if it was ours.

"No, it's not ours," I told them. "It belongs to a friend of ours. I'm just holding it for him. He's going to come back tomorrow to get it."

260

I'll Be Good *Tomorrow*

They'd searched my room, and thrown things all over the place. Then they made us empty out our pockets, and they searched us. Of course, they found the money from the poolroom on us, so they took us down to the stationhouse.

One of the things they were looking for was a watch. And, there it was in Lou's pocket. Lou had taken the man's watch after all! Even after Victor and I had gotten on him about it, that son of a bitch, Lou—who was unpredictable—had just reached down and taken the watch, anyway, right before we left. And he didn't tell Victor or me about it.

When we got down to the stationhouse, the man from the poolroom was there. The first thing he did was to identify his watch. And, he made it a point to let us know that if we hadn't taken his watch, he probably wouldn't have said anything. It was losing his watch that had upset him.

Now, since he knew he wasn't going to get his watch back unless he identified us, he told the cops, "Yeah, that's them. That's two of them. Two of the three guys who held me up."

They took Lou into one room and me into another. They asked me, "You stuck up the poolroom, didn't you?"

"No!" I said. "I didn't stick up any poolroom. I wouldn't do that. I don't know what you're talking about. I swear."

"Bullshit!" they said. "You stuck up that poolroom, and you took the guy's watch. He described it perfectly before we found it on you."

"Not on me," I said. "You didn't find that watch on me. I have my own watch, and that's not it. I don't know how my friend got that watch. I swear!"

But they kept saying, "Bullshit. Your friend already told us you stuck up this place."

I stuck to my story. I'd been through this so many times before.

I remembered one particular time when Orlando had taken a bicycle from a kid. He'd wanted to ride it and the kid didn't want him to, so Orlando just snatched it and rode off. The kid called a cop. The cops rounded up Manny, Tommy, and me, and drove us down to the stationhouse. They'd put me in one room and Manny in another.

They'd told me Manny said that I'd taken the bike. They'd told Manny I said he had taken the bike.

Now, these guys were using the same old trick of putting us in separate rooms, and telling each of us that the guy in the other room had already confessed. What these two detectives were trying to get me to say was, "I wasn't alone. He was with me." Or, they were trying to get Lou to say that.

And they were pretty convincing about it. A couple of times there I thought, *Holy shit, Lou really ratted me out.* But, I didn't believe it enough so I'd go for it. I figured I had nothing to lose. I wasn't going to cop out.

There's always one "good cop" and one "bad cop." This time Kavanaugh was the good guy. They took me into a little room with a cot and a couple of lockers. Kavanaugh's partner started hitting me in my side and on my head. But that didn't bother me. The Guinea and Huntley had hit me before with flashlights.

I was so intent on not confessing anything—on not having them pin this on me, on not having my mother know, on not having my neighbors know—I didn't even feel the beating he gave me.

After one of his punches, I dropped to the floor. One of the things I used to do when a cop was beating on me, was double up, fall over, and act like I was half knocked out. I would start gurgling, making noises with my mouth, like I was bleeding inside. I'd try anything to get him to ease up a little. So, I tried that tactic again.

But then he started kicking me in the side, and said, "You wise little prick. Get your ass up or I'll kick your fuckin' head off."

I got up on one knee and muttered, "I didn't do anything. I swear, I didn't do anything." Then I added, "I never saw that man before. Or that watch."

He grabbed me by the hair and said, "Your friend, your buddy there, said that's your gun, and that you stuck up that poolroom."

I said, "He said that about me? Gee, officer, I don't know why he'd say that. That guy is supposed to be my friend."

"Yeah, you lying prick. He said that about you," he yelled.

I'll Be Good *Tomorrow*

"I let him come to my room, officer," I repeated. "I was going to let him sleep there. And then he says this about me? Some friend he's turned out to be. I don't know. I swear, I don't know why he'd say that."

I just stuck to my story. I figured, *what the hell, they can beat me all night. I'm not going to change that, no way. Let them bring Lou in front of me and have him accuse me to my face.*

My answers irritated the cop. He could see his bullshit wasn't working on me. He got madder and hit me harder.

Then Kavanaugh came into the room and said, "Enough. Leave him alone."

He pulled me up and got me some water. "It's all right, kid," he said. "This guy's a mean bastard. Try to stay away from him. Don't get him irritated."

I'd been through this bullshit before, too. The Guinea and Huntley used to take turns doing this kind of act. One of them would put his arm around the guy they were questioning and say, "Oh man, this guy, he's really a mean bastard. Why don't you tell him what we wants so he won't hit you any more?"

After about three hours of their crap, and getting nowhere, they put Lou and me in a room together. Kavanaugh came in and looked at us, and said, "You know how we knew it was you guys, and knew where to find you?"

Lou and I looked at each other and shook our heads. We didn't know. We really didn't know how the hell they'd gotten us.

So he just looked at us and let us squirm for a minute. Then he said, "One fat little bastard gave us a tip. I won't tell you his name, but you'll figure it out. He's the one who turned you in."

We didn't know what or who he was talking about. I remember thinking, *Victor!* But, why would Victor turn us in? He'd been with us—and besides, he's not fat.

Then Kavanaugh took out a bullet, put it on the table, and left the room.

Lou grabbed the bullet and looked at it. He'd had the German

Luger with the two bullets for about a month, and every night he used to clean the Luger and the bullets. He knew every mark on those bullets. This was one of them.

He looked at me and said, "Johnny Loco! This is the one I gave Johnny Loco."

"Are you sure?" I asked.

"Yeah," he said. "See that scratch! This is the bullet I gave Johnny Loco. I'd know it anywhere. That son of a bitch ratted on us."

"Shit!" I said. "And from what Kavanaugh hinted at, Johnny's a rat. The neighborhood rat. That son of a bitch!"

I started thinking back, and it made sense. Johnny was the type. I remember those little stories all these years. Johnny never got busted for anything. Johnny was always out. If he got picked up, he'd always come around the next day, bragging, and bullshitting about how he'd beaten the rap. "They knock me around a bit," he'd say. "But you know me, I don't say nothing to them."

I figured out what must've happened. The cops would pick him up, knock him around a little, and he'd spill his guts out. I began remembering friends of mine who had been picked up and gotten busted.

There was that time with Manny's money. Manny had that $1,000. The Guinea and Huntley had been right on the spot, and the money disappeared. It was obvious to me now that Johnny Loco had been ratting guys out for quite a while.

I spent that night in a little cell in the police station on Amsterdam Avenue and 156th Street. They'd also picked Victor up. The next morning they took the three of us downstairs and put us in a paddy wagon for the ride downtown. It was the first time I'd ever been in one.

The paddy wagon was a paneled truck with two benches facing each other inside. The door in the back was a locked gate and there were two cops sitting there. They made stops at police stations along the way heading downtown, picking up guys.

On the way down, we were not allowed to talk to each other. It was silence—or else. That, of course, was long before any Miranda

I'll Be Good *Tomorrow*

Rights Legislation. So once a guy was caught, he had little, if any, rights. The cops could do or say anything they wanted.

Once the truck got downtown, they took us to the Manhattan Detention Center—the New York City prison—where they took our pictures and fingerprinted us. All, firsts for me. Then, Victor, Lou, and I were split up and we were taken to different floors.

I was now in the infamous New York City TOMBS—the nickname made popular in movies, newspapers, magazines, and dime novels. The same place where the brains of the mafia, Lucky Luciano, had once stayed.

RALPH B. LAO

CHAPTER 38

THE TOMBS

They took me and a couple of the other guys up in the elevator to one of the higher floors. A cop was there, guarding a large gate with steel bars. He unlocked it and we passed through. Then another set of gates with bars and another cop. When we passed through this gate, we were in a huge open area.

To the right was a small booth where the guard in charge stayed, kept his records, and answered the phone. Directly in front of the entrance were big windows, and to the right and left were long corridors filled with cells.

The corridors had steel-barred doors, one on the left, and one on the right, that slid open. The central area with the booth could be shut off so the guards could separate themselves from the prisoners if anything happened. They would be in the center, and we would be isolated on the sides.

A light-skinned black guard who was manning the small booth took my name and checked me in. He seemed like a pretty nice guy.

Soft-spoken and courteous. Then they took me through a gate to the corridor on the left.

That corridor had two tiers of cells, an upper and a lower, facing each other. These cells ran all the way to the end, with metal benches down the center. The benches were anchored to the floor, and ran the length of the corridor, with the cells on each side.

At the end of the corridor were two or three cells facing the entrance, connecting both rows of cells, like a giant U. The second tier had a platform with a railing where guys could stand, look down and across, and talk to each other.

They assigned me to one of the cells at the end of the corridor, facing the main door. That was a good location for me, because I could look all the way down the corridor to the main room where the guard's booth was. From my cell I could see everything that was going on. If a guy was in a cell by the benches, he was just facing the cells in front of him, and he couldn't see the guards going back and forth.

Each cell had a sliding door that covered half the front, consisting of bars running up and down. When opened, it slid over a stationary set of bars that made up the other half of the front. The back of each cell also had bars so the guards could look in and keep track of the occupant.

Every cell had bars on both the front and back, with metal walls on each side, separating one cell from the other. All along the back of every cell, both on the lower tier and the upper one, ran a catwalk, a walkway where the guards could patrol, look in, and keep an eye on everyone.

My section at the end of the corridor had its own catwalk, which connected to the other walkways.

At nine o'clock at night, the guards, or "hacks" as we called them, would call, "Lights out." Everyone was supposed to be quiet and go to sleep. No talking, although there were always guys who kept whispering back and forth, from one cell to the other.

But, if the hacks heard someone talking, they'd slip up behind him on the catwalk, and pour a bucket of cold water on him. They'd drench the guy—clothes, blankets, and all. Once the poor guy was wet, that's how he had to spend the night and try to sleep. That was the guard's way of keeping everyone quiet.

I whispered back and forth as much as everyone else did at night, but I was lucky, because I never got drenched. Of course, I was in a good location. I could look down the corridor and see if the guard was in the booth or not.

Usually there were two or three guards patrolling at night, but I could keep my eye on them and see when they were moving around. If I didn't see them in the booth, I'd suspect they were filling a bucket, and I'd be quiet. Sure enough, shortly after I'd hear, Splash! Someone had just gotten soaked.

The cells each had a toilet and a sink made of metal. There was no seat on the toilet, just a button on the wall that was pressed to flush. The sink also had a button that was pressed and water ran for about ten seconds. Cold water only. If a guy needed more, he pressed the button and got another ten seconds of cold water. Everyone was given soap and a towel.

The bunks consisted of bare springs with a steel frame around them that was welded to the wall. There was a chain at each end of the frame bolted to the wall from the outside corner of the frame to the wall, for extra support.

We also received two blankets, which were changed once a week, with a pillow (no pillowcase) full of straw. We were supposed to place one blanket under us, so we wouldn't have to sleep right on the bare springs, and the other blanket over us for warmth. These were not five star hotel accommodations—nor were they supposed to be.

This was 1955. Prison reform didn't really start until the mid-sixties, when the Tombs got some attention, and was finally shut down for good. So, I was there when things were nearly at their worst. And it was crowded.

One day they brought in a kid—a junkie—whose arm was so full of needle holes it looked like a necklace painted from his shoulder down. That night he hung himself. According to some of the old-timers, it wasn't the first time some junkie couldn't handle the "withdrawal" symptoms. Again, being the mid-fifties, there were no special cells for junkies to "kick the habit."

Every day we had to "brush down," either in the morning or right after lunch. That meant they handed out buckets of water, soap, and brushes. We had to brush down our cells and clean the bowl and the sink. But, they only had about ten brushes, so we had to take turns getting brushes and soaking them in the bucket. Afterwards the guards came around and inspected to make sure everything was clean.

There were a lot of black guys and Spanish guys in the Tombs, so I fit in right away. As soon as I got there, I got friendly with these guys, and I had no problems with anyone. That is, except for one particular Italian guy named Lennie, who bunked a couple of cells away from me. One day while I was waiting to clean my cell, I had a run-in with him. He was one of three Italian guys who always hung out together.

It was brush down time, and they handed out the usual ten brushes that had to be shared between fifty guys. But, Lennie had two brushes, one in each hand. I watched him dipping them into the water and brushing his cell down, using one brush at a time.

I went up to him and asked, "Lennie, can I have one of the brushes?"

"No," he said.

I thought he was kidding, since we'd joked around with each other a few times before. I laughed and reached for one of the brushes. With his other hand he swung out and caught me right on the side of the face with his fist holding the other brush.

I reeled back. The next thing I knew, we were fighting. I managed to get him down on the bench, but only got in one good shot to his face before the guards came over and broke it up.

They threw me into my cell and him into his. I sat there waiting for the worst. Every time anyone got into a fight, the guards would come a short time later and beat the shit out of him. They figured if a guy wanted to fight, okay, he could fight them.

Sure enough, three of them came walking down, opened the door to Lennie's cell, and stepped in. I could hear them knocking him around. Bam, bam! They repeated over and over, "You like to fight?

I'll Be Good *Tomorrow*

Okay, wise guy, fight. Come on, fight us!" They beat the crap out of him.

Then they closed his cell and headed down to mine. I thought, *Oh-oh, now it's my turn.*

The light-skinned black cop—the nice guy—called me over and asked, "Okay, what happened?"

"I reached for one of the two brushes Lennie had, and Bam! I got hit. It was stupid of me," I answered. "I should've known better than to reach for it before he said it was okay. My fault."

"Yes, you have to be more careful when you're in here," he said. "You're lucky it was him you were fighting with," he added. "If it'd been with anyone else, you'd have had the crap kicked out of you by us. It's routine. We don't put up with fighting in here."

They didn't do anything to me. As he was walking out of my cell, he added, "Watch yourself around him and his two friends. They don't seem to like Puerto Ricans or blacks. Actually, they don't seem to like anyone."

All the guards knew this. They watched us. They observed us. They could see that these three guys looked down on the Puerto Ricans and the blacks. So this was a chance for the guards to get him. Thus, I was spared.

At night in the Tombs I got into the habit of sleeping with only one blanket. I put it half under me and half over me. The second blanket was used to keep the rats out.

There was a space under my door, and at night rats would creep in looking for crumbs. I'd be lying there, trying to sleep, and suddenly I'd hear a scratching sound. It would be a goddamn rat in my cell looking for food.

So some of us used to roll up our blankets and put them at the base of the door to try to discourage the rodents from coming in to our cells. They couldn't just slip under the doors; they'd have to jump over the blanket barrier. When the rat would see that obstacle, he'd just move on to the next cell. Also, I made sure I didn't have any crumbs lying around.

I had a loathing for rats. They always made me think of my

cousin, Alicia. A pretty girl, blond, and beautiful, but on the back of her right hand she had a big ugly scar.

When she was only a couple of months old, her parents had left her in the crib while they were in another room. Suddenly they heard screams. She'd been drinking milk and some of the milk had spilled on her hand. They ran in to her room, and there was a big rat in the crib with her. The rat had smelled the milk, climbed up in the crib, and bit her hand. Alicia carried that scar the rest of her life.

When I saw those rats in the Tombs, that's all I could think of. I could just imagine one of those bastards climbing up and biting me in the middle of the night, and I wanted no part of it.

The food in the Tombs was atrocious, the worst I ever had. Worst tasting and worst looking. We'd get up in the morning and line up in the center corridor. They would roll in the food trays on a big cart. They gave us each a metal tray and a spoon, and then filled the tray with some steamed garbage. A lot of beans, and terrible, ugly-looking meat with white streaks running through it—nerves and crap.

The first time I saw it, I asked a guy next to me, "What the hell is this stuff?"

"It's the Sunday Special," he answered. "We call it 'slop,' and you don't just get it on Sundays. You get it almost every day. And don't be fooled by the steam coming out of the pot. It's not steam, it's just the smell trying to escape. Slop is never hot, it's always cold."

"Do they ever add gravy to make it taste better?" I asked. "Or at least some lettuce or something to make it look better?"

"Once in a while they'll throw in a ginger cookie that tastes a little better," he added. "But even then, it all still looks like crap and tastes like it. But you'd better eat it if you want to survive long enough for your court date."

So we'd get up in the morning, get our meal and eat, turn back our trays, and then clean up our cells. After that, we could stay out until lunchtime. The doors of the cells were open and we could choose between staying in our cell, hanging out with a couple of guys and bullshitting, or we could sit on the benches and play cards.

I'd been there almost a week when suddenly, during visiting

time, I got a call telling me I had a visitor. Great! It had to be Maureen. Good girl. By then she had to know I'd been caught. She was sure to go to my room and see that I wasn't around, or, even that the lock might have been changed. Then she would have gone to the manager to see what was going on.

The manager of the place would know what had happened, because the cops had to make a report and get my clothes. The apartment manager, an old guy who never bothered me, was pretty nice. I'd given him a bottle of whiskey and a carton of cigarettes once, so he liked me.

He'd probably told Maureen, and she'd come to see me. Maybe she'd even brought me money for cigarettes.

When a guy had a visitor in the Tombs, he'd step into a metal booth in a section of the building downstairs. In front of him would be a thick glass slot, about four or five inches high and maybe a foot wide. He'd look through this slot and could see his visitor on the other side. But they couldn't talk to each other freely. They had to talk through a telephone, one on each side of the wall.

I went downstairs, all excited. I'd been there close to a week and this was my first visitor. Maureen had finally come to see me! The guard in charge told me which booth to go to. But when I got to my booth, Maureen wasn't there.

It was my mother.

I'd always imagined that if I got into trouble, my mother would do the same thing she'd done that time at Brooklyn Tech. She'd yell at me and say, "You're on your own now. I don't care what you do anymore. You're just like your father."

After that experience with her, I had changed and I didn't give a crap about anything. If she didn't care, why should I?

I remembered telling Maureen, "If I ever get caught, just call my aunt and tell her I've gone back to Miami." I figured if my mother ever found out, either she wouldn't give a crap, or she'd start yelling at me, and go through one of her screaming fits.

But, now, my mother wasn't doing any of that. She was standing there, crying. When she looked at me, I could see her eyes were swollen. She couldn't hold back the tears. She looked at me with an expression of anguish, pain, and sorrow. I could see that she hadn't come to wash her hands of me. She hadn't come to yell, "I don't care about you. Do whatever you want."

It was nothing like that. Not even, "What am I going to tell the girls at work?" It was not at all what I had expected.

She wasn't yelling. She wasn't mad. She wasn't screaming. All she was concerned about was me. She asked, "How are you, Bobby? You look so thin. Did they hurt you? Did they hit you?" All the while, tears flowed down her cheeks.

"Oh, Mom. I'm okay. I'm fine. Please, I'm fine," I answered.

She sat there looking at me, like she didn't believe me.

"No, Mom, they didn't hit me. They didn't hurt me," I added. "If I look thin, it's because the food here's not very good, so I don't eat much."

"Bobby, why didn't you let me know right away? Why didn't you call? You could have asked Maria to get me. I'm your mother," she said.

"I know, Mom. I know," I answered. "But I didn't want you or Maria to worry about me. I kept thinking I would get out of here, and no one would know. Not you, not Maria, not Sasita—no one. I just didn't want to hurt you any more than I already had, so I didn't call."

I hadn't confessed to sticking up that poolroom...yet. When I first saw her, it flashed through my mind to just keep denying I'd done it. But, when I started talking to her and saw the pain on her face and in her voice, it didn't seem to matter to me anymore. I just couldn't imagine myself lying to her, so I was prepared to tell her the truth.

But, she didn't ask me if I had done it. If I was guilty, or not. Just, "How are you? Don't worry, we'll get you out of here."

She kept repeating, "Bobby, you're my son, I love you. Nothing else matters to me. Not Renaldo, not the girls at work, not anyone. I don't love anyone as much as I love you. You're my son. I've always loved you. You should know that."

I just stood there, stunned, not knowing what to say or what to do. I felt my throat closing up as I struggled to hold back my own tears.

Then she said, "I want you to know that a person doesn't have to keep telling other people that they love them, to really love them."

That did it. It was the first time since my father had left that I remember my mother saying—out loud—that she loved me.

As I started to choke up, all I could say was, "I've never heard you say that to me before, Mom. Never heard you say you love me. I guess I thought, after all these years, you didn't really care."

After my father had left us, things had changed. She'd never come right out and said, "Bobby, I love you." No reason to. She had to go out and work to support us. She felt she had to be both mother and father to me. It was as if the day my father left, my childhood days ended.

But that day in the Tombs, she told me over and over that she loved me. Her words and her tears made me realize she was really hurt and worried about me. I felt terrible because I was putting her through this.

That moment changed the direction of my life. That was my defining moment.

Everything that happened to me afterwards didn't affect what I did, or how I behaved. There was no need for "rehabilitation" for me later. None. I was rehabilitated that day, when I saw my mother there, with tears streaming down her cheeks.

Suddenly, it didn't matter what happened to me. Now, the only thing that mattered was what I was doing to her. And, the only thing that mattered to her now was what was happening to me.

All too soon, our time was up and she had to leave. They took me out of the booth and moved me into a holding pen until they were ready to take me upstairs. I sat in the corner of the pen, overcome with emotion, tears flowing down my cheeks, not caring or giving a damn who saw me. I couldn't control the tears. I couldn't hold them back any longer.

Although there were other inmates in there with me, no one bothered me. No one said anything to me. That was one thing about the Tombs back then. If you saw a guy sitting in a corner crying, tears streaming down his cheeks, you didn't mess with him. You left him alone. Saying the wrong thing was the quickest way to get killed. You just didn't risk it.

It wasn't a matter of fear. It was more an understanding. Everyone has his day, and we all knew that. If we saw a man sitting there like that, we knew it was "his day." And we left him alone.

This was my day. I couldn't control my tears, and I didn't care. But no one bothered me, or said anything. Finally, the guard came and took me back upstairs.

The next day I got a call to go down and see my lawyer. Before that, I hadn't gotten a lawyer, although I knew a Public Defender would be assigned to me sooner or later. But now, I had my own private attorney.

My mother had hired Mr. Ellman through her union, the International Ladies Garment Workers' Union. He told me I would be out that night. He had just posted bail for me. My mother had put up $125 cash, and the rest was pledged.

That night, while sitting in my cell, the guard came over and said, "Get your things together, you've made bail." And I went home.

I'll Be Good *Tomorrow*

CHAPTER 39

TOMORROW

A few days later I found out that the night my mother discovered I was in the Tombs, had been a double nightmare for her. In a single moment, she'd been to hell and back.

She and Renaldo, who were now married, were visiting Maria, my aunt, and Sasita, my grandmother, at 140th Street. Since I would show up at Maria's for dinner at least every other day, they were all worried because six days had gone by and they hadn't heard from me.

I didn't know it then, but my mother had been staying in constant touch with my aunt to know of my wellbeing. That night my mother was there to see why there was no news about me. While she was there, the phone suddenly rang and my aunt answered it.

A girl, who didn't want to give her name, told her, "If you want to find out about Bobby, call this number." She gave a number and hung up.

Right away my mother grabbed the phone and called the number. She didn't know it then, but it was the telephone at the dinette where Angelo worked.

RALPH B. LAO

Whenever Angelo answered the phone, he'd usually jokingly say something like, "Millie's Haberdashery," or "Charley's Steak House," or "Knickerbocker Hospital." This day when my mother dialed the number the girl had given, Angelo answered, "City Morgue."

My mother dropped the phone and fainted.

Concerned, Renaldo picked up the telephone and heard Angelo on the other end repeating, "Hello, hello, hello?"

Renaldo asked what was going on. Finally he got out of Angelo that this was a dinette, and he was just joking. Although Angelo was really apologetic, Renaldo cursed the hell out of him.

When my mother came to, Angelo was in the process of telling Renaldo that I'd been arrested for something, and was at the Tombs.

Days later, when I was out on bail, I ran into Angelo and he couldn't have been sorrier. He said, "Damn, Bobby, you and your stepfather cured me of answering the phone with a joke. Now, whenever I pick up the phone, I just say 'Hi, Al's Luncheonette'."

I never found out who had called my aunt's house. Maureen insisted it wasn't her, and I'm sure it wasn't. Had she called, my aunt would've recognized her voice. However, Maureen was smart enough to have a friend make the call for her. So I'm pretty sure she was behind it. I could feel it by the way she acted, looking away when she answered me.

Maureen knew I needed help, and the only way I could get it would be through my aunt, or my mother. She was not about to let me stay there, just sitting in the Tombs, so she'd had someone call my home.

My attorney, Mr. Ellman, tried to do everything he could for me. One night we went together to the National Guard Armory in my area to try and get a report from them.

I had joined, along with Manny and Richard, when I was seventeen. We'd gone to meetings once a week, and had gone to "Camp Drum" for a two-week training camp. While there, I'd earned a medal for rifle marksmanship, and my attorney wanted to get a copy of the medal.

The captain didn't want to give it to me when he found out what

278

I'll Be Good *Tomorrow*

had happened. My attorney explained that he wanted a report from him so he could use it in court.

The captain said, "See the clerk and you can get a standard report. But, you can't get the medal if you're in jail, or going through the court system." Well, that was that.

Mr. Ellman also thought it would be a good idea for me to join the army. I'd had a good record before all of this. I'd never been in trouble, and I had attended Brooklyn Tech—an elite school. He was sure my report from the state psychologist, together with other good character references, would all help me.

With all of this in hand, he could convince the judge to release me into the army. He planned to argue that military life would be the best thing for me, and would certainly straighten me out.

With that idea in mind, I went downtown, took a physical and a written test, and passed both with flying colors. Then, just like they said on their "We Want You!" posters, they wanted me.

But it wasn't the army. It was the marines. I'd decided that, if I was going to join, it had to be with the elite. It had to be as much of a challenge as I could muster. So I chose the United States Marines.

Another thing I needed to do while I was out on bail, was to get a job. So I applied at one of the jewelry exchanges downtown on Canal Street, and got hired. My job consisted of carrying expensive jewelry and diamonds, in a satchel, from one store to another.

That was kind of funny, because here I was on bail, and I was transporting thousands of dollars worth of jewelry every day. I had what would have been Orlando's dream job.

Unfortunately, I also had to stay away from 143rd Street and the dinette. My attorney thought it would be a bad idea for me to be seen there—by detective Kavanaugh, or anyone else who might be keeping tabs on me.

Unfortunately, that also included staying away from Maureen. That really hurt. Although I wasn't in love with her, I had grown very attached to her. I cared for her. Now that was over. We met, talked it over, and she understood. Besides, we both figured it was only until this trial thing was over, and then we'd be together again.

279

"Oh, hon, you're going to look great in a marine uniform," she said. "Just think, I won't be able to call you 'Young Bob' anymore. I'll have to start calling you 'Officer Bob.' MY Officer Bob—I can't wait." We both laughed.

But it was never to be. Shortly after saying goodbye to Maureen, I ran into Bernadette. One thing led to another and we fell madly in love—again. We realized we had never really stopped.

I told her what happened, and she felt terrible. "Bobby, Bobby, it's all my fault," she said. "If only I hadn't screwed up when you were working. If only I'd gotten a job after school, this never would've happened. I'm so sorry, Bobby. So sorry."

For a couple of weeks, it was the greatest romance in the world. Bernadette and me—together again. We spent another night at the Hamilton Place Hotel. Another night of love, just like old times.

I was going to go to the marines and we were going to get married. Bernadette would go with me after I spent my three months at "Paris Island," the marine boot camp. She would be a marine wife.

I just had to take care of this little business, and everything would be cool.

First, I had to appear in court to enter my plea. I was prepared to plead guilty, as were Lou and Victor. They each had their own public defender attorneys, and were both still in the Tombs. This was Victor's second offense, so he had a very high bail. Lou had a lower bail, but had no one to get him out.

The night before I was supposed to go down and plead the next afternoon, I told Bernadette I would see her the next day after work.

My attorney assured me, "This is just routine. You'll go before the judge and plead guilty. He'll ask you if you understand the charges, and you say 'yes, your honor.' That's it. He'll set a date on the calendar for this case, and you'll go home and wait until the sentencing date. No problem."

That morning I went to my job at the jewelry exchange and told them I had to leave early that afternoon. Then I went down to plead.

The judge looked at me, and asked my attorney, "Why is this one out on bail when the others aren't?"

I'll Be Good *Tomorrow*

Mr. Ellman said, "Your honor, his mother was very concerned over what happened and she posted bail. She had to borrow the money needed, but she thought that being in a loving home was better than him sitting in a jail cell."

But the judge didn't seem to care. Instead he said, "Bail revoked."

I couldn't understand what was going on. I started to turn to Mr. Ellman, to ask him, when one of the bailiffs grabbed me and headed me towards the door to the holding cells.

My attorney made a motion requesting to talk to me, and the judge gave him a few minutes with me. "I'm sorry," he said to me. "But the judge doesn't think you should be out on bail while Lou and Victor are sitting in jail cells. He thinks it's unfair to them, and that you should all be treated equally."

"What about the fact that my mother had to borrow the money for my bail, and I've only been out a short time?" I asked him.

"I told him," my attorney answered. "But this judge doesn't seem to care about that." There didn't seem to be anything Mr. Ellman could do. He was helpless.

That shook my confidence in him a bit, because I'd put a lot of faith in him. I figured he knew what he was talking about when he'd come up with the idea of me enlisting in the military and all the other crap. Now he was telling me there was nothing he could do. No motions, no appeals, nothing.

I couldn't believe it. I was heading straight back to the Tombs!

When I got there, I was assigned to the same section as before, and some of the guys I'd been with earlier, were still there.

Lennie, the guy I'd had the fight with during my earlier stay was one of them. He looked at me, gave me a friendly smile, and asked, "What the hell are you doing back here? What happened?"

I explained as best I could, adding, "Fucking lawyer let me down."

"Who'd you have?" he asked.

"An attorney from my mothers union. His name is Ellman, and he was supposed to be good," I answered.

"A union lawyer!" he said. "Shit, no wonder you're back here.

You needed a criminal attorney. Someone who knows the system. Not a business guy. Damn!"

"He's all my family could afford," I said.

"Sorry about that, man," he answered—and he really seemed to mean it.

I spent about four more months there, waiting for our sentencing date. I didn't get to see Bernadette again. On visiting days I could only see my mother.

Mr. Ellman collected my pay from the jewelry exchange, and gave it to my mother, telling her he would wait until I got out to collect his fee from me, not from her.

Sentencing day came. Again, my attorney seemed helpless.

He'd been sure I was going to get out on probation, both because of my good record and because the marines had accepted me. He showed the judge a letter I had just received, requesting me to show up downtown at marine headquarters for my swearing in.

But again, the judge didn't care. All he said was, "Are you all ready for sentencing?" It was almost as if the judge resented my lawyer, Mr. Ellman, being there for me.

I never got my probation. Instead, we were all sentenced to prison. Victor was given ten years at Sing Sing Prison, while Lou and I were both sent to the Elmira Reception Center, each receiving an indeterminate sentence—zip/five. That meant "one day to five years."

We had to do a total of five years, but for good behavior we could get out on parole any time before that.

The people in the courtroom became no more than blurs—faceless and shapeless. I felt a bailiff grab my arm and lead me through a door. It was almost as if time were standing still, frozen, while I was the only one moving. Being led through a fog—a blurry maze of shock and disbelief.

Somehow, I found myself back upstairs.

A day or two later, I removed the clothes they'd given me in the Tombs, and put on a suit my mother had brought me. I was then led downstairs, where they handcuffed me to another guy.

"Hi there," he said. It was Lou! He'd been on another floor.

I'll Be Good *Tomorrow*

Out of the twenty or thirty guys getting on the train for Elmira, Lou and I were handcuffed together.

Lou looked at me and said, "Not what I had ever expected—or wanted."

"I know, but at least we're both going to the same place," I told him. It was all I could think of to say, as I found myself feeling sorry for him all over again.

As they led us on to the train for Elmira, I looked around, and I realized:

Abuelita, It Is Tomorrow.

RALPH B. LAO

I'll Be Good *Tomorrow*

EPILOGUE

Once apprehended, Ralph determined to make the most of his prison term by turning it into a learning experience. He took advantage of the opportunities offered by the prison to complete his high school education and to learn a trade. Always an artist, he studied drafting and quickly became so proficient his instructor made him his assistant and assigned Ralph to help the other students.

On his release from prison, Ralph worked as a technical illustrator, and within a few years he established his own art studio, quickly rising to the top of his field of textbook illustration.

A few years after prison, he married a beautiful Puerto Rican girl and soon became the father of two children.

While operating his successful art studio in midtown Manhattan, Ralph acquired a Honda motorcycle to ease coping with New York City traffic. He quickly ran afoul of an inequitable NYC parking regulation and determined to fight it. He formed and led a 3000-member motorcyclists' organization, "The Metropolitan Cycle Association."

After a two-year fight, he met with then mayor of NYC, John Lindsay, who overturned the law. Thus, Ralph beat City Hall. His effort attracted considerable TV and newspaper coverage, including radio and television appearances, as well as a story in *Newsweek* magazine.

RALPH B. LAO

After several years of preparing artwork for NYC book publishers, and shortly after losing his mother to cancer, he moved his studio and his family to Palo Alto, California. There he resumed his training in Karate, which he had begun in New York, earning his black belt and becoming an instructor shortly thereafter.

After a few relatively quiet years he suddenly found himself fighting to save the life of his daughter, Marixa, who was diagnosed with a stage-4 cancer, Non-Hodgkin's Lymphoma. This battle led him to form a parents' self-help group at Children's Hospital at Stanford where she was being treated.

Through a letter that he wrote to the CBS news show, *60 Minutes*, he brought national attention to the problem of children's cancer. Morley Safer and his crew responded to Ralph's letter by coming to California and producing a sensitive story on the subject. The show, which aired in January 1977, was titled "Marixa." Their efforts were rewarded with an award from the America Cancer Society for the best news show of the year on cancer.

Marixa saw herself on television in January and again in August when the show was repeated. She enjoyed her newfound status as a minor celebrity only briefly, however, as she lost her valiant fight and succumbed to her illness in September 1977.

Down but not out, Ralph resumed the sports of sailing and whitewater rafting, which had given him and his family so much pleasure in happier years. He moved his family and studio to the heart of the California gold country to be closer to the rivers.

Never one to back down from a fight, he plunged almost immediately into the battle to save California's few remaining whitewater rivers. As a board member of the American River Recreation Association, he engaged in the struggle to prevent proposed dams on the lower South Fork of the American River. His efforts, per statements from the opposing landowners, led directly to a solution that united and satisfied all of the groups involved.

Shortly thereafter, the utility company servicing northern California raised their rates to a level that made it almost impossible for customers to afford the payments. After attending a local residents meeting, Ralph joined a county protest group and together they formed the "Consumers Coalition of CA."

Ralph was elected president of the group, and after a march on the capital in Sacramento, he and a handful of other members were invited to meet with then governor of California, Jerry Brown. This meeting resulted in a successful effort to lower utility rates to an affordable level for all Californians.

Ralph no longer belongs to any group or organization, and has vowed to "fight no more, forever." Instead, he spends his time with his second wife kayaking the lakes of southern Oregon, where he has made his home.

Ralph with Governor Jerry Brown

Me with my first wife, Criss

I'll Be Good *Tomorrow*

ACKNOWLEDGMENTS

I thank my first wife, Criss, for her patience while I locked myself in a room and recreated my past on paper, evening after evening. She not only kept our son Robert and our daughter Marixa from barging in on me and asking, "What are you doing Daddy?"— although sometimes unsuccessfully—but she made sure family routines were strictly kept, whether I struggled for privacy or not.

Unfortunately, our daughter's sudden illness forced me to stop before editing my first, and very rough version of this story.

Close to twenty years later, my second and present wife, Lois, unearthed, dusted off, and read a few chapters of the original rough draft. Her laughter at some of my early escapades, especially the one with Pearl in "The First Time," made her take on the job of Muse to my early efforts. She shared the chapters with a close friend who quickly joined her in encouraging me to finish what I had started years before.

A very special thanks to that friend, Karen Walther, who after reading some of the first few chapters, kept saying, " Ralph, you must finish this. You really have something worth sharing here."

However, she and Lois found my use of some words hilarious. Finally Karen asked me "Did you really use the words "penis" and "vagina" when you were in your teens?"

"No" I said, as I realized I had used words in my story that I now used as an adult. She convinced me to write what I actually said as a teenager. Karen not only added realism to my early years, but she kept pushing me for "more chapters."

Although I kept "fixing" and changing my early draft, Lois began sharing chapters with some of our fellow members in the "Aquatics Class" of our local YMCA. Together, with members of the staff, they encouraged me to continue, even through those moments of doubt and "writers block."

Another "very special thanks" has to go to Jo Johnston, a member of that aquatics class. Karen knew her as a published writer, a book editor, and a dear friend. After reading my story, both she and her husband, Ken Johnston agreed that a book was certainly the next step.

Jo soon became my editor, turning my efforts into a polished and finished product. I can still see her comments in my dreams. While I had described friends and life in the neighborhood, she made me relive each moment with her comment, "Needs more dialogue here." If her notes weren't enough, she had them printed on a gift cup to me—"More Dialogue."

She has also become, as Karen introduced her, "A Dear Friend." Without her efforts, you would not be reading this now. She showed me how to make the readers feel as if *THEY* were running the streets, sharing the love, and feeling the pain—while also making them say to themselves, *"I must read one more chapter."*

Opposite: Photos of Lois and me having fun together

I'll Be Good *Tomorrow*

RALPH B. LAO

Made in the USA
Columbia, SC
15 July 2019